Lingua Latina A2
Latin – English Interlinear Short Stories on Egyptian Myths

Latin A2 Reader

Brian Smith

Ortus Hori

Proditio Sethi

In Aegypto antiqua, ubi dei et homines inter se communicant, Osiris, rex sapientissimus et benignissimus, regnum suum cum aequitate et clementia gubernabat. Sed in corde Sethi, fratris sui, invidia et ira bulliebant propter potentiam et popularitatem Osiridis crescentem.

In ancient Egypt, where gods and humans communicated with one another, Osiris, the wisest and kindest king, ruled his kingdom with fairness and mercy. But in the heart of Seth, his brother, envy and anger boiled because of Osiris's growing power and popularity.

Quadam die, Seth, dolo plenus, consilium nefarium concepit ut fratrem deponeret. Ad cenam magnificam Osirim invitavit, ubi insidias ei paravit. "Frater carissime," Seth astute dixit, "convivium in honorem tuum paravi ut fraternitatem nostram celebremus." Osiris, nil suspicans, invitationem acceptavit.

One day, Seth, full of deceit, devised a wicked plan to overthrow his brother. He invited Osiris to a grand feast, where he laid a trap for him. "Dearest brother," Seth cunningly said, "I have prepared a banquet in your honour to celebrate our brotherhood." Osiris, suspecting nothing, accepted the invitation.

Cenae tempore, Seth, dolis usus, Osirim in arcam ligneam inclusit et eam clausit. Tum arcam in Nilo flumine iecit, ubi aquae eam ferrent incertum. Isis, uxor Osiridis, ubi de mariti sui fato audivit, dolore et maerore affecta est. "Quomodo sine te vivere possum, O carissime?" lacrimans dixit.

At the time of the feast, Seth, using trickery, trapped Osiris in a wooden chest and sealed it. He then threw the chest into the Nile, where the waters would carry it away to an unknown fate. When Isis, Osiris's wife, heard of her husband's fate, she was overcome with grief and sorrow. "How can I live without you, dearest one?" she cried.

Statim, Isis, determinata Osirim invenire, per Aegyptum iter fecit. Auxilio Nephthys, sororis Sethi, tandem corpus Osiridis repperit. Per artes magicas, Isis Osirim ad vitam breviter revocavit. "Isis, amor meus, regnum inferorum mihi nunc est," Osiris, reviviscens, susurravit. "Horus, filius noster, spes sola restat."

Immediately, Isis, determined to find Osiris, journeyed throughout Egypt. With the help of Nephthys, Seth's sister, she eventually found Osiris's body. Through magical arts, Isis briefly brought Osiris back to life. "Isis, my love, the kingdom of the underworld is now mine," Osiris, revived, whispered. "Horus, our son, is the only hope that remains."

Ita Osiris rex inferorum factus est, regnum mortuorum cum iustitia gubernans.

Thus Osiris became the king of the underworld, ruling the realm of the dead with justice.

Nativitas Hori

In paludibus delta Nili, locus secretus et tutus, Isis, dea prudens et amoris plena, se occultavit. Illic, longe a Sethi insidiis, Horum filium peperit, spem novam pro deis et hominibus portantem.

In the marshes of the Nile delta, a secret and safe place, Isis, the wise and loving goddess, hid herself. There, far from Seth's plots, she gave birth to her son Horus, carrying new hope for gods and humans alike.

"Hic, in hac tranquillitate, tu, Horus, sine timore crescere potes," Isis filio suo susurravit, cunabula ferens. Horus, oculis magnis et curiosis, mundum novum inspiciebat, naturae et divinitatis arcanis mox eruditus.

"Here, in this tranquillity, you, Horus, can grow without fear," Isis whispered to her son, as she carried his cradle. Horus, with wide and curious eyes, looked out at the new world, soon to be taught the secrets of nature and divinity.

Cum tempus processit, animalia paludis, tam parva quam magna, Horum amici et protectores fiebant. "Vos estis familia mea," Horus ad eos dixit, cum ludum inter arundines et aquas ageret.

As time passed, the animals of the marsh, both small and large, became Horus's friends and protectors. "You are my family," Horus said to them as he played among the reeds and waters.

Isis, magistra sapientissima, Horum de iustitia, virtute, et sapientia docebat. "Iustitia fundamentum est regni aequi," Isis explicavit, "et virtus est quae nos defendit contra iniuriam."

Isis, the wisest teacher, taught Horus about justice, virtue, and wisdom. "Justice is the foundation of a fair kingdom," Isis explained, "and virtue is what protects us against wrongdoing."

Inter somnia nocturna, Horus patrem suum vindicare et Sethi malitiam superare cogitabat. "Tempus veniet," Isis affirmavit, "cum paratus eris ad contendendum."

In his nightly dreams, Horus thought of avenging his father and overcoming Seth's wickedness. "The time will come," Isis assured, "when you will be ready to fight."

Thoth, deus scripturae et sapientiae, Horum visitavit, futurum regem conspiciens. "Ego te adiuvabo," Thoth promisit, "doctrina et consilio."

Thoth, the god of writing and wisdom, visited Horus, seeing in him a future king. "I will help you," Thoth promised, "with knowledge and guidance."

Militiae artes et strategemata, ab Isis et Thoth docta, Horum corroborabant, et, crescente, spem novam omnibus praebuit. Dei ipsi, e caelo spectantes, magnitudinem futuri eius agnoscebant.

The military skills and strategies taught by Isis and Thoth strengthened Horus, and as he grew, he offered new hope to all. Even the gods, watching from the heavens, recognised the greatness of his future.

Factus iuvenis robustus et determinatus, Horus, nunc ad ultionem patris et ad certamen contra Sethi tyrannidem paratus, ex paludibus exiit. "Tempus est," dixit, "ut iustitia restituatur et regnum meum recipiam."

Having become a strong and determined youth, Horus, now ready to avenge his father and to battle against Seth's tyranny, emerged from the marshes. "The time has come," he said, "for justice to be restored and for me to reclaim my kingdom."

Hoc modo, Horus, sub Isis matris et Thoth dei tutela, viam suam ad veram potentiam et sapientiam incepit, destinatus non solum ut patris sui mortem ulcisceretur sed etiam ut aequitatem et pacem in Aegypto restitueret.

In this way, Horus, under the protection of his mother Isis and the god Thoth, began his path towards true power and wisdom, destined not only to avenge his father's death but also to restore fairness and peace in Egypt.

Disciplina Hori

Ex paludibus delta Nili egressus, Horus, divinitatis iuvenis et spei portator, iter per Aegyptum incepit, ut mundum hominum et deorum exploraret. "Videamus quid ultra paludes iaceat," sibi dixit, in novam periculam progressurus.

Having emerged from the marshes of the Nile delta, Horus, the young deity and bearer of hope, began his journey through Egypt to explore the world of men and gods. "Let us see what lies beyond the marshes," he said to himself, ready to face new dangers.

Prima statio eius fuit in sacris Aegypti aris, ubi Anubis, deus mumificationis et post mortem vitae, eum exspectabat. "Salve, Horus. Ars protectionis et sanationis magna est sapientia," Anubis, capite canino, benevolenter dixit. Sub eius tutela, Horus artem curandi et protegendi didicit, vias antiquas ad vitam aegrotorum meliorem faciendas cognoscens.

His first stop was at the sacred temples of Egypt, where Anubis, the god of mummification and the afterlife, awaited him.

"Greetings, Horus. The art of protection and healing is a great wisdom," said Anubis, his head that of a jackal, kindly. Under his guidance, Horus learned the art of healing and protection, discovering the ancient ways to improve the lives of the sick.

Postea, Hathor, dea amoris et gaudii, Horum in lucem calidam et amabilem duxit. "Benedictiones meae tibi sint, Horus. Amor et sapientia te in tuis itineribus regant," Hathor, voce dulci et melodia, affirmavit. A Hathore, Horus discere potuit quomodo amor et sapientia in vita cuiusque momenti essent, et quomodo istae virtutes eum in futuris conflictibus sustinere possent.

Afterwards, Hathor, the goddess of love and joy, led Horus into a warm and welcoming light. "My blessings be upon you, Horus. Let love and wisdom guide you on your journeys," Hathor affirmed in a sweet and melodic voice. From Hathor, Horus was able to learn how love and wisdom were of utmost importance in life and how these virtues could sustain him in future conflicts.

Cum novis potestatibus divinis armatus, Horus per Aegyptum iter fecit, ubi varios labores et adversarios invenit. Hi congressus fortitudinem eius et audaciam probaverunt, eum ad proximos conflictus suos praeparantes. "Hae experientiae me fortiorem faciunt," Horus, post duram probationem, dixit. "Paratus sum ad proximum laborem."

Armed with new divine powers, Horus journeyed through Egypt, where he encountered various tasks and adversaries. These encounters tested his strength and courage, preparing him for his upcoming battles. "These experiences make me stronger," Horus said after a tough challenge. "I am ready for the next task."

In itinere suo, Horus etiam lectiones de iustitia, pace, et harmonia didicit. Intellexit quomodo haec omnia essentia essent ad Aegypti futurum sanum et prosperum creandum.

During his journey, Horus also learned lessons about justice, peace, and harmony. He understood how essential these were for creating a healthy and prosperous future for Egypt.

Denique, cum disciplina completa et novis potestatibus armatus, Horus ad Isis regressus est, paratus ad ultimum certamen contra Seth ad regnum suum recuperandum. "Mater, discipulus tuus paratus est," Horus, plenus virtute et sapientia, dixit.

At last, with his training complete and armed with new powers, Horus returned to Isis, ready for the final battle against Seth to reclaim his kingdom. "Mother, your student is ready," Horus said, full of virtue and wisdom.

Ita finitur Hori disciplina, iuvenis deus nunc ad magnam pugnam contra Seth paratus, non solum armis sed etiam mente et corde fortis.

Thus ends Horus's training, the young god now prepared for the great battle against Seth, strong not only in arms but also in mind and heart.

Certamen pro Throno

Cum tempus advenit, Horus, virtute et sapientia plenus, socios suos convocavit et exercitum paravit, regnum avitum recuperare destinatus. "Comites, venite! Pro Aegypto et iustitia pugnabimus!" Horus clare exclamavit.

When the time came, Horus, full of virtue and wisdom, called together his allies and prepared his army, determined to reclaim his ancestral kingdom. "Companions, come! We will fight for Egypt and justice!" Horus declared loudly.

Seth, nuntium de Hori reditu accipiens, suos etiam copias congregavit, paratus ad ultimum conflictum. "Horus nunquam regnabit," Seth minitabundus dixit, ferrum et flammam in oculis portans.

Seth, receiving news of Horus's return, also gathered his forces, ready for the final conflict. "Horus will never rule," Seth said menacingly, with steel and fire in his eyes.

Dei Aegyptii, spectantes, se in duas partes diviserunt: alii Horum, spei portatorem, alii Seth, potentiae avidum, sustinebant. Caelum et terra tensione vibraverunt, praeludium belli magnum indicans.

The Egyptian gods, watching, divided into two sides: some supported Horus, the bearer of hope, while others sided with Seth, hungry for power. Heaven and earth trembled with tension, heralding the great war to come.

Conflictus incepit, terrae Aegypti et caelis magicis proeliis testes. Horus et Seth in duellis magnificis et terribilibus sese invicem provocaverunt, viribus et artibus suis maxime contendentes.

The conflict began, with the lands of Egypt and the skies witnessing magical battles. Horus and Seth challenged each other in magnificent and terrifying duels, using all their strength and skills to the utmost.

In acie, Horus graviter vulneratus est, sed animus eius infractus mansit. "Non desistam," Horus, vulneribus laborans, susurravit.

On the battlefield, Horus was gravely wounded, but his spirit remained unbroken. "I will not give up," Horus whispered, struggling with his wounds.

Thoth, sapientiae deus, ad Hori latus venit, artibus suis eum sanans et in pugnam iterum mittens. "Vires tuae regnum liberabunt," Thoth ei dixit, medicamentis et verbis magicis utendo.

Thoth, the god of wisdom, came to Horus's side, healing him with his arts and sending him back into the fight. "Your strength will free the kingdom," Thoth said to him, using magic words and medicines.

In ultima pugna, Horus et Seth vires ultimas conflaverunt. Horus, superando dolores et fatigationem, Seth vicit, sed misericordia motus, vitam eius pepercit. "Iustitia, non ultio, regnum nostrum definiet," Horus victor dixit.

In the final battle, Horus and Seth summoned their last powers. Horus, overcoming pain and exhaustion, defeated Seth, but moved by mercy, spared his life. "Justice, not vengeance, will define our kingdom," the victorious Horus said.

Tum Horus, pro sua virtute et iustitia, rex legitimus Aegypti proclamatus est, ordine et iustitia restitutis. Dei hominesque, nova pace fruentes, regnum eius celebraverunt, spes in futurum renovata.

Then Horus, for his virtue and justice, was proclaimed the rightful king of Egypt, with order and justice restored. Gods and humans, enjoying a new peace, celebrated his reign, their hope for the future renewed.

Sic finitur narratio de Horo, qui, per multas difficultates et probationes, non solum regnum suum recuperavit sed etiam novam aetatem pacis et iustitiae in Aegypto inchoavit.

Thus ends the story of Horus, who, through many challenges and trials, not only reclaimed his kingdom but also began a new era of peace and justice in Egypt.

Iudicium Osiridis

Coniuratio Sethi

In Aegypti terra antiqua, ubi flumina Nili terras fertiles irrigant, Osiris, rex iustus et sapiens, regnavit. Frater eius, Seth, corde obscuro et invidia plenus, potentiam Osiris invidit.

In the ancient land of Egypt, where the rivers of the Nile irrigate fertile lands, Osiris, a just and wise king, ruled. His brother, Seth, with a dark heart and full of envy, coveted Osiris's power.

"Cur Osiris, non ego, Aegypti solium tenet?" Seth secum cogitavit. Itaque, astu malo, consilium cepit ut regnum fratris usurparet.

"Why does Osiris, not I, hold the throne of Egypt?" Seth thought to himself. So, with evil cunning, he devised a plan to usurp his brother's kingdom.

Festo die, Seth Osiridem ad convivium invitavit, reconciliationis specie. "Frater dilecte, veni et laetitia nostra fruamur," Seth callide dixit. Convivio parato, arcam splendidam ostendit, dicendo: "Donum cuique intranti dabo."

On a festival day, Seth invited Osiris to a banquet under the guise of reconciliation. "Beloved brother, come and enjoy our happiness," Seth slyly said. Once the banquet was prepared, he revealed a splendid chest, saying: "I will give a gift to whoever fits inside."

Osiris, nihil mali suspicatus, in arcam intravit. Seth cito arcam clausit et sigillavit, Osiridem insidiose intrappans. "Nunc regnum meum erit," Seth susurravit, arcam in Nili fluenta proiciens.

Osiris, suspecting no evil, entered the chest. Seth quickly closed and sealed the chest, trapping Osiris treacherously inside. "Now the kingdom will be mine," Seth whispered, throwing the chest into the Nile's currents.

Isis, Osiridis uxor dilecta, mariti desiderio moesta, consilium invenit. "Osiridem meum inveniam," dixit, Nephthys adiuvante. Per

Aegyptum ambulaverunt, usque ad deltae ripas ubi arcam invenerunt.

Isis, Osiris's beloved wife, sorrowful with longing for her husband, made a plan. "I will find my Osiris," she said, with the help of Nephthys. They travelled across Egypt, until they reached the banks of the delta where they found the chest.

Isis, lacrimis commota, arcam aperuit et Osiridis corpus repperit. Arte magica usa, Osirim ad vitam breve tempus revocavit. "Regnum inferorum nunc tuum est," Isis flens dixit.

Moved by tears, Isis opened the chest and found Osiris's body. Using magic, she brought Osiris back to life for a short time. "The kingdom of the underworld is now yours," Isis said, weeping.

Osiris, vita ad inferos reditus, iudex mortuorum factus est, animas ponderans.

Osiris, returned to the underworld, became the judge of the dead, weighing their souls.

Hic narratio incepit, fabula de deis, amore, invidia, et iustitia aeterna.

Thus begins the story, a tale of gods, love, envy, and eternal justice.

Isidis Quaestus

Isis, luctu et dolore confecta ob amissionem Osiridis, qui nunc regnum inferorum tenet, in solitudine flens inventa est. Subito, mirabilem nuntium proprio sensu cognovit: se gravidam esse filio Osiridis, Horo futuro.

Isis, overwhelmed with grief and sorrow over the loss of Osiris, who now rules the underworld, was found weeping in solitude. Suddenly, she sensed a miraculous message: she was pregnant with Osiris's son, the future Horus.

Determinata filium suum a Sethi malitia protegere, in mariscis delta Nili se celavit. Horus, nescius sui patrimonii regalis, sub matris cura crescebat.

Determined to protect her son from Seth's wickedness, she hid in the marshes of the Nile delta. Horus, unaware of his royal heritage, grew up under his mother's care.

"Patris tui historia plena est iustitiae et potentiae," Isis Horo narravit, "et tu, fili mi, eius viam sequi debes." Isis Horum arte magica et divinitatum scientia erudiebat, sperans eum paratum ad futuros conflictus facere.

"Your father's story is filled with justice and power," Isis told Horus, "and you, my son, must follow his path." Isis educated Horus in magical arts and divine knowledge, hoping to prepare him for future conflicts.

Interea, Seth, semper inimicus, heredis perniciem machinabatur, sed Isis, magica arte utendo, eius consilia frustrabat. Horus, robur et determinationem ex matris exemplis trahens, in virum iuvenem evasit, paratus ad patris ultionem.

Meanwhile, Seth, always the enemy, plotted the heir's demise, but Isis, using her magical skills, thwarted his plans. Horus, drawing strength and determination from his mother's example, grew into a young man, ready to avenge his father.

"Veritatem de Seth scio, et patrem meum vindicabo," Horus, animo firmo, iuravit. Isis tunc revelavit Horum destinatum esse Aegypti regem.

"I know the truth about Seth, and I will avenge my father," Horus vowed with a determined heart. Isis then revealed that Horus was destined to be the king of Egypt.

Horus, sapientiam et fortitudinem adquirendi causa, iter incepit, varios deos conveniens qui eum docebant et sustentabant. Quisque deus aliquid pretiosum Horo tradidit, eum magis ac magis paratum ad finale certamen faciens.

Horus, in search of wisdom and strength, began his journey, meeting various gods who taught and supported him. Each god bestowed something valuable upon Horus, making him more and more prepared for the final battle.

Isis, filii sui victoria confidens, diem exspectabat cum ordo in Aegypto restitueretur. "Mea fides in te magna est, Horus. Tu Aegypti spes es," Isis, spe plena, filio suo dixit.

Isis, confident in her son's victory, awaited the day when order would be restored in Egypt. "My faith in you is great, Horus. You are Egypt's hope," Isis said to her son, full of hope.

Sic Horus, divinorum auxiliorum et matris amoris fulcitus, ad ultimum bellum contra Seth paratus erat, Aegyptum ad iustitiam et pacem ducere destinatus.

Thus, Horus, supported by the help of the gods and his mother's love, was ready for the final battle against Seth, destined to lead Egypt to justice and peace.

Duellum Deorum

Cum tempus venisset, Horus, thronum Aegypti vindicare paratus, provocavit Sethum ad pugnam. Dei omnes ad spectaculum conveniunt, partibus divisi et favoribus distinctis.

When the time came, Horus, ready to claim the throne of Egypt, challenged Seth to a fight. All the gods gathered to witness the spectacle, divided into sides and distinct in their support.

"Seth, callidus et potens, magnus adversarius es," Horus in campo certaminis exclamat, "sed iustitiam pro patre meo et Aegypto restituam."

"Seth, cunning and powerful, you are a great adversary," Horus exclaimed on the battlefield, "but I will restore justice for my father and for Egypt."

Seth, risu maligno respondet: "Audaciam tuam, Horus, agnosco, sed non superabis me. Vim et artem magicam meam experieris!"

Seth, with a malicious laugh, responded: "I acknowledge your audacity, Horus, but you will not defeat me. You will experience my strength and magical art!"

Pugna ferociter incipit, vi magica et corporea mixta. Horus, fortiter pugnans, vulneratur, sed animus eius firmus manet.

The battle began fiercely, with magical and physical forces intertwined. Horus, fighting bravely, was wounded, but his spirit remained strong.

Isis, mater, suis potestatibus sanationis utendo, Horum curat. "Fili mi, tua virtus intus est, noli succumbere," Isis suaviter dicit.

Isis, his mother, used her healing powers to tend to Horus. "My son, your strength is within, do not give in," Isis said softly.

Refectus, Horus rursus in pugnam ingreditur, hac vice intensius. Sapientia deorum duce, in certamine praevalit.

Restored, Horus returned to the battle, this time with greater intensity. Guided by the wisdom of the gods, he prevailed in the contest.

Denique, Seth superatus est. Horus, victoria in manu, tamen clementiam ostendit. "Seth, vitam tuam servabo, exilium tuum decretum est," Horus iudicat.

Finally, Seth was defeated. Horus, with victory in hand, nevertheless showed mercy. "Seth, I will spare your life, but exile is your sentence," Horus declared.

Deorum concilium Horum regem legitimum Aegypti proclamat. Seth, tyrannide sua finita, in exilium mittitur.

The council of gods proclaimed Horus the rightful king of Egypt. Seth, his tyranny ended, was sent into exile.

Pax et iustitia, Osiridis exemplo secutae, per Horum in Aegypto restituuntur. Osiris, ex inferis, regnum filii sui benedicit.

Peace and justice, following the example of Osiris, were restored in Egypt through Horus. Osiris, from the underworld, blessed his son's kingdom.

Dei hominesque novam harmoniam celebrant. Horus, spes et renovatio Aegypti, symbolum omnium fit.

Gods and humans alike celebrated the new harmony. Horus, the hope and renewal of Egypt, became a symbol for all.

Haec fabula cor Aegypti per millennia movet, Horus et eius pugna contra Sethum aeternum exemplar iustitiae et virtutis praebentes.

This story has moved the heart of Egypt for millennia, with Horus and his battle against Seth serving as an eternal example of justice and virtue.

Oculus Hori

Amisso Oculi

Horus, iuvenis et fortis bellator, sub tutela deorum Aegyptiorum crescebat, virtutis et pugnae artibus eruditus. Interim Seth, frater invidus et aemulus, destructionem Hori semper quaerebat, zelo motus ob potentiam et honorem qui Horo concedebantur.

Horus, a young and strong warrior, grew up under the protection of the Egyptian gods, trained in the arts of virtue and combat. Meanwhile, Seth, his envious and rival brother, always sought Horus's destruction, driven by jealousy of the power and honour granted to Horus.

Conflictatio inevitabilis erat. In campo proelii, ubi terra et caelum testes erant, Horus et Seth ad extremum duellum convenere. "Hodie finis tui adventus est, Horus!" Seth clamavit, gladio in manu fulgens. Horus, non timens, respondit: "Numquam cedam, Seth! Pro iustitia et patris memoria pugnabo!"

A confrontation was inevitable. On the battlefield, where earth and sky bore witness, Horus and Seth met for the final duel. "Today marks your end, Horus!" Seth shouted, with a gleaming sword in hand. Horus, unafraid, replied: "I will never yield, Seth! I fight for justice and in memory of my father!"

Pugna ferox et crudelis erat, vi et magia inter se mixta. In tumultu, Seth insidiose oculum sinistrum Hori eripuit, clamore victoriae exsultans. Horus, dolore et ira superatus, in terram cecidit, vulneratus sed non victus.

The battle was fierce and brutal, with strength and magic intertwined. Amid the chaos, Seth treacherously ripped out Horus's left eye, exulting with a shout of victory. Horus, overcome by pain and anger, fell to the ground, wounded but not defeated.

Isis, dolorosa, ad filium suum festinavit, eius statum afflictum cernens. "Thoth, sapientissime deorum, veni ad filium meum adiuvandum!" Isis precata est. Thoth, dei sapientia et magia praeditus, advenit et dixit: "Artem meam adhibebo, ut Horus sanetur."

Grieving, Isis rushed to her son, seeing his afflicted state. "Thoth, wisest of the gods, come and help my son!" Isis prayed. Thoth, endowed with the wisdom and magic of the gods, arrived and said: "I will use my skills to heal Horus."

Licet Thoth sua magia Horum sanaverit, oculus originalis amissus erat. Tamen, Thoth ingenio magico usus, novum oculum creavit, potentia veterem superantem. Horus, gratia motus, novum oculum Osiridi dedit, ut vitalitas in regno infero restauraretur. "Pater, hoc donum tibi vitam novam dabit," Horus dixit.

Though Thoth healed Horus with his magic, the original eye was lost. However, using his magical ingenuity, Thoth created a new eye, one more powerful than the original. Moved by gratitude, Horus gave the new eye to Osiris, to restore vitality in the underworld. "Father, this gift will give you new life," Horus said.

Osiris, munere accepto, potentior in suo regno factus est. Hoc gesto, oculus Hori non solum ut symbolum protectionis sed etiam sacrificii et renovationis habebatur.

Osiris, having accepted the gift, became more powerful in his kingdom. From that moment, Horus's eye was regarded not only as a symbol of protection but also of sacrifice and renewal.

Sic incipit saga de Oculo Hori, symbolo aeterni vigoris, protectionis, et luminis contra tenebras.

Thus begins the saga of the Eye of Horus, a symbol of eternal strength, protection, and light against darkness.

Virtus Oculi

Postquam oculus Hori amissus est, nova potentia inter homines Aegyptios orta est. Oculus ille, magica arte recreatus, non modo symbolon protectionis sed etiam potentissimum amuletum factus est.

After Horus's eye was lost, a new power arose among the Egyptian people. That eye, recreated through magical art, became not only a symbol of protection but also a most powerful amulet.

Aegyptii, oculi virtute cognita, imaginem eius in omnia sua protegenda rebus coeperunt uti. "Hoc oculo nos a malis defendimus," cives inter se dicebant, amuleta et imagines per domos et templa diffundentes.

The Egyptians, knowing the power of the eye, began using its image to protect all their belongings. "With this eye, we defend ourselves from evil," the citizens would say to each other, spreading amulets and images throughout their homes and temples.

Horus, nunc ut deus custos contra malum veneratus, in omnium Aegyptiorum precationibus aderat. Templa eius effigie oculi sui decorabantur, ut loca sacra protectionis divinae praeberent.

Horus, now worshipped as the guardian god against evil, was present in the prayers of all Egyptians. Temples were adorned with the image of his eye, offering sacred spaces of divine protection.

Amuleta oculi formam habentia ubique portabantur. "In hoc amuleto, oculus Hori me custodit," vir Aegyptius, amuletum collo gestans, affirmabat. Sic, per haec signa, Horus ipsorum vitas quotidie protegebat.

Amulets shaped like the eye were worn everywhere. "In this amulet, the eye of Horus protects me," an Egyptian man, wearing an amulet around his neck, would declare. Thus, through these symbols, Horus protected their lives daily.

Pugnae contra chaos et tenebras sine fine erant, sed Horus, oculo magico praeditus, victorias multas reportabat. Seth, licet victus, tamen in tenebris suis insidias parabat. "Numquam desistam," Seth in umbra murmurabat.

The battles against chaos and darkness were unending, but Horus, armed with his magical eye, won many victories. Seth, though defeated, continued to plot in his shadowy lair. "I will never stop," Seth muttered in the shadows.

Horus, sapientia et potentia oculi sui usus, veritatem a mendacio secernere poterat. "Nullae insidiae me fallunt," Horus, oculum ad veritatem revelandam adhibens, dicebat.

Horus, using the wisdom and power of his eye, could separate truth from lies. "No deception can fool me," Horus would say, as he used the eye to reveal the truth.

Populus Aegyptius, in Horum fiducia, eius auxilium in omnibus periculis invocabat. "O Horus, nos protege," preces ad altaria portabant.

The Egyptian people, confident in Horus, called upon his aid in all dangers. "Oh Horus, protect us," their prayers carried to the altars.

Navigatores, in maria vasta et periculosa se committentes, oculi imaginem in navibus suis pictam ferebant, credentes se ita tutiores esse in fluctibus.

Sailors, venturing into vast and dangerous seas, painted the image of the eye on their ships, believing they were safer in the waves with its protection.

Pharaones, regni sui legitimam potestatem ostendere volentes, coronas oculo Hori insignitas gestabant. "Per hunc oculum, regnum meum confirmatur," pharao, corona capite imposita, proclamabat.

Pharaohs, wishing to display the legitimacy of their power, wore crowns marked with the eye of Horus. "Through this eye, my kingdom is affirmed," the pharaoh would proclaim, with the crown placed upon his head.

Oculus etiam in sarcophagis pictus erat, mortuos in itinere ad alteram vitam protegens. Medicinae artes, oculi virtute auxiliatae, aegrotis salutem et sanationem ferebant.

The eye was also painted on sarcophagi, protecting the dead on their journey to the afterlife. The medical arts, aided by the power of the eye, brought health and healing to the sick.

Sic oculus Hori, lumine tenebras vincens, symbolon unitatis, protectionis, et virtutis in Aegypto fiebat, per aetates omnes veneratus et in corde culturae Aegyptiae manens.

Thus, the Eye of Horus, overcoming darkness with light, became a symbol of unity, protection, and virtue in Egypt, venerated through all ages and remaining at the heart of Egyptian culture.

Hæreditas Oculi

In Aegypto antiqua, Horus inter deos maxime colitur, eius historia et virtus per aetates narratur. Oculus eius, symbolon potentiae et protectionis, in omnium corde Aegyptiorum vivit.

In ancient Egypt, Horus is greatly revered among the gods, and his story and virtue are told through the ages. His eye, a symbol of power and protection, lives in the hearts of all Egyptians.

"Pueri, audite fabulam Oculi Hori, quod amissum et recuperatum est, nobis virtutem et tutelam semper affert," magister iuvenibus discipulis narrabat. Per haec verba, generatio post generationem fortitudinis et sacrificii momenta discebat.

"Children, listen to the tale of the Eye of Horus, which was lost and recovered, always bringing us strength and protection," the teacher told his young students. Through these words, generation after generation learned the significance of strength and sacrifice.

Artifices, novis imaginibus inspirati, oculum in variis mediis recreabant. "Per artem meam, Oculi Hori legatum perpetuo manet," pictor, novam tabulam pingens, dicebat.

Artists, inspired by new visions, recreated the eye in various mediums. "Through my art, the legacy of the Eye of Horus endures," said the painter, while creating a new painting.

Carmen et musica victoriam Hori super Seth celebrabant, populum ad virtutes antiquas memorandas excitantes. "Canamus de Horo, deo invicto, qui malum superavit," citharoedus in foro canebat.

Songs and music celebrated Horus's victory over Seth, encouraging the people to remember ancient virtues. "Let us sing of Horus, the undefeated god, who overcame evil," sang a lyre player in the marketplace.

Sacerdotes, in templis sacris, spiritualis oculi significatum docebant. "Oculus Hori nos in tenebris ducit et protegit," sacerdos adstantibus explicabat.

Priests, in sacred temples, taught the spiritual meaning of the eye. "The Eye of Horus guides and protects us in the darkness," a priest explained to the gathered crowd.

Festivitates magnae in honorem Hori et oculi eius celebrabantur, populo conveniente ut deum suum laudarent. "Hodie, Horum et eius oculum veneramur," cives in festo clamabant.

Great festivals were held in honour of Horus and his eye, with people gathering to praise their god. "Today, we worship Horus and his eye," the citizens shouted at the festival.

Eruditi, arcanis oculi studentes, eius virtutes magicas et sanativas investigabant. "Oculus Hori, præter protectionem, etiam salutem nobis offert," scholaris in bibliotheca legens affirmabat.

Scholars, studying the mysteries of the eye, researched its magical and healing powers. "The Eye of Horus, beyond protection, also offers us health," a scholar reading in the library declared.

Vates, futuro praevidere volentes, oculi auxilio utebantur. "Per Oculum Hori, quae futura sunt, intuemur," vates, signa interpretans, dicebat.

Prophets, seeking to foresee the future, used the power of the eye. "Through the Eye of Horus, we gaze upon what is to come," said a seer, interpreting signs.

Militares, ante proelia, oculi virtutem invocabant. "O Horus, da nobis victoriam!" dux ante aciem suorum militum exclamabat.

Warriors, before battles, invoked the power of the eye. "Oh Horus, grant us victory!" the commander shouted before his army.

Nobilium sepulcra, oculi imaginibus ornata, testabantur ad protectionem etiam in morte credentium. "In hoc tumulo, Oculus Hori me custodit," inscriptio in sarcophago nobilis legebatur.

The tombs of nobles, adorned with images of the eye, bore witness to their belief in protection even in death. "In this tomb, the Eye of Horus guards me," read the inscription on a noble's sarcophagus.

Architectura regalis et sacra, oculo Hori insignita, divinam protectionem et aestheticam pulchritudinem demonstrabat. "In hac aula, Oculus Hori nos omnes spectat," architectus, novum templum designans, dicebat.

Royal and sacred architecture, marked by the Eye of Horus, demonstrated divine protection and aesthetic beauty. "In this hall, the Eye of Horus watches over us all," said the architect, as he designed a new temple.

Fabri, preciosa ornamenta creantes, oculo inspirati sunt. "Hoc monile, Oculum Hori gerens, fortunam et tutelam fert," aurifex, gemmam sculpiens, explicabat.

Craftsmen, creating precious ornaments, were inspired by the eye. "This necklace, bearing the Eye of Horus, brings fortune and protection," explained the goldsmith, as he carved a gem.

In ritibus transitionis, benedictiones per Oculum Hori dabuntur, vitae momenta sacra sanctificantes. "Per hunc ritum, Oculi Hori benedictione te munimus," sacerdos adulescenti ritum inchoanti dicebat.

In rites of passage, blessings were given through the Eye of Horus, sanctifying the sacred moments of life. "Through this rite, we bestow upon you the blessing of the Eye of Horus," said the priest to the young person beginning the ceremony.

Sic legatum Oculi Hori, symboli fortissimi protectionis et unitatis Aegyptiae, per aeternitatem perseverat, vitas Aegyptiorum in omni aspectu tangens.

Thus, the legacy of the Eye of Horus, the strongest symbol of Egyptian protection and unity, endures through eternity, touching the lives of Egyptians in every aspect.

Anubis et Ars Mumificandi

Origo Mumificationis

Anubis, deus mumificationis et rituum funerariorum, in Aegypto antiqua maxime veneratus est. Capite canis, qui custos et protector est, repraesentatus, Anubis modum invenit mortuos in aeternum conservandi.

Anubis, the god of mummification and funeral rites, was greatly revered in ancient Egypt. Represented with the head of a dog, who acts as a guardian and protector, Anubis discovered the way to preserve the dead for eternity.

"Corpora post mortem servare debemus ut in vita post mortem floreant," Anubis sacerdotibus, artem embalsamationis docens, dixit. Aegyptii, aeternitatem animae post mortem credentes, corporis conservationem essentialem putabant.

"We must preserve bodies after death so that they may flourish in the afterlife," Anubis said to the priests, teaching the art of embalming. The Egyptians, believing in the eternity of the soul after death, considered the preservation of the body essential.

Herbis aromatibusque, corpora mortuorum curabant ut contra temporis detrimentum defenderentur. "Haec unguenta corpora a corruptione servabunt," sacerdos, ritu embalsamandi perficiendo, affirmavit.

With herbs and aromatic oils, the bodies of the dead were cared for to protect them against the ravages of time. "These ointments will preserve the bodies from decay," a priest affirmed while performing the embalming ritual.

Cor, quod sedes sensus et intellectus esse credebatur, in corpore relinquebatur. "Cor nostrum nos definit, etiam in morte," Anubis, animas mortuorum ad inferos ducens, explicabat.

The heart, believed to be the seat of emotion and intellect, was left inside the body. "Our heart defines us, even in death," Anubis explained, as he guided the souls of the dead to the underworld.

Corpora linteis involuta et amuletis inter fascias positis, ut defunctos in itinere ad alteram vitam tuerentur. "Haec amuleta te in via protegent," Anubis ad animam defuncti, iudicium parantem, loquebatur.

The bodies were wrapped in linen, and amulets were placed between the wrappings to protect the deceased on their journey to the afterlife. "These amulets will protect you on your way," Anubis said to the soul of the deceased, preparing for judgment.

Si cor levius esset qua penna Maat, anima ad aeternam vitam transire poterat. "Iustitia tua te liberabit," Anubis, cor ad penna Maat appendens, dicebat.

If the heart was lighter than the feather of Maat, the soul could pass into eternal life. "Your justice will set you free," Anubis said, as he weighed the heart against Maat's feather.

Imagines Anubis sepulcris insculptae erant, aeternam protectionem promittentes. "Anubis, custodi eum in pace," familia dolens in oratione dixit.

Images of Anubis were carved into tombs, promising eternal protection. "Anubis, keep him in peace," the grieving family said in prayer.

Arte mumificationis, Aegyptii non solum mortuos honore afficiebant sed etiam deorum mundum et humanum arctius conectebant. "Per hanc artem, aeternitatis portas aperimus," sacerdos, ceremoniam finiens, pronuntiavit.

Through the art of mummification, the Egyptians not only honoured the dead but also brought the divine and human worlds closer together. "Through this art, we open the gates to eternity," the priest declared, as he concluded the ceremony.

Sic, Anubis magister et dux in arte mumificationis, initium huius artis sacrae Aegyptiis tradidit, quae non solum corpora sed etiam animas ad vitam aeternam conservare potest.

Thus, Anubis, the master and guide in the art of mummification, passed down this sacred craft to the Egyptians, which could preserve not only bodies but also souls for eternal life.

Ritus Mumificationis

Processus mumificationis, arte sancta et meticulosa, septuaginta dies ad completum exigit. Sacerdotes, vultus Anubis gestantes, mysteria mortis et vitae aeternae tractant.

The process of mummification, a sacred and meticulous art, requires seventy days to complete. Priests, wearing the face of Anubis, handle the mysteries of death and eternal life.

"In his aquae Nili lustrationibus, corpus purificamus et sanctificamus," sacerdos, corpus lavans, dixit. Aqua sacra Nili, quae vitam fertilitatemque Aegypto praestat, in ritu purificationis essentiale est.

"In these lustrations with Nile water, we purify and sanctify the body," said the priest, washing the body. The sacred water of the Nile, which gives life and fertility to Egypt, is essential in the purification ritual.

Viscera, corde excepto, caute extrahuntur et in canopis, vasibus sacris, reponuntur. "Haec organa in aeternum servabuntur," alter sacerdos, organa removens, explicavit.

The internal organs, except for the heart, are carefully removed and placed in canopic jars, sacred vessels. "These organs will be preserved for eternity," explained another priest, as he removed the organs.

Corpus, natrone impletum, exsiccatum est ut corruptionem vitaret. Postea, unguentis sacris liniebatur ut flexibilitatem retineret. "Haec olea corpus aeternum conservabunt," sacerdos, corpus ungens, susurravit.

The body, filled with natron, was dried to avoid decay. Afterwards, it was anointed with sacred oils to retain its flexibility. "These oils will preserve the body for eternity," whispered the priest, as he anointed the body.

"Scientia anatomica nobis est necessaria ut ritum perficiamus," sacerdos ad discipulum suum dixit, mysteria corporis humani revelans.

"Anatomical knowledge is necessary for us to complete the ritual," the priest said to his disciple, revealing the mysteries of the human body.

Magicae voces et carmina, mortem superare posse credita, per ritum recitabantur. "Per haec verba magica, spiritum in aeternum protegemus," sacerdos, librum mortuorum tenens, affirmavit.

Magical chants and spells, believed to conquer death, were recited throughout the ritual. "Through these magic words, we will protect the spirit for eternity," affirmed the priest, holding the Book of the Dead.

Sarcophagus, dignitate defuncti congruens, diligenter eligitur. "In hoc sarcophago, aeternitatis domum inveniet," sacerdos, sarcophagum inspiciens, dixit.

The sarcophagus, befitting the dignity of the deceased, is carefully chosen. "In this sarcophagus, they will find a home for eternity," said the priest, inspecting the sarcophagus.

In tumulis, thesauri et utensilia quotidiana collocantur, credentibus Aegyptiis haec in vita altera usui fore. "Haec dona defuncto in altera vita proderunt," sacerdos, tumulum ornans, explicavit.

In tombs, treasures and everyday items are placed, as Egyptians believed these would be useful in the afterlife. "These gifts will benefit the deceased in the next life," the priest explained while decorating the tomb.

Ritus apertionis oris, ut defunctus in altera vita loqui et spirare possit, cum summa reverentia peragitur. "Per hanc ceremoniam, vox et spiritus tibi in aeternum manebunt," sacerdos, ritum perficiens, promisit.

The Opening of the Mouth ritual, so the deceased could speak and breathe in the afterlife, is performed with the utmost reverence. "Through this ceremony, your voice and spirit will remain with you for eternity," promised the priest as he completed the ritual.

Anubis, omnium custos et dux in viis inferorum, ritum observat ne quid amissum sit. "Sub mea protectione, omnia secundum morem procedent," Anubis, invisibiliter praesens, susurravit.

Anubis, the guardian and guide of all in the paths of the underworld, observes the ritual to ensure nothing is missed. "Under my protection, everything will proceed according to tradition," whispered Anubis, invisibly present.

Familia, honorem defuncto reddens, convivium celebrat, memoriam eius in terra viventium colentes. "Hodie, vitam et virtutes eius celebramus," pater familias, festum inchoans, dixit.

The family, paying honour to the deceased, holds a feast, celebrating their memory in the land of the living. "Today, we celebrate their life and virtues," said the head of the family, as the feast began.

Cum omnibus ritibus religiose peractis, defunctus, Anubis ductu, ad vitam aeternam transire paratus est. "Per haec sacra, via tua ad aeternum aperta est," sacerdos, ultima verba dicens, conclamavit.

With all the rites performed religiously, the deceased, under Anubis's guidance, is ready to pass into eternal life. "Through these sacred rites, your path to eternity is open," the priest proclaimed in his final words.

Sic, per manus sacerdotum Anubidis et per artem mumificationis, Aegyptii mortem non ut finem, sed ut transitionem ad vitam alteram intellegebant, aeternitatis promissionem corde tenentes.

Thus, through the hands of Anubis's priests and the art of mummification, the Egyptians understood death not as an end but as a transition to another life, holding the promise of eternity in their hearts.

Legatum Anubis

Anubis, custos sepulcrorum et dux animarum ad inferos, per Aegyptum totam veneratur. Templa magnifica in eius honorem exstructa sunt, ubi fideles convenire possunt ad preces et sacrificia offerenda.

Anubis, the guardian of tombs and guide of souls to the underworld, is worshipped throughout Egypt. Magnificent temples have been built in his honour, where the faithful can gather to offer prayers and sacrifices.

"In hoc templo, Anubim, protectorem nostrum colimus," sacerdos, ad altare stans, ad populum dixit. Sacerdotes Anubis, pro sua peritia in artibus funerariis et mumificatione, magna cum reverentia tractantur.

"In this temple, we worship Anubis, our protector," the priest said to the people, standing at the altar. The priests of Anubis, for their expertise in funeral arts and mummification, are treated with great reverence.

Cultura mumificationis, ab Anubis instituta, non solum in Aegypto manet sed etiam ad alias culturas diffunditur. "Haec sapientia, a deo Anubi nobis tradita, nunc per orbem terrarum cognoscitur," eruditus in concilio loquebatur.

The culture of mummification, instituted by Anubis, remains not only in Egypt but also spreads to other cultures. "This wisdom, given to us by the god Anubis, is now known throughout the world," a scholar said in a council.

Anubis, in iudicio mortuorum, non tantum protector sed etiam iustitiae symbolum in aeternum manet. "Per Anubim, aequitas in vita altera servatur," sacerdos in ritu explicabat.

Anubis, in the judgment of the dead, remains forever not only a protector but also a symbol of justice. "Through Anubis, fairness is maintained in the afterlife," a priest explained during the ritual.

Fabulae de Anubis, artes et litteras inspirant. Sculptores, pictores, et poetae deum in operibus suis immortalizant. "Per hanc

*statuam, Anubim, iustitiae et protectionis deum, aeternus erit,"
sculptor, opus suum finiens, dixit.*

Tales of Anubis inspire art and literature. Sculptors, painters,
and poets immortalise the god in their works. "Through this statue,
Anubis, the god of justice and protection, will be eternal," the
sculptor said, as he finished his work.

*Amuleta Anubis formam gerentia ab Aegyptiis ad defensionem
gestantur. "Hoc amuletum me in omnibus periculis proteget," civis,
amuletum collo suspendens, affirmavit.*

Amulets bearing the form of Anubis are worn by Egyptians for
protection. "This amulet will protect me in all dangers," said a
citizen, hanging the amulet around their neck.

*Processiones solemnes per vias Aegyptiarum urbium aguntur in
Anubis honorem, fideles canentes et preces offerentes. "Hodie,
Anubim, deum nostrum veneramur," chorus in processione
cantabat.*

Solemn processions move through the streets of Egyptian cities
in honour of Anubis, with the faithful singing and offering prayers.
"Today, we worship Anubis, our god," the choir sang during the
procession.

*Historici, Anubis mumificationis methodos scrutantes,
antiquam sapientiam adhuc magis revelant. "Haec studia nobis
permittunt profundiora Anubis mysteria intellegere,"
historiographus in academia loquebatur.*

Historians, studying Anubis's methods of mummification,
continue to reveal ancient wisdom. "These studies allow us to
understand the deeper mysteries of Anubis," a historian said in an
academic discussion.

*Mumiae Aegyptiae, mundum fascinantes, ad scientiam et
admirationem provocant. "Hae mumiae, per Anubis artem
conservatae, nobis antiquae Aegypti vitam revelant,"
archaeologus, expositionem ducebat.*

Egyptian mummies, fascinating the world, provoke both
knowledge and admiration. "These mummies, preserved through

the art of Anubis, reveal to us the life of ancient Egypt," said an archaeologist, guiding an exhibition.

Musea, artefacta et mumias exhibentia, culturae Aegyptiae testimonium praebent. "Per haec artefacta, legatum Anubis per saecula manet," curator, visitatores per museum ducens, explicabat.

Museums, displaying artefacts and mummies, provide testimony to Egyptian culture. "Through these artefacts, the legacy of Anubis endures through the ages," explained the curator, leading visitors through the museum.

Pelliculae et libri, thema Anubis tractantes, fabulam eius ad novas generationes portant. "Hac in historia, Anubis, aeterni custos, iterum ad vitam venit," scriptor, novum opus praesentans, dixit.

Films and books that explore the theme of Anubis bring his story to new generations. "In this story, Anubis, the eternal guardian, comes to life once again," said the writer, presenting his new work.

Ritus funerarii Aegyptii, usque ad hodiernum diem, modernas exequias influunt, legatum Anubis per aetates extendentes. "Etsi temporum fluxu mutamur, Anubis nos adhuc docet de morte et vita post mortem," anthropologus in colloquio loquebatur.

Egyptian funeral rites, to this day, influence modern funerals, extending the legacy of Anubis through the ages. "Although we change with the passage of time, Anubis still teaches us about death and life after death," an anthropologist said during a conference.

Anubis, aeternum in Aegyptiae cultura eminens, non solum deus praeteriti sed etiam aeterni legati portator manet, humanitatis memoriae et spiritualitatis custos.

Anubis, eternally prominent in Egyptian culture, remains not only a god of the past but also a bearer of an eternal legacy, the guardian of human memory and spirituality.

Iter Solis per Infernum

Proficiscens Ra

Ra, divinitas solis, caelum terramque dominatur, lucis et vitae fons. Cum nox advenit, Ra mundum inferum ingreditur, per tenebras iter faciens ut novum diem renasci possit.

Ra, the god of the sun, rules the sky and the earth, the source of light and life. When night falls, Ra enters the underworld, journeying through the darkness so that a new day may be born.

"Ego, Ra, rursus ad tenebras descendo ut lucem et vitam renovem," Ra, in navem solarem ascendens, dixit. Deus, magni splendoris et potestatis, non solus iter facit; comitatus est a coetu deorum qui eum in periculis protegunt.

"I, Ra, descend once more into the darkness to renew light and life," Ra said, boarding the solar barque. The god, of great splendour and power, does not journey alone; he is accompanied by a host of gods who protect him from dangers.

Inferus mundus, Apophis, ingentem serpentem et mortalem inimicum Ra, monstris daemonibusque plenus est, praeceps. "Hac nocte, Ra, te exspecto," Apophis, in tenebris latens, sibilavit.

The underworld is filled with Apophis, a huge serpent and mortal enemy of Ra, as well as monsters and demons, perilous and treacherous. "Tonight, Ra, I await you," Apophis hissed, lurking in the darkness.

Aegyptii, de periculis itineris scientes, pro Ra salutem precabantur. "Ra, te custodiant dii in itinere tuo," sacerdos, ad aram stans, oravit.

The Egyptians, aware of the dangers of Ra's journey, prayed for his safety. "Ra, may the gods protect you on your journey," a priest prayed, standing at the altar.

"Duodecim portas transire debeo, unamquamque horae nocturnae assignatam," Ra, iter suum praeparans, enuntiavit. Portae, a deis daemonibusque custoditae, singulae sui generis pericula offerebant.

"I must pass through twelve gates, each assigned to an hour of the night," Ra declared, preparing for his journey. The gates, guarded by gods and demons, each presented their own unique dangers.

"Magia mea utar ut impedimenta superem," Ra, confidenter, affirmavit, scilicet vias securas per insidias invenire posse.

"I will use my magic to overcome the obstacles," Ra affirmed confidently, knowing he could find safe paths through the traps.

In cordibus Aegyptiorum spes refulgebat, diem novum et Ra reditum exspectantes. "Ra, in te confidimus," populus, ad templum congregatus, susurravit.

Hope shone in the hearts of the Egyptians as they awaited the new day and Ra's return. "Ra, we trust in you," the people whispered, gathered at the temple.

Sacerdotes, sacris ritibus perficiendis, viam Ra facilitare studebant, preces et incantationes ad deum dirigentes. "Per haec sacra, o Ra, tibi vires damus," sacerdos, sacra peragens, pronuntiavit.

The priests, performing sacred rites, sought to ease Ra's path, offering prayers and incantations to the god. "Through these sacred rites, O Ra, we give you strength," the priest proclaimed while conducting the rituals.

Narrationes de itinere Ra per inferos in parietibus tumulorum inscriptae sunt, aeternam luctam inter lucem et obscuritatem commemorantes. "Haec gesta, pro posteris scripta, nostram fidem et spem aeternam demonstrant," scriptor, historiam delineans, explicavit.

Stories of Ra's journey through the underworld were inscribed on tomb walls, commemorating the eternal struggle between light and darkness. "These deeds, written for future generations, demonstrate our faith and eternal hope," the scribe explained, outlining the story.

Cum prima luce, Ra, superatis omnibus periculis, renascitur, victoria lucis super tenebras significans. "Ecce, novus dies! Ra victor!" Aegyptii, solis ortum salutantes, clamaverunt.

With the first light, Ra, having overcome all dangers, is reborn, signifying the victory of light over darkness. "Behold, a new day! Ra is victorious!" the Egyptians shouted, greeting the sunrise.

Ita incipit fabula de Ra, deo solis, qui noctu per infernum navigat, vitam et ordinem contra chaos et tenebras defendens, aeternum Aegyptiis spem et securitatem praebens.

Thus begins the tale of Ra, the god of the sun, who sails through the underworld by night, defending life and order against chaos and darkness, providing eternal hope and security to the Egyptians.

Proelia in Mundo Infero

Vix Ra in tenebrosos inferni mundi recessus descendit, statim Apophim, serpentem immanem, invenit. Certamen inter deum solis et monstrum horrendum initium cepit.

As soon as Ra descended into the dark recesses of the underworld, he immediately encountered Apophis, the immense serpent. A battle between the god of the sun and the terrifying monster began.

"Apophis, hodie finem tuae malitiae ponam!" Ra, lumine suo coruscante, clamavit. Apophis, sibilans et ira plenus, ad pugnam se paravit.

"Apophis, today I will put an end to your evil!" Ra shouted, with his light flashing. Apophis, hissing and full of rage, prepared for battle.

Dei comitantes, Ra adiuvantes, in proelium se intulerunt. "Tecum sumus, Ra!" Thoth, deus sapientiae, exclamavit, magias adhibens ut Ra auxilium ferret.

The accompanying gods, aiding Ra, joined the battle. "We are with you, Ra!" Thoth, the god of wisdom, exclaimed, using magic to assist Ra.

Ra, solis potestate usus, tenebras dispellere conatus est. "Luce mea, tenebras fugabo!" Ra, lumine intensissimo emisso, pronuntiavit.

Ra, using the power of the sun, tried to drive away the darkness. "With my light, I will banish the darkness!" Ra declared, emitting an intense light.

Ad quamque portam perveniens, Ra nomen secretum pronuntiare debebat. "Verba potentiae, me admittere," Ra, ad portas mysticas accedens, susurravit. Nomina arcana a sacerdotibus custodita et viva voce tradita sunt.

At each gate he reached, Ra had to pronounce a secret name. "Words of power, admit me," Ra whispered as he approached the mystical gates. The secret names were guarded by the priests and passed down orally.

Monstra inferi, Ra audaciam probantia, in itinere eius obstabant. "Me non terrebis, creaturae inferi!" Ra, contra monstra pugnans, dixit.

The monsters of the underworld, testing Ra's courage, blocked his path. "You will not scare me, creatures of the underworld!" Ra said, fighting against the monsters.

In itinere, animas errantes et perditas sanabat. "Pace fruere, anima," Ra, misericordia motus, ad umbras locutus est.

During his journey, he healed the lost and wandering souls. "Rest in peace, soul," Ra, moved by compassion, said to the shadows.

Iter longum et plenum periculis erat, sed Ra, indefessus et fortis, pergebat. "Non deficiam, dum lux superat tenebras," Ra, animo confirmato, monebat.

The journey was long and full of dangers, but Ra, tireless and strong, continued onward. "I will not falter, as long as light triumphs over darkness," Ra, with a determined spirit, declared.

Cantus sacerdotum, in mundo vivorum resonantes, Ra sustentabant. "O Ra, vires tibi damus!" sacerdotes, sacra cantilena peragentes, clamabant.

The chants of the priests, resonating in the world of the living, supported Ra. "O Ra, we give you strength!" the priests cried out as they performed sacred chants.

Ra, in infero mundo iustorum animabus lucem afferebat. "Hæc lux vobis est signum spei," Ra, ad iustas animas loquens, pronuntiavit.

In the underworld, Ra brought light to the souls of the righteous. "This light is a sign of hope for you," Ra said, speaking to the just souls.

Animae malae, luce Ra superatae, fugiebant. "A mea luce recedite, spiritus obscuri!" Ra, contra umbras malas, exclamavit.

The wicked souls, overcome by Ra's light, fled. "Depart from my light, dark spirits!" Ra shouted against the evil shadows.

Ra semper docebat iustitiam et veritatem victores esse. "In fine, iustitia et veritas praevalent," Ra, doctrinam suam prædicans, affirmavit.

Ra always taught that justice and truth would prevail. "In the end, justice and truth will triumph," Ra affirmed, preaching his doctrine.

Daemonibus magia Ra superatis, ultimum concessum est. "Tua magia nos superavit, Ra," daemones, victi, susurraverunt.

With the demons defeated by Ra's magic, the final obstacle was overcome. "Your magic has defeated us, Ra," the vanquished demons whispered.

Cum ultima porta aderat, Ra, auroram nuntians, ad finem itineris sui appropinquabat. "Ecce, aurora prope est, et meum iter finit," Ra, ultimam portam transiens, dixit.

When the final gate appeared, Ra, heralding the dawn, was approaching the end of his journey. "Behold, the dawn is near, and my journey is ending," Ra said, passing through the final gate.

Sic Ra, per inferos iter faciens, non solum mundum subterraneum purgavit sed etiam animabus iustis lucem et spem attulit, aeternam luctam inter lucem et tenebras iterum superans.

Thus, as Ra journeyed through the underworld, he not only purified the subterranean world but also brought light and hope to the righteous souls, once again triumphing in the eternal struggle between light and darkness.

Reditus Solis

Cum primum lumen aurorae in caelo apparuit, Ra, victoriosus et gloriosus, ex mundo infero emersit. Totus mundus, lucis et caloris reditum celebrans, in novum diem gratulabatur.

As the first light of dawn appeared in the sky, Ra, victorious and glorious, emerged from the underworld. The whole world, celebrating the return of light and warmth, rejoiced in the new day.

"Gratias tibi, Ra, pro tutela et luce renovata!" Aegyptii, ad templa convenientes, deo soli gratias agebant. Orationes et sacrificia ut immensum gratiae signum offerebantur.

"Thank you, Ra, for your protection and renewed light!" The Egyptians, gathering at the temples, gave thanks to the sun god. Prayers and sacrifices were offered as a great sign of gratitude.

Ciclus mortis et renascentiae Ra, aeternitatis symbolon, mentes Aegyptiorum implebat. "Per Ra, aeternitas et vita iterum affirmantur," sacerdos, ad altare stans, populo praedicavit.

The cycle of Ra's death and rebirth, a symbol of eternity, filled the minds of the Egyptians. "Through Ra, eternity and life are reaffirmed," the priest preached to the people, standing at the altar.

Secreta mundi inferi, a Ra revelata, sacerdotibus sacra erant. "Haec arcana, a Ra nobis tradita, sapientiam nostram augent," sacerdos, discipulis suis secretum docens, explicavit.

The secrets of the underworld, revealed by Ra, were sacred to the priests. "These mysteries, given to us by Ra, increase our wisdom," the priest explained, teaching the secret to his disciples.

Leges Aegypti, iustitiae doctrina Ra inspiratae, in aequitate et veritate fundabantur. "Per exemplum Ra, leges nostrae iustitiam omnibus praestant," iudex, in foro loquens, affirmavit.

The laws of Egypt, inspired by Ra's teachings on justice, were founded on fairness and truth. "Through Ra's example, our laws ensure justice for all," a judge declared, speaking in the forum.

Artifices, ab itineribus Ra moti, nova opera creabant. "Hac pictura, Ra, solis deus, aeternum iter suum celebramus," pictor, opus suum demonstrans, dixit.

Artists, inspired by Ra's journeys, created new works. "With this painting, we celebrate Ra, the god of the sun, and his eternal journey," said the painter, showing his work.

Infantes, fortitudinis et perseverantiae fabulis Ra eruditi, magnanimitatem discebant. "Audite, pueri, de Ra et eius victoria contra chaos," magister, ad circulum discipulorum narrans, invitavit.

Children, taught by the stories of Ra's strength and perseverance, learned about greatness. "Listen, children, to the story of Ra and his victory over chaos," the teacher invited, narrating to his group of students.

Templa Ra, solis ortu illuminata, divinae praesentiae testimonia praebebant. "In hoc templo, Ra, solis deus, nos benedicat," sacerdos, ad congregatos orans, petivit.

The temples of Ra, illuminated by the rising sun, bore witness to divine presence. "In this temple, may Ra, the sun god, bless us," the priest prayed to the gathered crowd.

Pharaones, ut terrae Ra incarnationes, populi et deorum nexus repraesentabant. "Ut Ra in caelo, sic pharao in terra regnat," consiliarius, ad regem loquens, affirmavit.

Pharaohs, as incarnations of Ra on earth, represented the connection between the people and the gods. "As Ra reigns in the sky, so the pharaoh reigns on earth," the advisor declared, speaking to the king.

Fides Aegyptiorum in vita altera, per Ra iter confirmata, animos sustentabat. "Ra nobis viam ad aeternitatem monstrat," sacerdos, ad populum docens, confirmavit.

The Egyptians' faith in the afterlife, confirmed by Ra's journey, sustained their spirits. "Ra shows us the way to eternity," the priest affirmed, teaching the people.

Matutini ritus Ra redeuntem in caelum salutabant. "Hac luce, Ra, te in caelum redeuntem celebramus," chori, hymnos canentes, resonabant.

Morning rituals welcomed Ra's return to the sky. "With this light, we celebrate you, Ra, as you return to the heavens," the choirs resounded, singing hymns.

Iter Ra, quotidiana victoria super chaos, spem et securitatem Aegyptiis praestabat. "Per Ra, quotidie chaos superamus," philosophus, in schola disputans, docebat.

Ra's journey, a daily victory over chaos, provided hope and security to the Egyptians. "Through Ra, we conquer chaos every day," a philosopher taught, debating in the school.

Ra, ut protectio, in itineribus et novis inceptis invocatus, populum in omni via tuebatur. "Sub Ra protectione, secure ambulamus," mercator, ad viam inchoandam, deum invocabat.

Ra, invoked as a protector on journeys and new ventures, guarded the people in all their paths. "Under Ra's protection, we walk safely," a merchant invoked the god before starting his journey.

Sic Ra, solis deus, Aegyptum numquam desinit custodire, promittens novum diem et aeternam lucem contra tenebras et chaos, Aegyptiorum corda spe et gratitudine implens.

Thus Ra, the sun god, never ceases to watch over Egypt, promising a new day and eternal light against darkness and chaos, filling the hearts of the Egyptians with hope and gratitude.

Narratio Duorum Fratrum

Discessio

Olim in Aegypto, duo fratres, Anubis maior et Bata minor, vivebant. Anubis, frater providus et custos, iuvenem fratrem suum protegebat.

Once in Egypt, two brothers, Anubis the elder and Bata the younger, lived. Anubis, a careful and protective brother, guarded his younger sibling.

Bata, pro sua virtute et audacia laudatus, una cum Anubi in agris laborabat, vitam cotidianam communicans. "Una fortes sumus," Anubis ad Batam dixit, operam dantes.

Bata, praised for his bravery and courage, worked in the fields alongside Anubis, sharing everyday life. "Together we are strong," Anubis said to Bata as they worked.

Quadam die, uxor Anubis Batam seducere conata est. Bata, tamen, invitationem repudiavit. "Hoc non fieri potest," Bata, recusans, respondit.

One day, Anubis's wife attempted to seduce Bata. However, Bata refused the invitation. "This cannot happen," Bata said, rejecting her.

Bata, fide plenus, ad Anubim confugit, sed uxor Anubis, mendacium texens, Batam accusavit. Anubis, ira et dolore captus, fratrem occidere statuit.

Filled with faith, Bata fled to Anubis, but Anubis's wife, weaving a lie, accused Bata. Anubis, overcome with anger and pain, decided to kill his brother.

"Bata, cur me prodidisti?" Anubis, iratus, exclamavit. Bata, veritatem defendens, in fugam vertit, divinum auxilium implorans.

"Bata, why did you betray me?" Anubis exclaimed angrily. Bata, defending the truth, fled, imploring divine help.

Dei, fratrum discordiam videntes, fluvium crocodilis plenum inter eos creaverunt ut Batam tuerentur. "Hoc flumen me proteget," Bata, gratias agens, dixit.

The gods, seeing the discord between the brothers, created a crocodile-filled river between them to protect Bata. "This river will protect me," Bata said, giving thanks.

Bata, promittens se unum diem reversurum, in Vallem Cedrorum secessit, novam vitam solus incipiens. "In hac valle, novum initium faciam," Bata, sibi pollicitus, constituit.

Bata, promising that he would one day return, retreated to the Valley of the Cedars, beginning a new life alone. "In this valley, I will make a new beginning," Bata vowed to himself.

Bata, divinum signum si in periculo esset petens, deis supplicavit. Dei, Batae precibus commoti, ei potestatem magicam dederunt.

Bata, seeking a divine sign if he were in danger, prayed to the gods. Moved by Bata's prayers, the gods gave him magical power.

Bata, cor suum excidens, in cedro condidit, vitam suam arbori ligans. "Dum hoc cor in arbore manet, vivam," Bata, sacrum perficiens, susurravit.

Bata, cutting out his heart, placed it in a cedar tree, binding his life to the tree. "As long as this heart remains in the tree, I will live," Bata whispered, completing the ritual.

Sic incipit tristis narratio duorum fratrum, Anubis et Bata, quorum vita et amor fraternus probantur, divinis machinationibus et humanis affectibus intertexti.

Thus begins the sad tale of two brothers, Anubis and Bata, whose lives and brotherly love are tested, woven with divine schemes and human emotions.

Tentatio et Renascentia

Anubis, paenitentia plenus, fraternam reconciliationem quaerit. "Quomodo fratrem meum offendere potui?" Anubis, corde fracto, sibi quaerebat.

Anubis, filled with remorse, seeks reconciliation with his brother. "How could I have wronged my brother?" Anubis, with a broken heart, asked himself.

Interea, uxor Anubis, secretum Batae cognoscens, cedrum, vitae eius nexum, delere statuit. "Hac arbori finem imponam," illa, consilium nefarium molita, susurravit.

Meanwhile, Anubis's wife, learning of Bata's secret, decided to destroy the cedar, the link to his life. "I will put an end to this tree," she whispered, plotting her wicked scheme.

Anubis, veritate revelata, uxorem pro mendaciis punit. "Tua falsitas hoc pretium habet," Anubis, iustitia motus, decrevit.

Anubis, after discovering the truth, punished his wife for her lies. "Your deceit comes at this cost," Anubis declared, driven by justice.

Bata, cedri interitu debilitatus, moritur, sed eius magia vitam novam affert. "Etsi cado, iterum surgam," Bata, in novam formam renatus, spem tenuit.

Bata, weakened by the destruction of the cedar, died, but his magic brought him new life. "Though I fall, I will rise again," Bata, reborn into a new form, held onto hope.

Nova specie, Bata in Aegyptum redit, Anubim requiriturus. "Frater meusne es?" Anubis, Batam non agnoscens, interrogavit.

In a new form, Bata returned to Egypt, seeking Anubis. "Are you my brother?" Anubis, not recognising Bata, asked.

Amicitia inter eos cito reflorescit, et Bata, signo magico, veram identitatem revelat. "Ego sum Bata, tuus frater," Bata, miraculum demonstrans, Anubi revelavit.

Friendship between them quickly blossomed again, and Bata, with a magical sign, revealed his true identity. "I am Bata, your brother," Bata revealed to Anubis, demonstrating a miracle.

Fratres, post revelationem, reconciliantur et fidem aeternam sibi iurant. "Numquam rursus divellamur," Anubis, Bata amplexus, promisit.

The brothers, after the revelation, reconciled and swore eternal loyalty to each other. "We shall never be separated again," Anubis, embracing Bata, promised.

Bata, principem ducens uxorem, vir potens et honoratus evadit. "Tecum, Aegypti fortunas augebo," Bata, sponsam suam aspiciens, affirmavit.

Bata, marrying a princess, became a powerful and honoured man. "With you, I will increase Egypt's fortunes," Bata declared, looking at his bride.

Una, Anubis et Bata, patriae bono laborant. "Manu in manu, Aegyptum defendemus," Bata, consilia cum Anubi partiens, dixit.

Together, Anubis and Bata worked for the good of their homeland. "Hand in hand, we will defend Egypt," Bata said, sharing plans with Anubis.

Rex Aegypti, Batae virtute atque sapientia captus, ei locum eminentem in regno offert. "Tua praestantia regno nostro inserviat," rex, Batam honorans, decrevit.

The king of Egypt, impressed by Bata's virtue and wisdom, offered him a high position in the kingdom. "May your excellence serve our kingdom," the king decreed, honouring Bata.

Fratres Aegyptum contra invasiones et fames tutantur. "Nos, custodes huius terrae, sumus," Anubis, ad Batam stans, dixit.

The brothers protected Egypt against invasions and famine. "We are the guardians of this land," Anubis said, standing beside Bata.

Di, pro eorum fidelitate et virtute, Anubim et Batam benedicunt. "Vestra acta laudamus," di, super eos aspicientes, pronuntiaverunt.

The gods, for their loyalty and virtue, blessed Anubis and Bata. "We praise your deeds," the gods declared, looking down upon them.

Ita, fabula duorum fratrum, Anubis et Bata, per saecula transmittitur, exemplar fraternitatis, redemptionis, et constantiae praebens. "Haec narratio, per generationes docebitur," sacerdos, ad iuvenes loquens, confirmavit.

Thus, the tale of the two brothers, Anubis and Bata, is passed down through the ages, offering an example of brotherhood, redemption, and perseverance. "This story will be taught for generations," the priest affirmed, speaking to the young.

Hereditas Fraterna

Tempore progresso, Anubis et Bata in Aegypti mythologia heroas legendarios evaserunt. "Eorum fabula exemplar fraternitatis et redemptionis est," magister ad discipulos narravit.

As time passed, Anubis and Bata became legendary heroes in Egyptian mythology. "Their story is an example of brotherhood and redemption," the teacher told the students.

In honorem duorum fratrum, templa magnifica exstructa sunt. "Hic locus sacro Anubi et Batae cultui dicatus est," sacerdos, templum ingressus, explicavit.

Magnificent temples were built in honour of the two brothers. "This place is dedicated to the sacred worship of Anubis and Bata," the priest explained, entering the temple.

Pueri et puellae, eorum historia audita, veritatis iustitiaeque momenta discunt. "Haec fabula vos docet semper ad veritatem et iustitiam aspirare," paedagogus in schola dixit.

Boys and girls, hearing their story, learn the importance of truth and justice. "This tale teaches you always to aspire to truth and justice," the teacher said in school.

Artifices, ab eorum gestis inspirati, novas artes creaverunt. "Per hoc opus, Anubis et Batae gestas celebro," pictor, tabulam pingens, affirmavit.

Artists, inspired by their deeds, created new works. "Through this piece, I celebrate the deeds of Anubis and Bata," the painter affirmed, as he worked on his painting.

Festivitates ad eorum memoriam reconciliatam celebrantur. "Hodie, fraternam Anubi et Batae concordiam laetamur," civis, festo participans, exclamavit.

Festivals are held to celebrate their reconciled memory. "Today, we rejoice in the brotherly harmony of Anubis and Bata," a citizen exclaimed, participating in the festival.

Sacerdotes, in sacris caerimoniis, duorum fratrum historiam enarrant. "Per hanc narrationem, divinam fraternitatem commemoramus," sacerdos, ad altare stans, praedicavit.

Priests, during sacred ceremonies, recount the story of the two brothers. "Through this tale, we commemorate divine brotherhood," the priest preached, standing at the altar.

Amuleta, quae Anubim et Batam repraesentant, ad tutelam geruntur. "Hoc amuletum nos a periculis defendat," fidelis, amuletum manu tenens, oravit.

Amulets representing Anubis and Bata are worn for protection. "May this amulet defend us from danger," the devotee prayed, holding the amulet in their hand.

Eruditi, eorum contum perscrutantes, morales lectiones eliciunt. "Ex hac fabula, multa de vita et moribus discere possumus," doctus in academia disputavit.

Scholars, studying their tale closely, draw moral lessons. "From this story, we can learn much about life and character," a learned scholar argued in the academy.

Exploratores, Vallis Cedrorum vestigia quaerentes, spem habent Batae praesentiam invenire. "Forsitan hic, Batae vestigia reperire possimus," explorator, in vallem ingressus, dixit.

Explorers, searching for traces of the Valley of the Cedars, hope to find Bata's presence. "Perhaps here, we may discover Bata's footprints," an explorer said, entering the valley.

Fabulae theatricae, duorum fratrum acta narrantes, audientiam delectant. "Per hanc scenam, Anubis et Batae spiritum reviviscimus," actor, in scaena stans, pronuntiavit.

Theatrical plays, telling the deeds of the two brothers, delight the audience. "Through this scene, we revive the spirit of Anubis and Bata," an actor declared, standing on stage.

Carmine, fraternitatis et sacrificii laudes celebrantur. "Hoc poëmate, Anubis et Batae fidelitatem canimus," poëta, carmen recitans, dixit.

In song, praises of brotherhood and sacrifice are celebrated. "In this poem, we sing of the loyalty of Anubis and Bata," the poet said, reciting the verse.

Ut protectores familiarum et fraternitatum, Anubis et Bata venerantur. "Sub eorum protectione, nostra familia tutamur," paterfamilias, prece familiari, dixit.

As protectors of families and brotherhoods, Anubis and Bata are revered. "Under their protection, we safeguard our family," the head of the family said in prayer.

Eorum legenda, per totam Aegyptum, audaciam et fidem inspirat. "Eorum exemplum nos ad meliores actus hortatur," iuvenis, ad monumentum fratrum stans, cogitavit.

Their legend, throughout all of Egypt, inspires courage and faith. "Their example urges us to greater deeds," a young man thought, standing by the brothers' monument.

Ita, duorum fratrum fabula, culturae et spiritualitatis Aegyptiae fundamentum, aeternas fraternitatis, iustitiae, et fortitudinis valores docet, perpetuo in cordibus Aegyptiorum vivens.

Thus, the tale of the two brothers, a foundation of Egyptian culture and spirituality, teaches eternal values of brotherhood, justice, and strength, living on forever in the hearts of the Egyptians.

Isis et Septem Scorpii

Fuga Isis

Isis, magiae dea, a persecutoribus mariti sui Osiridis fugit. Filius eius, Horus, ab ea occultatus est ut tutaretur. Septem scorpii protectores, Tefen, Befen, Mestet, Mestetef, Petet, Theteth, et Setet nomine, eam comitabantur. Unusquisque scorpii potestatem unicam ad Isidem et Horum protegendos habebat.

Isis, the goddess of magic, fled from the persecutors of her husband Osiris. Her son, Horus, was hidden by her to be protected. Seven protective scorpions, named Tefen, Befen, Mestet, Mestetef, Petet, Theteth, and Setet, accompanied her. Each scorpion had a unique power to protect Isis and Horus.

Per Aegyptum, dea et custodes eius clam iter faciebant, variis hominibus occurrentes, quidam benigni, alii metuentes. Nocte quadam, in urbe perfugium quaerebant, sed a divite femina repulsi sunt. Paupera sola eos hospitio accepit.

Throughout Egypt, the goddess and her protectors traveled in secret, meeting various people—some kind, others fearful. One night, they sought refuge in a city but were turned away by a wealthy woman. Only a poor woman offered them shelter.

Scorpiones, ira commoti, divitem feminam punire decreverunt. Venenum suum combinarunt ut ictum letalem crearent. Tefen, potentissimus, ad perficiendum consilium electus est. Femina divitis, ictu affecta, graviter aegrotavit.

The scorpions, angered, decided to punish the wealthy woman. They combined their venom to create a deadly sting. Tefen, the most powerful, was chosen to carry out the plan. The rich woman, struck by the sting, became gravely ill.

Isis, hoc cognoscens, intervenire decidit. Magia sua, feminam sanavit, magnanimitatem suam demonstrans. "Etsi iniuria facta est, tamen misericordia praevalebit," Isis, divina voce, dixit.

Isis, upon learning of this, decided to intervene. Using her magic, she healed the woman, demonstrating her magnanimity.

"Though harm was done, mercy shall prevail," Isis said in her divine voice.

Ita incipit fabula de Iside et septem scorpionibus, narratio de fuga, protectione, et potestate sanandi, quae pericula et inimicitias superat, misericordiae et magiae virtutem ostendens.

Thus begins the tale of Isis and the seven scorpions, a story of flight, protection, and the power of healing, which overcomes dangers and enmity, showing the strength of mercy and magic.

Virtus Sanandi

Sanatio mulieris ab Iside facta famam eius late diffundit. Homines, potentiam eius admirantes, eam simul venerantur et timent. "Isis, tua virtute nos omnes salvasti," populus, gratus, exclamat.

The healing of the woman by Isis spread her fame far and wide. People, admiring her power, both revered and feared her. "Isis, you have saved us all with your power," the grateful people exclaimed.

Isis, misericordiam et iustitiam docens, exemplar virtutis praebet. "Per compassionem et aequitatem, veram sapientiam invenire potestis," Isis, ad homines loquens, suadet.

Isis, teaching mercy and justice, sets an example of virtue. "Through compassion and fairness, you can find true wisdom," Isis urged, speaking to the people.

Scorpiones, fideles custodes, Isidem et Horum in itinere suo protegunt. "Sub nostra custodia, tuti eritis," scorpiones, circa deam et filium eius congregati, affirmant.

The scorpions, faithful protectors, guarded Isis and Horus on their journey. "Under our protection, you will be safe," the scorpions, gathered around the goddess and her son, affirmed.

Isis, arcanis magiae utens, indigentibus opem fert. "Magia mea ad auxilium vocatur," Isis, manus extendens, sanationem operatur.

Isis, using her mystical magic, offers help to those in need. "My magic is called upon to aid," Isis said, extending her hands to perform healing.

Tandem, Isis et Horus locum tutum inveniunt ubi habitare possunt. "Hic, in pace vivemus," Isis, novam domum inspectans, dicit.

At last, Isis and Horus found a safe place to live. "Here, we will live in peace," Isis said, inspecting their new home.

Isis amuleta creare incipit, quae gestantes contra scorpii ictus tutantur. "Haec amuleta vos in salute conservabunt," Isis, amuleta fabricans, promittit.

Isis began to create amulets that protected those who wore them from scorpion stings. "These amulets will keep you safe," Isis promised, as she crafted the amulets.

Amuleta cito apud Aegyptios populares fiunt. "Per haec amuleta, Isis nos protegit," civis, amuletum gestans, gaudet.

The amulets quickly became popular among the Egyptians. "Through these amulets, Isis protects us," a citizen rejoiced, wearing the amulet.

Scorpiones, ob eorum protectionem, magni fiunt et coluntur. "Scorpiones nostri protectores sunt," puer, ad scorpionem parvum spectans, miratur.

The scorpions, for their protection, became revered and honoured. "The scorpions are our protectors," a young boy marvelled, looking at a small scorpion.

Isis, docens ut plantae medicinales adhibeantur, scientiam suam communicat. "Hae plantae vobis salutem ferent," Isis, herbas demonstrans, erudit.

Isis, teaching how to use medicinal plants, shared her knowledge. "These plants will bring you health," Isis instructed, showing the herbs.

Perseverans, Isis eos qui morbis vel morsibus affliguntur, sanat. "Tua infirmitas mea magia sanabitur," Isis, aegrotum curans, susurrat.

Persevering, Isis healed those afflicted by illness or bites. "Your sickness will be healed by my magic," Isis whispered, tending to the sick.

Nexus inter Isidem et septem scorpiones symbolon protectionis efficitur. "Una, invincibiles sumus," Isis, ad scorpiones suos spectans, affirmat.

The bond between Isis and the seven scorpions became a symbol of protection. "Together, we are invincible," Isis affirmed, looking at her scorpions.

Fabulae de Iside et scorpiis per Aegyptum diffunduntur, eorum gesta celebrantes. "Isis et scorpiones eius magnam virtutem nobis ostendunt," narratores, historias populis narrantes, dicunt.

Tales of Isis and the scorpions spread throughout Egypt, celebrating their deeds. "Isis and her scorpions show us great virtue," storytellers said, recounting the tales to the people.

Templa Isidi dedicata eriguntur, ubi homines ad sanitatem et protectionem petendam conveniunt. "In hoc templo, a Iside benedicimur," fidelis, ad templum accedens, orat.

Temples dedicated to Isis were built, where people gathered to seek health and protection. "In this temple, we are blessed by Isis," a devotee prayed, approaching the temple.

Isis et Horus, in tranquillitate viventes, sciunt se vitas multorum mutavisse. "Per nostra facta, mundum meliorem fecimus," Isis, ad Horum spectans, cum gaudio loquitur.

Isis and Horus, living in tranquillity, knew they had changed many lives. "Through our deeds, we have made the world better," Isis said with joy, looking at Horus.

Sic fabula Isidis et potestatis sanationis non solum de magia et miraculis narrat sed etiam de amore, custodia, et communitatis virtute docet, aeternas virtutes quae adhuc Aegyptiis et omnibus hominibus carae sunt.

Thus, the tale of Isis and her power of healing speaks not only of magic and miracles but also of love, guardianship, and the strength of community, eternal virtues that are still dear to the Egyptians and all people.

Hereditas Isis

Historia de Iside et septem scorpionibus in legendam vertitur. Sacerdotes sacerdotaeque Isidis praecepta eius persequuntur, eius vias sanandi et protegendi docentes.

The story of Isis and the seven scorpions becomes a legend. The priests and priestesses of Isis follow her teachings, instructing others in her ways of healing and protection.

"Festivitates in honorem Isis, benignae deae, agimus," sacerdos populo congregato annuntiat, diem festum celebrans. Artifices, inspiratione accepta, imagines Isidis scorpionibus circumdatae creant, ostendentes eius potentiam et protectionem.

"We hold festivals in honour of Isis, the kind goddess," the priest announces to the gathered people, celebrating the feast day. Artists, inspired by this, create images of Isis surrounded by scorpions, showing her power and protection.

"Pueri puellaeque, audite fabulas de Iside et scorpionibus, quae virtutem et misericordiam docent," magister ad discipulos suos narrat, historiam tradens. Nomina scorpionum memorantur, una cum singulorum virtutibus, ut exempla fortitudinis et fidei.

"Boys and girls, listen to the tales of Isis and the scorpions, which teach virtue and mercy," the teacher tells his students, passing on the story. The names of the scorpions are remembered, along with their individual virtues, as examples of strength and loyalty.

"Per vias longinquas ambulantes, amuleta Isidis gestamus, ut nos tueantur," viator, amuletum collo gerens, dicit, securitatem in

itinere quaerens. Medicus, remedia parans, Isidis auxilium invocat, "O Isis, da nobis scientiam ad sanandum," preces effundens.

"Walking along distant roads, we wear the amulets of Isis to protect us," says a traveller, wearing an amulet around his neck, seeking safety on his journey. A physician, preparing remedies, invokes the help of Isis, "O Isis, grant us the knowledge to heal," he prays.

Scorpiones, olim timore visi, nunc ut protectores venerantur. "Hi scorpiones, qui Isidem tuebantur, nunc nobis auxilium ferunt," incola, scorpionem in via videns, reflectit.

Scorpions, once feared, are now revered as protectors. "These scorpions, who protected Isis, now bring us aid," reflects a local, seeing a scorpion on the road.

In sanctuariis Isidis, homines salutem et solacium quaerunt. "Hic, in templo Isidis, curatio et pacem invenimus," aegrotus, ad altare accedens, confitetur. Rituum sollemnitas, Isidis et scorpionum memoriam celebrans, in praxi religiosa integratur.

In the sanctuaries of Isis, people seek health and solace. "Here, in the temple of Isis, we find healing and peace," confesses a sick man, approaching the altar. The solemn rituals, celebrating the memory of Isis and the scorpions, are integrated into religious practice.

"Doctrina Isis de cura et tutela per generationes traditur," sacerdos, adulescentibus praecepta tradens, docet. Fabulae de Iside homines adiuvant ut metus superent et virtutem internam inveniant.

"The teachings of Isis about care and protection are passed down through generations," a priest teaches, passing on the precepts to the young. The stories of Isis help people to overcome fear and find inner strength.

"In Iside, magiae, sanationis, et protectionis dea, fiduciam et amorem ponimus," mulier, in oratione, exprimit. Isis, ut magica sanatrix, in arte, litteris, et quotidiana vita celebratur.

"In Isis, the goddess of magic, healing, and protection, we place our trust and love," a woman expresses in prayer. Isis, as a magical healer, is celebrated in art, literature, and everyday life.

Ita, narratio de Iside et septem scorpionibus, eius benignitate et potentia testificans, aeternus hereditatis thesaurus manet, praecepta amoris fraterni, iustitiae, et resistentiae docens.

Thus, the story of Isis and the seven scorpions, bearing witness to her kindness and power, remains an eternal treasure of heritage, teaching the lessons of brotherly love, justice, and resilience.

Thoth et Luna

Certamen Caelestis

In aethere nocturno, Thoth, deus sapientiae et magiae, stellas et lunam contemplatur. Luna, mysterii et luminis fons, clare in caelo nocturno splendet. Subito, inter deos contentio oritur de dominatu lunae. Quidam deorum, potentiam lunae cupientes, inter se disputant. Thoth, semper sapiens, ad controversiam solvendam accedit.

In the night sky, Thoth, the god of wisdom and magic, gazes at the stars and the moon. The moon, a source of mystery and light, shines brightly in the night sky. Suddenly, a dispute arises among the gods over the dominion of the moon. Some gods, desiring the power of the moon, argue amongst themselves. Thoth, ever wise, approaches to resolve the controversy.

"Cur non," inquit Thoth, "certamina constituimus ut verus dominus lunae eligatur?" Propositum eius sapientem omnes deos movet. Decernuntur igitur certamina, quae ingenium, fortitudinem, et astutiam deorum probant. Thoth, sua calliditate, omnes provocationes superat.

"Why don't we," said Thoth, "establish competitions to choose the true ruler of the moon?" His wise suggestion impresses all the gods. Thus, competitions are decided, testing the intellect, strength, and cunning of the gods. Thoth, with his cleverness, overcomes all the challenges.

Ceteri dei, eius ingenio atque sapientia commoti, ei ius regendi lunam concedunt. Thoth, potestate sua utens, cyclis lunae influere incipit. Calendarium, quod lunae phasibus innititur, creat, quo Aegyptii tempus metiri incipiunt.

The other gods, moved by his intellect and wisdom, grant him the right to rule the moon. Thoth, using his power, begins to influence the cycles of the moon. He creates a calendar based on the phases of the moon, by which the Egyptians start to measure time.

Homines de importancia lunae in vitis suis docet, lunaque sapientiae et renovationis symbolum fit. In honorem Thoth et lunae, templa aedificantur.

He teaches people about the importance of the moon in their lives, and the moon becomes a symbol of wisdom and renewal. Temples are built in honour of Thoth and the moon.

In hac nova era, Thoth, nunc lunae dominus, noctibus praesidet. Luna luce sua viatores errantes ducit, agricolae lunares cyclis secundum seminant et metunt.

In this new era, Thoth, now the lord of the moon, presides over the nights. The moon, with its light, guides wandering travellers, and farmers plant and harvest according to the lunar cycles.

Thoth amuleta lunaria ad nocturnam tutelam fabricat. Sub lumine lunae, poetae et artifices inspirationem inveniunt, et Thoth lites solvit.

Thoth crafts lunar amulets for protection at night. Under the moonlight, poets and artists find inspiration, and Thoth settles disputes.

Preces ad Thoth in plenilunio potentiores habentur, festa lunaria sapientiam et magiam eius celebrant. Secreta nocturna revelat, sanatoresque lunae energia ad remedia confirmanda utuntur.

Prayers to Thoth during the full moon are considered more powerful, and lunar festivals celebrate his wisdom and magic. He reveals the secrets of the night, and healers use the moon's energy to strengthen their remedies.

Somnia plenilunio Thoth adiuvante interpretantur, et Thoth naturae respectum docet. Nautae lunae lumine navigant, amantes sub ea vota faciunt, lunaque spem et renascentiam symbolizat.

Dreams during the full moon are interpreted with Thoth's guidance, and Thoth teaches respect for nature. Sailors navigate by the moon's light, lovers make vows beneath it, and the moon symbolizes hope and renewal.

Cultus Thoth et lunae diffunditur, scribae et eruditi Thoth patronum venerantur, calendarii lunares in vita cotidiana essentiales fiunt. Fabulae de Thoth et luna generationes inspirant, templa lunaria scientiae et magiae centra evadunt.

The cult of Thoth and the moon spreads, scribes and scholars revere Thoth as their patron, and lunar calendars become essential in daily life. Tales of Thoth and the moon inspire generations, and lunar temples become centres of knowledge and magic.

Astronomi in honorem Thoth caelum nocturnum scrutantur, ritus lunares ad Thoth invocandum fiunt. Horti templorum secundum lunares cycli plantantur, festa lunaria communitates ad celebrationem congregant.

Astronomers study the night sky in honour of Thoth, and lunar rituals are performed to invoke him. Temple gardens are planted according to lunar cycles, and lunar festivals bring communities together in celebration.

Preces ad Thoth sapientiam, directionem, claritatemque petunt. Exploratio mysteriorum lunae pergit, et historiae Thoth aequilibrium harmoniamque docent.

Prayers to Thoth seek wisdom, guidance, and clarity. The exploration of the moon's mysteries continues, and the stories of Thoth teach balance and harmony.

Luna potentem scientiae et mutationis symbolum manet, Thoth et luna in mythologia Aegyptia aeternum coniuncti, humanitatem per tenebras ad scientiae lucem ducunt.

The moon remains a powerful symbol of knowledge and change, and Thoth and the moon, eternally linked in Egyptian mythology, guide humanity through darkness to the light of wisdom.

Lunae Benedictiones

Sub regno Thoth, deus lunae, noctes tutantur. Luna, viatorum dux, errantes ad destinatum ducit. "Luce tua," Thoth ad lunam dicit, "homines per tenebras viam inveniant."

Under the reign of Thoth, god of the moon, the nights are protected. The moon, a guide for travellers, leads wanderers to their destination. "By your light," Thoth says to the moon, "let people find their way through the darkness."

Agricultores, lunae cyclis sequentes, tempora sementis et messis cognoscunt. Ad pericula nocturna arcenda, Thoth amuleta lunaria creat. "Hae res," inquit, "vos noctu tuebuntur."

Farmers, following the lunar cycles, know the times for planting and harvest. To ward off the dangers of the night, Thoth creates lunar amulets. "These items," he says, "will protect you during the night."

Poetae et artifices, lunae pulchritudine capti, nova opera concipiunt. "O luna," poeta exclamat, "tu inspirationis fons es!" Thoth, intercedens in litibus sub luna ortis, concordiam restituit. "In lumine tuo," Thoth ad homines dicit, "veritas et concordia reperiuntur."

Poets and artists, captivated by the beauty of the moon, conceive new works. "O moon," exclaims the poet, "you are a source of inspiration!" Thoth, intervening in disputes that arise under the moon, restores harmony. "In your light," Thoth says to the people, "truth and harmony are found."

In plenilunio, preces ad Thoth potentiores feruntur. Festivitates lunares, sapientiam et magiam Thoth celebrantes, per totam terram fiunt. "Hac nocte," sacerdos populum adhortatur, "Thoth magis propinquus est."

During the full moon, prayers to Thoth are more powerful. Lunar festivals, celebrating the wisdom and magic of Thoth, take place across the land. "Tonight," the priest urges the people, "Thoth is closer."

In obscuritate, Thoth arcana revelat. "Nihil," inquit, "in tenebris abscondi potest." Guerissores, lunae energia utentes, remedia potentiora conficiunt. "Luna," medicus ait, "vires nostras auget."

In darkness, Thoth reveals secrets. "Nothing," he says, "can be hidden in the dark." Healers, using the energy of the moon, prepare more potent remedies. "The moon," says the healer, "increases our strength."

Somnia, plenilunio Thoth auxiliante, interpretantur. "Per somnia," Thoth explicat, "mens humana nobiscum loquitur." Naturae respectum docens, Thoth homines ad harmoniam cum universo hortatur.

Dreams are interpreted with Thoth's assistance during the full moon. "Through dreams," Thoth explains, "the human mind speaks with us." Teaching respect for nature, Thoth encourages people to live in harmony with the universe.

Marinari, lunae lumine navigantes, tuta itinera per maria inveniunt. "Luna," nauta dicit, "nostra stella ducens est." Sub luna, amantes vota faciunt, spem et amoris aeternitatem promittentes. "In tua luce aeternum amorem invenio," amans ad amicam suam dicit.

Sailors, navigating by the light of the moon, find safe routes across the seas. "The moon," says the sailor, "is our guiding star." Under the moon, lovers make vows, promising hope and eternal love. "In your light, I find eternal love," the lover says to his beloved.

Luna, spes et renovationis symbolo evadens, in cordibus hominum locum tenet. "Luna," Thoth omnibus declarat, "vitae cursus et initium et finis est. Eius lumine, spes semper renovatur."

The moon, becoming a symbol of hope and renewal, holds a place in people's hearts. "The moon," Thoth declares to all, "is the cycle of life, both beginning and end. By its light, hope is always renewed."

Ita, sub Thoth regimine, luna non solum caeleste corpus, sed etiam vitae, amoris, et sapientiae fons fit. Templa Thoth et lunae dedicata, ubi homines ad preces et gratiarum actiones conveniunt, per Aegyptum eriguntur.

Thus, under Thoth's rule, the moon becomes not only a celestial body but also a source of life, love, and wisdom. Temples dedicated to Thoth and the moon, where people gather for prayers and thanksgiving, are built throughout Egypt.

Thoth, deus lunae, non modo noctes illuminat sed etiam corda hominum sapientia et magia replet.

Thoth, the god of the moon, not only lights up the night but also fills the hearts of people with wisdom and magic.

Sic finitur capitulum de lunae benedictionibus, in quo Thoth, magister sapientiae et lunae dominus, hominibus viam per tenebras ad lucem et scientiam monstrat.

Thus ends the chapter on the blessings of the moon, in which Thoth, master of wisdom and lord of the moon, shows people the way through darkness to light and knowledge.

Hereditas Lunaris

Tempore progresso, cultus Thoth et lunae per Aegyptum late diffunditur. Scribae eruditionem Thoth, magistri sapientiae, ut patronum colunt, eiusque in lunae dominatu fundamenta in vita quotidiana profundius insidunt.

As time passed, the cult of Thoth and the moon spread widely across Egypt. Scribes honoured the wisdom of Thoth, the master of knowledge, as their patron, and his dominion over the moon became deeply rooted in daily life.

Calendarii lunares, ad vitam agricolae et civitatis ordinandam necessarii, in usum veniunt. Narrationes de Thoth et luna, generationes novas ad sapientiam et imaginationem provocantes, per ora hominum vivae manent.

Lunar calendars, essential for organising the life of farmers and the city, came into use. Stories of Thoth and the moon, inspiring new generations towards wisdom and creativity, remained alive on people's lips.

In templis, quae lunae et Thoth dedicantur, magia et scientia florent. Pueri lunae phasium scientiam acquirunt, eorumque significatio in agris et mare navigando discitur. "Videte," praeceptor aliquando dicit, "quam lunae cursus nos in vita regat et adiuvet."

In the temples dedicated to the moon and Thoth, magic and knowledge flourished. Children learned about the phases of the moon, and its significance was understood in farming and sea navigation. "Look," a teacher might say, "how the course of the moon governs and helps us in life."

Astronomi, caelum nocte scrutantes, Thoth honorem dant, eiusque sapientiam in astris legere conantur. "Per lunam," inquiunt, "Thoth nos ad astra ducit, eiusque mysteria nobis paulatim revelat."

Astronomers, studying the night sky, honour Thoth and attempt to read his wisdom in the stars. "Through the moon," they say, "Thoth leads us to the stars, gradually revealing their mysteries to us."

In ritualibus lunae, Thoth invocatus, communitates protectionem et prosperitatem quaerunt. Horti templorum, lunaris cycli observantia plantati, ubertatem soli demonstrant. "Luna," sacerdos in ritu dicit, "nos in crescendo et renovando iuvat."

During lunar rituals, Thoth is invoked, and communities seek protection and prosperity. The temple gardens, planted in observance of the lunar cycle, demonstrate the fertility of the soil. "The moon," the priest says in the ritual, "helps us grow and renew."

Festivitates lunares, ubi communitas congregatur, Thoth laudem et gratitudinem exprimunt. Preces ad Thoth, pro sapientia, directione, et perspicuitate, feruntur, omnibus in plenilunio potentiores visae.

Lunar festivals, where the community gathers, express praise and gratitude to Thoth. Prayers to Thoth for wisdom, guidance, and clarity are offered, and are seen as more powerful during the full moon.

Mysteria lunae, semper nova, ad explorationem provocant. "Quid nobis luna," explorator noctis aliquis cogitat, "adhuc celare potest?"

The mysteries of the moon, ever new, provoke exploration. "What can the moon still be hiding from us?" a night explorer wonders.

Fabulae de Thoth, equilibrio et harmonia docentes, per aetates traduntur, lunae potentiam in mutatione et cognitione demonstrantes. "Thoth," magister ad discipulos suos dicit, "nos docet ut in vita et in universo harmoniam quaeramus."

Stories of Thoth, teaching balance and harmony, are passed down through the ages, demonstrating the moon's power in change and knowledge. "Thoth," the teacher says to his students, "teaches us to seek harmony in life and the universe."

Luna, symbolo potentis scientiae et mutationis, in corde Aegyptiae cultus manet, Thoth et luna, mythologiae Aegyptiae aeterno nexu coniuncti, humanitatem per tenebras ad scientiae lucem ducunt. "Per Thoth et lunam," sacerdos in templo loquitur, "a tenebris ad lucem, a ignorantia ad scientiam semper movemur."

The moon, as a symbol of powerful knowledge and transformation, remains at the heart of Egyptian culture. Thoth and the moon, eternally linked in Egyptian mythology, guide humanity through the darkness to the light of knowledge. "Through Thoth and the moon," the priest says in the temple, "we always move from darkness to light, from ignorance to wisdom."

Ita, hereditas Thoth et lunae, in Aegypti terra perpetuo vivit, generationes ad sapientiam, innovationem, et harmoniam cum natura ducens.

Thus, the legacy of Thoth and the moon lives on forever in the land of Egypt, guiding generations towards wisdom, innovation, and harmony with nature.

Hathor, Dea Gaudii

Adventus Hathoris

In caelo Aegypti, Hathor, dea amoris, pulchritudinis, musicaeque nascitur. Filia Solis, dei Ra, ubique gaudium et festivitatem ferens celebratur. Aegyptii templa in eius honorem aedificant, picturis et auro ornata. Hathor artem musicae saltationisque hominibus docet, saepe cornibus bovis et disco solari depicta.

In the sky of Egypt, Hathor, the goddess of love, beauty, and music, is born. Daughter of the Sun, the god Ra, she is celebrated everywhere, bringing joy and festivity. The Egyptians build temples in her honour, adorned with paintings and gold. Hathor teaches the art of music and dance to humans and is often depicted with cow horns and a solar disc.

Per Aegyptum iter faciens, amorem felicitatemque diffundit, mulieribus in amoris rebus adiuvandis et liberis protegendis. Festivitates Hathoris cantu saltationeque plenae sunt, eiusque carminibus magicis sanandi potestatem habent.

Travelling through Egypt, she spreads love and happiness, helping women in matters of love and protecting children. The festivals of Hathor are filled with song and dance, and her magical songs hold the power to heal.

Fossoribus et artificibus pro protectione veneratur, et formam bovis, maternitatis fertilitatisque symbolum, assumere potest. Peregrini templa eius ad benedictiones accipiendas visitant, et Hathor etiam ut dea occidentis, mortuos in alium mundum ducens, colitur. Celebritates eius honoris inter Aegyptios laetissimae sunt.

She is worshipped by miners and artisans for protection and can take the form of a cow, a symbol of motherhood and fertility. Travellers visit her temples to receive blessings, and Hathor is also honoured as the goddess of the west, guiding the dead into the afterlife. Celebrations in her honour are the most joyful among the Egyptians.

"O Hathor," mulier Aegyptia in templo orans dicit, "tuam benedictionem petimus, ut amor in vita nostra floreat et musicae tuae dulcedine corda nostra sanentur."

"O Hathor," says an Egyptian woman praying in the temple, "we seek your blessing, that love may flourish in our lives and our hearts may be healed by the sweetness of your music."

Hathor, benigna et misericors, respondet: "Meis donis gaudii, amoris, musicaeque utamini. In vestris festivitatibus, in artibus colendis, in quotidiana vita, semper praesens ero."

Hathor, kind and merciful, replies: "Use my gifts of joy, love, and music. In your festivals, in cultivating the arts, in your daily life, I will always be present."

Templa Hathoris, loca gaudii puraeque felicitatis, fiunt ubi homines artes discunt, deis orant, et in communitatibus suis festum agunt. "Per Hathor," sacerdos adstantibus pronuntiat, "discimus quod vita sine amore, sine musica, sine pulchritudine, non est vita plena."

The temples of Hathor become places of pure joy and happiness, where people learn the arts, pray to the gods, and celebrate in their communities. "Through Hathor," the priest announces to those present, "we learn that life without love, without music, without beauty, is not a full life."

Ita Hathor, per Aegyptum iter faciens, non solum dea amoris et musicae, sed etiam dea vitae plenae gaudiique efficitur. Eius cultus, ab antiquis temporibus usque ad hodiernum diem, lumina gaudii in tenebris mundi accendit, monens nos de potentia amoris, artis, et festivitatis in vita humana.

Thus, Hathor, travelling through Egypt, becomes not only the goddess of love and music but also the goddess of a life filled with joy. Her cult, from ancient times to the present day, lights the lamps of joy in the darkness of the world, reminding us of the power of love, art, and celebration in human life.

Praecepta Hathoris

Hathor, dea gaudii amorisque, non solum festivitatem sed etiam vitae cotidianae pulchritudinem docet. In templis et domibus vivunt eius praecepta, quae homines ad vitam pleniorem ducunt.

Hathor, the goddess of joy and love, teaches not only festivity but also the beauty of everyday life. Her teachings live in temples and homes, guiding people towards a fuller life.

"Pulchritudo in omnibus rebus est," Hathor discipulis suis dicit, "non solum in arte sed etiam in actis quotidie. Musica quoque animos potest lenire, tristitiam superare." Sub eius tutela, artifices et musici florent, opera magnifica creantes.

"Beauty is in all things," Hathor tells her students, "not only in art but also in everyday actions. Music too can soothe the soul, overcoming sadness." Under her guidance, artisans and musicians flourish, creating magnificent works.

Artifices, Hathoris inspiratione ducti, gemmas et artefacta pulchra fabricant. "Hathor nos docet," artifex quidam in officina sua loquitur, "ut in opere nostro amor et pulchritudo reflectantur." Musica per Aegyptum resonat, corda hominum ad gaudium movens.

Artisans, led by Hathor's inspiration, craft beautiful gems and artefacts. "Hathor teaches us," says an artisan in his workshop, "that love and beauty should be reflected in our work." Music echoes throughout Egypt, moving people's hearts towards joy.

Familiae, Hathoris monitu, amorem et unitatem colunt. "In amore familiae," mater filiis narrat, "Hathoris spiritus invenitur." Hathor etiam per vias mortis suaviter ducit, animas ad lucem aeternam comitans.

Families, guided by Hathor's teachings, cultivate love and unity. "In the love of family," a mother tells her children, "the spirit of Hathor is found." Hathor also gently guides through the paths of death, accompanying souls to eternal light.

"Mater expectans," inquit mulier gravida ante aram Hathoris, "tua praesentia partum facilem efficiat, quaeso." Hathor

respectum naturae omniumque viventium docet, festa communitatis vincula firmant.

"Expecting mother," says a pregnant woman before Hathor's altar, "may your presence make the birth easy, I pray." Hathor teaches respect for nature and all living things, and festivals strengthen the bonds of community.

"Hathor, civilisationis ductrix," explorator ad amicos explicat, "etiam in terris longinquis cultum nostrum extendit." Arcana siderum et futuri, per Hathoris sapientiam, revelantur. Sacerdotes eius ritus salutares exercent; fabulae et legenda dea inspirata ad poesim scriptaque incitant.

"Hathor, the guide of civilisation," an explorer explains to his friends, "extends our culture even to distant lands." The secrets of the stars and the future are revealed through Hathor's wisdom. Her priests perform healing rituals; stories and legends inspired by the goddess incite poetry and writing.

"In difficilibus temporibus," dicit aliquis in luctu, "Hathoris solacium quaerimus." Nuptiae sub eius benedictione celebrantur, promissiones amoris et felicitatis ferentes.

"In difficult times," someone in mourning says, "we seek the comfort of Hathor." Marriages are celebrated under her blessing, bringing promises of love and happiness.

Ita Hathor, per sua praecepta et exempla, non solum Aegyptum sed etiam mundum docet. Pulchritudo vitae, musicae vis, amor in familia, respectus naturae, et vincula communitatis, omnia sub Hathoris signo florent. Eius hereditas, per saecula durans, hominibus viam ad maiorem comprehensionem et harmoniam ostendit.

Thus Hathor, through her teachings and examples, educates not only Egypt but also the world. The beauty of life, the power of music, love in family, respect for nature, and the bonds of community all flourish under Hathor's sign. Her legacy, enduring through the ages, shows humanity the path to greater understanding and harmony.

Hereditas Hathoris

In Aegypto, templa Hathoris culturae sapientiaeque foci evaserunt, ubi homines et mulieres artium pulchritudinem discunt. Statuae et amuleta eius, ut talismani pretiosi, in domibus templisque servantur, protectionem et felicitatem promittentes.

In Egypt, the temples of Hathor became centres of culture and wisdom, where men and women learn the beauty of the arts. Her statues and amulets, as precious talismans, are kept in homes and temples, promising protection and happiness.

Per urbes, sollemnes processiones ad Hathoris honorem fiunt, gaudium ubique diffundentes. "Videte," praeco in via clamat, "Hathoris festum appropinquat!" Cives cum floribus et cantibus conveniunt, deae gratias agentes.

Throughout the cities, solemn processions in honour of Hathor take place, spreading joy everywhere. "Look," the herald cries in the street, "the festival of Hathor approaches!" Citizens gather with flowers and songs, giving thanks to the goddess.

Hathor non solum in Aegypto colitur sed etiam trans fines terrae eius nomen et virtutes celebrantur. Historici et archaeologi antiquos ritus eiusque cultum explorant, magnas revelationes de antiqua religione aperiunt.

Hathor is not only worshipped in Egypt but her name and virtues are celebrated beyond the borders of the land. Historians and archaeologists explore her ancient rites and cult, uncovering great revelations about ancient religion.

Musea orbis terrarum thesauros Hathori dedicatos exhibent, visitatores ad admirationem artis eius invitant. "Quam pulchra haec statua Hathoris est!" visitator in museo exclamat, opus admirans.

Museums around the world exhibit treasures dedicated to Hathor, inviting visitors to admire her art. "How beautiful is this statue of Hathor!" a visitor exclaims in a museum, admiring the work.

Eruditi influentiam Hathoris in artibus et studiis spiritualibus scrutantur, eius symbola in contemporanea societate inveniunt. Hathor ut feminitatis, pulchritudinis, et interioris fortitudinis symbolum manet, hodiernis mulieribus inspirationem praebens.

Scholars study Hathor's influence on the arts and spiritual studies, finding her symbols in contemporary society. Hathor remains a symbol of femininity, beauty, and inner strength, providing inspiration to modern women.

Festivitates modernae, Hathoris antiquis celebrationibus inspiratae, communitates ad gaudium et unitatem convocant. In meditationis et sanationis praxi, eius antiqua energia adhibetur, mentes curantes et spiritus elevantes.

Modern festivals, inspired by Hathor's ancient celebrations, bring communities together in joy and unity. In practices of meditation and healing, her ancient energy is used, healing minds and uplifting spirits.

Poetae et musicae scriptores hodierni Hathoris imaginem adhibent, amorem harmoniamque in operibus suis promovendo. "Per Hathoris inspirationem," poeta dicit, "carmina de amore et vita scribo."

Modern poets and songwriters use the image of Hathor, promoting love and harmony in their works. "Through Hathor's inspiration," a poet says, "I write songs about love and life."

Organisationes, mulierum iura defendentes, Hathoris exemplum sequuntur, eius virtutes ad aequitatem et protectionem advocantes. "In Hathoris spiritu," dux feminarum dicit, "pro dignitate et amore laboramus."

Organisations defending women's rights follow Hathor's example, advocating her virtues for equality and protection. "In Hathor's spirit," a women's leader says, "we work for dignity and love."

Ita Hathor, per saecula culta, non solum in Aegypto sed etiam in toto mundo, ut dea gaudii amorisque perpetuo veneratur. Eius legatum, in artibus, celebrationibus, et vita cotidiana vivum, homines ad meliorem futurum ducit, semper nos monens de amoris et pulchritudinis potentia.

Thus, Hathor, worshipped for centuries, not only in Egypt but also throughout the world, is forever honoured as the goddess of joy and love. Her legacy, alive in the arts, celebrations, and daily life, leads people towards a better future, always reminding us of the power of love and beauty.

Ra et Humanitatis Perditio

Regnum Solis Ra

In antiqua Aegypti terra, Ra, deus solis, imperabat, omnium deorum potentissimus et a cunctis habitantibus veneratus. Tempore progresso, Ra senescere coepit, viresque eius minui. Homines, Ra regnandi capacitate dubitantes, paulatim fiduciam in eum amittere coeperunt. Nonnulli homines rebellare incipiebant, eius imperiis non parere eligentes.

In the ancient land of Egypt, Ra, the god of the sun, ruled, the most powerful of all gods and venerated by all inhabitants. As time passed, Ra began to age, and his strength diminished. People, doubting Ra's ability to rule, gradually began to lose trust in him. Some people even began to rebel, choosing not to obey his commands.

"Cur Ra nos adhuc regere potest?" quidam inter se susurrabant, eius debilitatem notantes. Ra, hominum verba audiens, dolore affectus est. Deus solis alios deos convocavit ut de rebellionis humanae consilium caperent. Isis, Osiris, Thothque, sapientes consiliarii, aderant.

"How can Ra still rule over us?" some whispered among themselves, noting his weakness. Ra, hearing the words of the people, was hurt. The sun god summoned the other gods to take counsel on the human rebellion. Isis, Osiris, and Thoth, wise advisors, were present.

"Humanitas pro insolentia puniri debet," Ra decrevit, ira commotus. Sekhmet, dea leonina irae et ultionis, creata est ut vindictam eius exsequeretur. Cum terram petivit, homines interficere coepit, terrorem ubique diffundens. Flumina sanguine victimarum rubefacta sunt, et homines, desperatione capti, ad Ra preces miserunt ut caedem finiret.

"Humanity must be punished for their insolence," Ra decreed, overcome with anger. Sekhmet, the lioness goddess of wrath and vengeance, was created to carry out his revenge. When she descended to the earth, she began killing people, spreading terror everywhere. Rivers were stained with the blood of victims, and the people, driven to despair, prayed to Ra to end the slaughter.

Ra, vastationem contemplans, poenitentia motus est. "Quid feci?" secum cogitavit, destructionis magnitudine perterritus.

Ra, watching the devastation, was filled with remorse. "What have I done?" he thought to himself, terrified by the scale of the destruction.

Hoc capitulum Ra regnum illustrat, deum solis potentem sed vulnerabilem ostendens. Rebellionis humanae et divinae poenitentiae narratio non solum de ira et ultione sed etiam de sapientia et misericordia agit. Ra, in suo maximo errore, humanitatis pretium intellexit, et quamvis deus esset, ad humanam fragilitatem et divinam clementiam respicere doctus est.

This chapter illustrates the reign of Ra, showing the sun god as powerful but also vulnerable. The story of human rebellion and divine remorse is not only about anger and vengeance but also about wisdom and mercy. In his greatest error, Ra understood the value of humanity, and although he was a god, he learned to reflect on human fragility and divine compassion.

Misericordia Ra

Ra, solis deus, magna cum sollicitudine cogitabat quomodo Sekhmet, iram suam in humanos effundentem, sistere posset sine aliis deorum offensione. Tandem, consilium cepit: iussit cerevisiam cum granato mixtam parari, quae sanguini simillima videretur. Haec potio in campis proeliis, ubi Sekhmet pugnabat, effusa est.

Ra, the sun god, with great concern, pondered how to stop Sekhmet, who was pouring out his anger upon humans, without offending the other gods. Finally, he came up with a plan: he ordered a mixture of beer and pomegranate to be prepared, which looked very similar to blood. This drink was poured over the battlefields where Sekhmet fought.

Sekhmet, potione pro sanguine habita, eam aviditate bibit et mox ebrietate capta est. Eius furor lenitus, in somnum altum incidit. Ra, hoc momento usus, Sekhmet in Hathorem, deam amoris, transformavit.

Sekhmet, mistaking the drink for blood, drank it eagerly and soon became intoxicated. Her fury was calmed, and she fell into a deep sleep. Ra, seizing this moment, transformed Sekhmet into Hathor, the goddess of love.

Cum Hathor experrecta est, confusa sed sine ullo occidendi desiderio, Ra ei mandavit ut deinceps humanos protegeret. Humanitas, hoc miraculo liberata, gratias Ra egit, promittentes se denuo eum veneraturos.

When Hathor awoke, confused but without any desire to kill, Ra commanded her to protect humans from that moment forward. Humanity, freed by this miracle, thanked Ra, promising to worship him again.

Ra, eventus contemplans, misericordiae et intellectus magnitudinem agnovit, discens poenam non semper primam actionem esse debere. Sic, di immortales et mortales novam pacis et mutualis respectus aetatem inierunt. Ra, sapientia nova instructus, mansuetiore modo regnare pergebat.

Ra, contemplating the events, acknowledged the greatness of mercy and understanding, learning that punishment need not always be the first action. Thus, the immortal gods and mortals entered a new age of peace and mutual respect. Ra, now equipped with newfound wisdom, continued to reign in a gentler manner.

Templa in honorem Ra et Hathor constructa sunt, ubi homines diis gratias agebant pacemque celebrabant. Aegyptus, sub divina custodia, iterum floruit, doctrina de misericordia et comprehensione per saecula mansura.

Temples were built in honour of Ra and Hathor, where people gave thanks to the gods and celebrated peace. Egypt, under divine protection, flourished once again, and the teachings of mercy and understanding endured through the ages.

Hoc capitulum docet etiam deos, tam potentes quam sint, errorem agnoscere et emendare posse. Ra, per actus suos, exemplar clementiae et sapientiae praebuit, monstrans veram potentiam in indulgentia et amoris propagatione sitam esse.

This chapter teaches that even the gods, as powerful as they are, can acknowledge and correct their mistakes. Ra, through his actions, set an example of mercy and wisdom, showing that true power lies in forgiveness and the spreading of love.

Disciplinae Doctae

Fabula de Ra et Sekhmet in legendam Aegyptiorum vertit, ut humilitatis respectusque magnitudo doceretur. Pueri puellaeque discebant deos quoque errare posse, templaque loca fiebant ubi de compassionis et veniae valoribus meditabantur.

The story of Ra and Sekhmet turned into an Egyptian legend, teaching the greatness of humility and respect. Boys and girls learned that even gods could make mistakes, and temples became places where people reflected on the values of compassion and forgiveness.

"Sic Ra se mutavit," sacerdos in templo narrabat, "et nos docuit etiam potentes errare et mutare." Festivitates Hathori, amoris laetitiaeque symbolo, celebrabantur, ubi omnes gaudio et caritate fruebantur.

"Thus, Ra changed himself," the priest in the temple would tell, "and he taught us that even the powerful can make mistakes and change." Festivals for Hathor, the symbol of love and joy, were celebrated, where everyone enjoyed joy and kindness.

Artifices imagines Sekhmet, quae in Hathorem transformata est, creabant, mirabilem mutationem demonstrantes. "Vide," artifex ad spectatorem dicebat, "quomodo ira in amorem vertitur." Scribae historiae in papyro scribebant, futuris generationibus legenda.

Artisans created images of Sekhmet, who was transformed into Hathor, showing the miraculous change. "Look," the artist would say to the onlooker, "how anger turns into love." Scribes wrote the story on papyrus, ensuring the legend would pass on to future generations.

Mercatores, fabulam per terras portantes, lectiones pretiosas diffundebant. 'Ra nos docuit sapientia et iustitia regere,' princeps, consilio suo dicente, Ra exemplum sequens.

Merchants carried the story across lands, spreading its valuable lessons. "Ra taught us to rule with wisdom and justice," said a prince, following Ra's example in his counsel.

Societas, veniae et evolutionis capacitate aestimata, ad pacem et concordiam aspirabat. "Discamus," magister ad discipulos suos inquit, "alterum intellegere et confligere sine vi."

Society, valuing the capacity for forgiveness and growth, aspired to peace and harmony. "Let us learn," a teacher said to his students, "to understand others and resolve conflicts without violence."

In religiosis ceremoniis, preces pro pace et harmonia fiebant, totam communitatem ad concordiam vocantes. "Per Ra et Hathor," sacerdos in oratione dicebat, "pacem et unitatem petimus."

In religious ceremonies, prayers for peace and harmony were offered, calling the whole community to unity. "Through Ra and Hathor," the priest said in prayer, "we seek peace and unity."

Haec fabula etiam ad politica movebat, diplomatem et iustam gubernationem incitans. Aegyptus, his doctrinis unita, florebat, magnam civitatem prosperam sub divina et humana sapientia demonstrans.

This story also influenced politics, inspiring diplomacy and just governance. Egypt, united by these teachings, flourished, showing itself as a great and prosperous civilisation under divine and human wisdom.

Ita, Ra et Sekhmet historia non solum de divina ira et misericordia narrabat sed etiam de humana capacitate ad discendum, mutandum, et per difficilia tempora meliores fieri. Aegyptiis haec fabula lumen in tenebris, viam ad meliorem futurum monstrabat.

Thus, the story of Ra and Sekhmet was not only about divine anger and mercy but also about humanity's ability to learn, change, and become better through difficult times. For the Egyptians, this story was a light in the darkness, showing the way to a better future.

Nocturnus Iter Bastetis

Excessus Bastetis

In antiquis Aegypti finibus, dea domus, fertilitatis, feliumque venerata, Bastet nomine, vitam deorum linquebat noctu ut in mortalium mundum descenderet. Propositum eius erat domos protegere et spiritus malignos pugnare. Ante discessum, in felis formam se convertebat ut inter mortales minime innotesceret. Alii dii eam salutabant et felicem iter optabant.

In the ancient lands of Egypt, Bastet, the goddess of the home, fertility, and cats, would leave the realm of the gods at night to descend into the mortal world. Her purpose was to protect homes and fight evil spirits. Before her departure, she would transform into the form of a cat to remain unnoticed among mortals. The other gods would greet her and wish her a safe journey.

Cum silentium urbes tegeret, Bastet per vias quietas ambulabat, oculi eius in tenebris micantes. Sensibus acutis utebatur ad omne periculum sentiendum. Felium urbis exercitus eam tacite sequi solebat, quasi cognitio ipsa eam duceret.

When silence covered the cities, Bastet would walk through the quiet streets, her eyes gleaming in the darkness. She used her keen senses to detect any danger. The city's army of cats would silently follow her, as if guided by some instinctive knowledge.

Primum, domos infirmorum ac liberorum visitabat ut protectionem praeberet. Serpentes scorpionesque venabatur, focos tutos servans. Etiam super messes vigilabat, eas a rodentibus protegens.

First, she would visit the homes of the sick and children to provide protection. She hunted snakes and scorpions, keeping the hearths safe. She also watched over the harvests, protecting them from rodents.

Nocte progressa, eius praesentia solatium adferebat iis qui eam videbant. Pax et securitas post eam manebant. Ante auroram, ad regnum deorum redibat. Primi solis radii eius iter concludebant, eius reditum nocte sequenti promittentes.

As the night progressed, her presence brought comfort to those who saw her. Peace and security followed in her wake. Before dawn, she would return to the realm of the gods. The first rays of the sun would mark the end of her journey, promising her return the following night.

Conversatio inter Bastet et alium deum:

Bastet: "Nocte hac iterum exeo ut mortales protegam." *Deus:* "Tua virtus nos omnes superat, Bastet. Felices sumus quod tu nostri custos es."

Bastet: "Omnem vim meam adhibebo ne malum prevalere possit. Vobiscum est mei animi fortitudo."

Deus: "Bona fortuna, Bastet. Tua praesentia in terra valde necessaria est."

Conversation between Bastet and another god:

Bastet: "Tonight I once again go forth to protect the mortals." God: "Your strength surpasses us all, Bastet. We are fortunate that you are our guardian."

Bastet: "I will use all my power to prevent evil from prevailing. My strength is with you."

God: "Good luck, Bastet. Your presence on earth is greatly needed."

Ita Bastet nocturnas expeditiones coepit, semper vigilans et praesidium ferens. Felium amor et mortalium tutela eius perpetua missio erat. Sub lunae lumine, iter suum pergebat, silentium noctis cum pace et tutela implebat.

Thus, Bastet began her nightly expeditions, always vigilant and offering protection. The love of cats and the guardianship of mortals were her eternal mission. Under the light of the moon, she continued her journey, filling the silence of the night with peace and protection.

Certamina Bastetis

Nocte quadam, Bastet malum praesens insolitum sensit, vi maiore quam umquam antea. Spiritus malignus, mundorum limites transcendens, in terris chaos diffundebat. Bastet conscia erat se daemonem invenire debere ante lucem, ut mortales tueretur. Omnes felium circumiacentium copias convocavit, ut daemonem localizaret.

One night, Bastet sensed an unusual presence of evil, stronger than ever before. A malevolent spirit, crossing the boundaries of worlds, was spreading chaos on earth. Bastet knew she had to find the demon before dawn to protect the mortals. She summoned all the surrounding cats to locate the demon.

Spiritus malignus, interea, corda hominum metu iraque corrumpere conabatur. Sub lunae spectaculo, Bastet cum daemone in proelio epico conflixit. Magia sua utens, daemonem repulit, quamquam pugna acerrima erat. Felium auxilio, fortibus et fidelibus, proelium sustinebat.

Meanwhile, the malevolent spirit tried to corrupt the hearts of men with fear and anger. Under the spectacle of the moon, Bastet clashed with the demon in an epic battle. Using her magic, she pushed the demon back, though the fight was fierce. With the help of the cats, strong and loyal, she held the line in the battle.

Post multum certamen, Bastet daemonem in amuletum inclusit. Hoc amuletum sacerdoti tradidit, ut ille illud in templo celaret. Dea vulneratos sanavit et terrefactos consolata est. Eius facta heroica a sacerdotibus habitantibusque celebrata sunt.

After much struggle, Bastet trapped the demon in an amulet. She handed the amulet to a priest, so that he could hide it in the temple. The goddess healed the wounded and comforted the terrified. Her heroic deeds were celebrated by priests and inhabitants alike.

Magna erat felium honoratio, ut protectores focorum laudarentur. Bastet pollicita est, quamdiu vigilet, nullum malum praevalere. Pace restituta, iter nocturnum resumpsit, semper mortales custodiens.

Great was the honour given to the cats, praised as protectors of the hearth. Bastet promised that as long as she kept watch, no evil would prevail. With peace restored, she resumed her nightly journey, always guarding the mortals.

Conversatio inter Bastet et sacerdotem:

Bastet: "Hoc amuletum, daemonis carcer, in loco sacro custodiendum est."

Sacerdos: "Tua mandata servabo, o divina Bastet. Hic in templo, tutum erit."

Bastet: "Vigilate super eo; potentia eius magna est. Nolumus umquam redire possit."

Sacerdos: "Promitto, omni diligentia custodiam. Tuorum beneficiorum grati sumus."

Bastet: "Una stamus. Malum superare nostrum commune propositum est."

Conversation between Bastet and the priest:

Bastet: "This amulet, the demon's prison, must be guarded in a sacred place."

Priest: "I will obey your command, O divine Bastet. Here in the temple, it will be safe."

Bastet: "Keep watch over it; its power is great. We do not want it to ever return."

Priest: "I promise, I will guard it with utmost diligence. We are grateful for your blessings."

Bastet: "We stand together. Overcoming evil is our shared purpose."

Ita Bastet, cum fidelitate felium suorum et auxilio divino, tenebras superavit, pacem terris reportans. Suum iter nocturnum, signum indefessae vigilantis, pergit, semper in amore et tutela humani generis et felium.

Thus, Bastet, with the loyalty of her cats and divine aid, overcame the darkness and brought peace back to the lands. She continues her nightly journey, a sign of her tireless watchfulness, always in the love and protection of humankind and cats.

Gloria Bastetis

Multis temporibus postea, Bastet inter mortales quasi legenda celebrabatur. In fenestris domuum statuae felium eius honori collocabantur. Liberi somniabant se noctu eius coruscantes oculos visuros esse, sperantes. Noctu, Bastet vinculum inter deos hominesque confirmabat.

Many times later, Bastet was celebrated among mortals as a legend. In the windows of homes, cat statues were placed in her honour. Children would dream, hoping to see her gleaming eyes at night. By night, Bastet strengthened the bond between gods and humans.

Domus et familiae doctrinam tutelae tradebant. Sacerdotes orationes ei dedicabant, eius benedictionem rogantes. Artifices, eius gestis inspirati, ea pingebant. Fabulae de itineribus eius ex generatione in generationem narrantur.

Homes and families passed down the teaching of protection. Priests dedicated prayers to her, asking for her blessing. Artists, inspired by her deeds, painted her. Stories of her journeys were told from generation to generation.

Bastet benignitas, vis, protectioque personabat. Iter eius nocturnum cyclum vitae, mortis, renascentiaeque significabat. Stellae in caelo ut duces eius habebantur. Aurora cum ad regnum deorum redibat, pacis sensus mundum tegebat.

Bastet's kindness, strength, and protection were renowned. Her nightly journey symbolised the cycle of life, death, and rebirth. The stars in the sky were considered her guides. When dawn returned her to the realm of the gods, a sense of peace covered the world.

Mortales se ab Bastet amatos tutosque sciebant. Amor eius erga homines et felium aeternus et immotus erat. Bastet pergit iter nocturnum facere, custos aeterna in umbra manens.

Mortals knew they were loved and protected by Bastet. Her love for humans and cats was eternal and unchanging. Bastet continues her nightly journey, remaining an eternal guardian in the shadows.

Conversatio inter Bastet et puerum:

Puer: "Bastet, num te hodie nocte videre possum?" *Bastet:* "Forsitan, parve puer. Si cor tuum purum est, in tenebris oculos meos invenire poteris."

Puer: "Te in somniis meis semper video, protegens nos." *Bastet:* "Et ego semper adero, tuam familiam tuens. Somnia tua vera sunt, nam in umbra custodio."

Conversation between Bastet and a child:

Child: "Bastet, will I be able to see you tonight?" Bastet: "Perhaps, little one. If your heart is pure, you will find my eyes in the darkness."

Child: "I always see you in my dreams, protecting us." Bastet: "And I will always be there, guarding your family. Your dreams are true, for I watch over you in the shadows."

Ita Bastet, amore infinito et protectione indefessa, inter mortales quasi lumina noctis fulgebat. Eius praesentia, etiam invisibilis, sensum securitatis et amoris omnibus praebat. Eius legenda, per aetates perpetua, cor hominum et felium semper tetigit.

Thus Bastet, with infinite love and tireless protection, shone among mortals like a light in the night. Her presence, even invisible, gave everyone a sense of security and love. Her legend, eternal through the ages, always touched the hearts of humans and cats.

Origo Mundi Aegypti

Initium

In principio, nihil nisi Chaos et aquarum infinitarum expansio, Nun nomine, erant. In medio Nuni, tumulus quidam apparuit, vitae signum primum. Super hunc tumulum, deus Atum se manifestavit, sui ipsius creator.

In the beginning, there was nothing but Chaos and the vast expanse of water, called Nun. In the midst of Nun, a mound appeared, the first sign of life. On this mound, the god Atum manifested himself, the creator of himself.

Atum, Shu, deum aeris, et Tefnut, deam humiditatis, evomuit. Shu et Tefnut in Chaos profecti sunt ut explorarent et se perdiderunt. Atum oculum suum misit ut eos reperiret, et, cum redierunt, lacrimis gaudii effusis est.

Atum vomited forth Shu, the god of air, and Tefnut, the goddess of moisture. Shu and Tefnut ventured into Chaos to explore and became lost. Atum sent his eye to find them, and when they returned, he shed tears of joy.

Eius lacrimae, in terram cadentes, primos homines feminasque creaverunt. Shu et Tefnut Geb, deum terrae, et Nut, deam caeli, genuerunt. Geb et Nut quattuor liberos habuerunt: Osirim, Isidem, Sethum, et Nephthys.

His tears, falling to the earth, created the first men and women. Shu and Tefnut gave birth to Geb, the god of the earth, and Nut, the goddess of the sky. Geb and Nut had four children: Osiris, Isis, Seth, and Nephthys.

Osiris terrae rex factus est et Isidem, suum aeternum amorem, in matrimonium duxit. Seth, invidia motus, contra Osirim conspiravit ut thronum occuparet. Mundus inter diem, a sole Ra gubernatum, et noctem divisus erat.

Osiris became the king of the earth and married Isis, his eternal love. Seth, moved by jealousy, conspired against Osiris to take the throne. The world was divided between day, governed by the sun god Ra, and night.

Ra per caelum in sua solari nave iter faciebat, lucem afferens. Dii Maat creaverunt, principium ordinis et aequilibrii. Ita ordo ex Chaos creatus est, creationis initium notans.

Ra journeyed across the sky in his solar boat, bringing light. The gods created Maat, the principle of order and balance. Thus, order was created from Chaos, marking the beginning of creation.

Conversatio inter Atum et Osirim:

Atum: "Fili mi, Osiris, tu nunc terrae rex es. Curam et iustitiam populo tuo praebe."

Osiris: "Pater, tua mandata servabo et Aegyptum in prosperitatem ducam."

Atum: "Maat tene, et noli oblivisci: aequilibrium inter omnia est maximi momenti."

Osiris: "Promitto, pater, me Maat semper custodire, ut ordo et pax in regno maneant."

Conversation between Atum and Osiris:

Atum: "My son, Osiris, you are now the king of the earth. Provide care and justice for your people."

Osiris: "Father, I will follow your commands and lead Egypt to prosperity."
Atum: "Hold to Maat, and do not forget: balance in all things is of utmost importance."

Osiris: "I promise, father, I will always uphold Maat, so that order and peace remain in the kingdom."

Sic fabula mundi origo narratur, ubi deorum actiones et hominum creatio inter se coniungunt, universi ordinationem et vitae sensum aeternum efficiens.

Thus the story of the world's origin is told, where the actions of the gods and the creation of humanity are intertwined, establishing the order of the universe and giving eternal meaning to life.

Ordo Mundi Constituitur

Osiris, regnans, artes agriculturae et civilisationis hominibus docuit. Isis, regina, scientiam magicam et sanationem communicavit. Eorum imperio, Aegyptus florebat, regnum fertile evadens.

Osiris, while ruling, taught the people the arts of agriculture and civilisation. Isis, the queen, shared magical knowledge and healing. Under their rule, Egypt flourished, becoming a fertile kingdom.

Seth, tamen, potentiam et gloriam fratris sui concupivit. Osirim prodidit, occidit, corpusque eius per Aegyptum dispersit. Isis, corde fracto, mariti corporis fragmenta quaesivit. Magica potentia utendo, Osiridis corpus reconstituit et ad vitam revocavit.

Seth, however, coveted the power and glory of his brother. He betrayed Osiris, killed him, and scattered his body across Egypt. Isis, heartbroken, searched for the fragments of her husband's body. Using her magical power, she reassembled Osiris's body and brought him back to life.

Osiris, factus est deus regni mortuorum, animas iudicans. Horus, Osiridis et Isis filius, patrem ulcisci iuravit. Horus et Seth in proeliis epicis conflixerunt. Tandem, Horus Sethem vicit et in throno Aegypti iure suo successit.

Osiris became the god of the underworld, judging souls. Horus, the son of Osiris and Isis, swore to avenge his father. Horus and Seth clashed in epic battles. Finally, Horus defeated Seth and rightfully succeeded to the throne of Egypt.

Per hanc victoriam, ordo et iustitia restituti sunt, Maat corroborante. Dies noctesque et tempora anni stabilizata sunt. Dii super Aegyptum vigilabant, prosperitatem et harmoniam garantentes. Creationis mythi in templis et inter populum celebrabantur.

Through this victory, order and justice were restored, reinforced by Maat. Day and night, as well as the seasons, were stabilised. The gods watched over Egypt, ensuring prosperity and harmony. The myth of creation was celebrated in temples and among the people.

Conversatio inter Horum et Sethem:

Horus: "Proditionem tuam nunquam ignoscem, Seth. Iustitia pro patre meo restituenda est."

Seth: "Numquam regnum Aegypti obtinere poteris, Horus. Me vincere non potes."

Horus: "Deorum virtute et iustitiae causa, te superabo et thronum Aegypti recuperabo."

Post multas pugnas, Horus victor extitit, verba sua probans.

Conversation between Horus and Seth:

Horus: "I will never forgive your betrayal, Seth. Justice for my father must be restored."

Seth: "You will never obtain the throne of Egypt, Horus. You cannot defeat me."

Horus: "By the strength of the gods and for the sake of justice, I will overcome you and reclaim the throne of Egypt."

After many battles, Horus emerged victorious, proving his words.

Sic, deorum voluntate et actis heroicis, mundus ex chaos in ordinem ductus est, cum Maat fundamentum esset cui omnis vita Aegyptia innitebatur. Haec narratio non solum de diis et mortalibus est sed etiam de aeterno ordine iustitiaque quaerendo.

Thus, by the will of the gods and through heroic deeds, the world was brought from chaos into order, with Maat as the foundation upon which all Egyptian life rested. This story is not only about gods and mortals but also about the eternal quest for order and justice.

Posteritas

Templa in honorem deorum ut loca cultus extructa sunt. Sacerdotes ritus ad deos honorandos et Maat conservandam perficiebant. Festivitates historias deorum et temporum anni celebrabant.

Temples were built in honour of the gods as places of worship. Priests performed rituals to honour the gods and preserve Maat. Festivals celebrated the stories of the gods and the seasons of the year.

Artifices opera, a mythis creationis inspirata, creabant. Scribae historias sacras in papyris scribebant. Moralia et valores per deorum legendas docebantur. Iustitia per leges et iudicia Osiridis in regno ducebat.

Artists created works inspired by the creation myths. Scribes wrote sacred stories on papyri. Morals and values were taught through the legends of the gods. Justice was guided by the laws and judgments of Osiris in the kingdom.

Stellae et constellationes nominibus deorum appellabantur. Inundatio Nili, quae est vitalis agriculturae, ut donum deorum laudabatur. Pharaones habebantur ut directi descendentes deorum. Constructio pyramidum et monumentorum credentiam in vitam post mortem reflectebat.

Stars and constellations were named after the gods. The flooding of the Nile, essential for agriculture, was praised as a gift from the gods. Pharaohs were regarded as direct descendants of the gods. The construction of pyramids and monuments reflected the belief in life after death.

Amuleta et talismani ad divinam protectionem invocandam utebantur. Preces et oblationes cotidie deis offerebantur. Mythi origines mundi explicabant et vitam Aegyptiorum ducebant. Ita mythus creationis culturam, religionem, societatemque Aegypti formabat.

Amulets and talismans were used to invoke divine protection. Prayers and offerings were made daily to the gods. Myths explained the origins of the world and guided the lives of Egyptians. Thus, the creation myth shaped the culture, religion, and society of Egypt.

Conversatio inter sacerdotem et civem:

Sacerdos: "Hodie deos colimus ut Maat in vita nostra conservetur."
Civis: "Quomodo possumus deorum benevolentiam assequi?"
Sacerdos: "Puris mentibus et sinceris oblationibus. Dei nostri amoris et fidei signa requirunt."

Civis: "Ergo, ad templum ibo ut preces meas offeram et gratias agam."
Sacerdos: "Bene facis. Deorum favor per pietatem et devotionem quaeritur."

Per haec acta, Aegyptus sensum divinitatis et profunditatem culturalem expressit, quae per aetates perdurant. Posteritas deorum in vita quotidiana manifestabatur, societatemque in viis moralibus et spiritualibus informabat.

Through these actions, Egypt expressed a sense of divinity and cultural depth, which endures through the ages. The legacy of the gods manifested in everyday life and shaped society in moral and spiritual ways.

Isidis in Quaerendo Osiride

Proditio Sethi

Seth, fratri suo Osiridi invidens ob potentiam et influentiam eius, nefarium consilium concepit ut eum exstingueret et thronum occuparet. Convivium sub reconciliationis praetextu Osiridi proposuit, ubi sarcophagum splendidum ostendit, promittens id donaturum ei qui perfecte conveniret. Osiris, dolo deceptus, in sarcophagum decubuit ut experiretur.

Seth, envious of his brother Osiris's power and influence, devised a wicked plan to destroy him and take the throne. He proposed a banquet under the pretext of reconciliation, where he displayed a splendid sarcophagus, promising to give it to the one who fit perfectly inside. Osiris, deceived by the trick, lay down in the sarcophagus to try it out.

Seth cum complicibus sarcophagum clausit atque in Nilum proiecit. Isis, Osiridis uxor dilectissima, de eius amissione devastata, statuit maritum carissimum quaerere ut ad vitam revocaret. In avem mutata, per Aegyptum volavit quaerens Osiridis reliquias.

Seth, along with his accomplices, sealed the sarcophagus and threw it into the Nile. Isis, Osiris's beloved wife, devastated by his loss, decided to search for her dear husband to bring him back to life. Transformed into a bird, she flew across Egypt searching for Osiris's remains.

Post longas inquisitiones, sarcophagum in arbore Bybli adhaerentem invenit. Isis corpus in Aegyptum reportavit, mortem eius deflens et sequentis consilii praeparationem faciens. Corpus in deltam Nili abscondit ut a Seth protegeretur.

After a long search, she found the sarcophagus clinging to a tree in Byblos. Isis brought the body back to Egypt, mourning his death and preparing her next steps. She hid the body in the Nile Delta to protect it from Seth.

Seth corpus Osiridis invenit et, ira commotus, in quattuordecim partes secuit easque per Aegyptum dispersit. Isis, firma proposito, omnes mariti corporis partes colligere coepit. Auxilio Nephthys, sororis suae, suum sacrum iter incepit.

Seth found Osiris's body and, in a fit of rage, cut it into fourteen pieces and scattered them across Egypt. Determined, Isis began to gather all the parts of her husband's body. With the help of her sister Nephthys, she started her sacred journey.

Conversatio inter Isidem et Nephthyn:

Isis: "Soror, adiuvare me debes, partes Osiridis coniungere ut eum ad vitam revocem."

Nephthys: "Tecum ero, Isis. Quocumque iter nos ducet, partes fratris nostri quaeremus."

Isis: "Magia nostra coniuncta, nulla nobis erit in re difficili insuperabilis."

Ita narratio Isidis, qua dea per Aegyptum peregrinatur ut dilectum suum Osiridem reconstituat, incipit. Haec fabula non solum de amore et fidelitate agit, sed etiam de resurrectionis potentia et aeterni vitae promissione.

Thus begins the story of Isis, as the goddess journeys across Egypt to restore her beloved Osiris. This tale is not only about love and loyalty but also about the power of resurrection and the promise of eternal life.

Quaestio Isidis

In vastis terris Aegypti, Isis, dea potentissima, per campos et flumina iter faciebat, quaerens reliquias dilecti sui Osiridis. Usura magia sua antiqua, conabatur singulas partes corporis dispersi invenire. Cum inveniret, ritu sacro eas conservabat, spe mota fore ut Osiridis formam pristinam restitueret.

In the vast lands of Egypt, Isis, the most powerful goddess, travelled across fields and rivers, searching for the remains of her beloved Osiris. Using her ancient magic, she tried to find each piece of his scattered body. When she found them, she preserved them with sacred rituals, moved by the hope that she could restore Osiris to his original form.

"O deae et dii, auxilium vestrum imploro," Isis in oratione dixit, caelum aspiciens. "Sine vestra benevolentia, Osiris numquam integrum restitui poterit."

"O goddesses and gods, I implore your help," Isis said in prayer, looking to the sky. "Without your benevolence, Osiris can never be restored to his full self."

Ad haec verba, Anubis, deus embalsamationis, apparet. "Isis," inquit, "arte mea te adiuvabo, ut corpus Osiridis aeternum conservetur."

At these words, Anubis, the god of embalming, appeared. "Isis," he said, "with my skill, I will help you so that the body of Osiris can be preserved for eternity."

"Gratias tibi ago, Anubis. Tua scientia nobis essetialis est," Isis respondit, gratitudine plena.

"Thank you, Anubis. Your knowledge is essential to us," Isis responded, full of gratitude.

Interim, Thot, deus sapientiae, advenit, magicae suae potentia adiuturus. "Magica mea et scientia tecum sunt, Isis. Quod quaeris, fieri potest," Thot affirmavit.

Meanwhile, Thoth, the god of wisdom, arrived to help with his magical power. "My magic and knowledge are with you, Isis. What you seek can be achieved," Thoth affirmed.

Cum omnibus partibus, praeter unam quae in Nilo amissa erat, collectis, Anubis Isidi artes embalsamationis docebat. Corpus sic praeparatum aeternitati erat destinatum.

With all the parts collected, except for one that was lost in the Nile, Anubis taught Isis the art of embalming. The body, thus prepared, was destined for eternity.

Deficiente parte una, Isis magiam suam adhibuit, creans simulacrum eius quod deerat. His actis, Osiridis corpus, nunc integrum, coram ea iacebat.

With one part missing, Isis used her magic to create a replica of what was lost. With this done, Osiris's body, now whole, lay before her.

"Tunc," Isis susurravit, "per hanc magiam, spiritum vitae in te insufflem." Et ventos vocavit, qui vitalitatem in Osiridem inspirarent.

"Then," Isis whispered, "through this magic, I breathe the spirit of life into you." And she called upon the winds to inspire vitality into Osiris.

Miraculo, Osiris ad vitam rediit, sed regnum mortuorum ei destinatum erat, ubi dominus fieret, vivis non amplius intermixtus.

By a miracle, Osiris returned to life, but the kingdom of the dead was now his destiny, where he would reign, no longer mingling with the living.

Ex hac unione, Horus natus est, qui patris ultionem ferret. Osiris, etiamsi in regno mortuorum, Horum in artibus belli et regendi erudiebat.

From this union, Horus was born, who would avenge his father. Even in the kingdom of the dead, Osiris taught Horus the arts of war and rulership.

Isis, interim, Horum a Sethi insidiis protegebat, donec ad ultionem patris paratus esset. Eius fortitudo et determinatio non solum familiam suam conservavit sed etiam aequitatem in mundo restituit.

Meanwhile, Isis protected Horus from Seth's schemes until he was ready to avenge his father. Her strength and determination not only preserved her family but also restored justice to the world.

Per haec omnia, Isis exemplar amoris, fortitudinis, et sapientiae manet, memoria eius in aeternum celebrata inter mortales et immortales.

Through all this, Isis remains an example of love, strength, and wisdom, her memory eternally celebrated among mortals and immortals.

Hereditas Isidis

In antiqua Aegypto, ubi fluenta Nili terras fecundant, cultus Isidis, deae magiae, maternitatis, ac fidelitatis, floruit. Amor eius erga Osirim et devotio non solum legendarii facti sunt sed etiam exemplum aeternum praebuerunt.

In ancient Egypt, where the Nile's waters enriched the lands, the worship of Isis, goddess of magic, motherhood, and loyalty, flourished. Her love for Osiris and her devotion became not only legendary but also an eternal example.

"Isis, nostra protectrix," populus in templis sacris clamabat, "tua sapientia nos ducat, tua magia nos servet."

"Isis, our protector," the people cried in the sacred temples, "may your wisdom guide us, may your magic save us."

Templa magnifica, artibus et religione plena, in honorem Isidis exstructa sunt. Sacerdotes et sacerdotissae, veste sacra induti, mysteria deae invocabant, eius benedictionem et protectionem quaerentes.

Magnificent temples, filled with art and religion, were built in honour of Isis. Priests and priestesses, dressed in sacred garments, invoked the goddess's mysteries, seeking her blessing and protection.

"Per ritus et preces, Isidis spiritum advocemus," sacerdos templi proclamavit, turibulum incensi circumferens.

"Through rituals and prayers, let us call upon the spirit of Isis," proclaimed the temple priest, carrying a censer of incense.

Historiae de Isidis quaestione, periculis superatis, et amore indefesso inspirationem praebebant omnibus qui adversis temporibus obviam ibant. "Isidis fortitudo nos docet nunquam desistere," mater filio suo narrabat, stellas nocturnas sub caelo Aegyptio contemplantes.

The stories of Isis's search, the dangers she overcame, and her unwavering love inspired all those who faced difficult times. "The strength of Isis teaches us never to give up," a mother told her son as they gazed at the stars under the Egyptian sky.

Isis, magistra vitae et mortis post resurrectionem, aeterna mysteria docebat. "In vita et in morte, renovatio est," docebat, "nihil vere perit, sed mutatur."

Isis, the teacher of life and death after resurrection, taught eternal mysteries. "In life and in death, there is renewal," she taught, "nothing truly perishes, but it changes."

Quae protectrix liberorum et mulierum erat, Isis in omni domo venerabatur. Amuleta, imaginem eius ferentia, pro protectione gestabantur. "Hoc amuletum te custodiat," pater filiae suae dicens, signum Isidis collo eius suspendebat.

As the protector of children and women, Isis was worshipped in every home. Amulets bearing her image were worn for protection. "May this amulet protect you," a father said to his daughter, placing Isis's symbol around her neck.

Festivitates Isidis, gaudio et spiritualitate plenae, communitates congregabantur. Cantus et orationes ad deam elevabantur, petentes sanitatem et benedictiones. "Isis, nobis viam ad pacem et prosperitatem ostende," chori canebant, lumina et flores ad altaria portantes.

Festivals in honour of Isis, full of joy and spirituality, brought communities together. Songs and prayers were raised to the goddess, asking for health and blessings. "Isis, show us the way to peace and prosperity," the choirs sang, carrying lights and flowers to the altars.

Scribae magna diligentia adventuras Isidis in papyris et parietibus tomborum scribebant, eius sapientiam et virtutes aeternum conservantes. "Haec gesta ne obliviscamur," scriba, calamo in papyro movente, murmuravit.

Scribes, with great care, wrote the deeds of Isis on papyri and tomb walls, preserving her wisdom and virtues for eternity. "Let us not forget these deeds," murmured a scribe, moving his pen across the papyrus.

Influentia Isidis, fines Aegypti transcensens, per Mediterraneum diffundebatur, eius cultus in terris longinquis celebratus. Figura eius materna et protectoria, in corde multorum, solacium et inspirationem offerebat.

The influence of Isis, extending beyond the borders of Egypt, spread across the Mediterranean, with her worship celebrated in distant lands. Her maternal and protective figure offered comfort and inspiration to many hearts.

Mythos Isidis et Osiridis, qui mortis et renascentiae cyclum reminiscent, naturae eternitatis echo erat. "Per Isidem, mysteria vitae et mortis melius intellegimus," philosophus in foro disputans dicebat, "et quamvis corpora nostra pereant, spiritus in aeternum vivit."

The myth of Isis and Osiris, recalling the cycle of death and rebirth, echoed the nature of eternity. "Through Isis, we better understand the mysteries of life and death," a philosopher argued in the forum, "and though our bodies perish, the spirit lives on forever."

Ita Isidis legenda, per saecula mansura, non solum deorum mythologiae pars erat sed etiam cotidianae vitae fundamentum, homines ad meliorem futurum ducens.

Thus, the legend of Isis, destined to endure through the ages, was not only part of the mythology of the gods but also a foundation of daily life, guiding people towards a better future.

Certamen pro Solio Aegypti

Hereditas Osiridis

In terra Aegypti, ubi flumina Nili terras fecundant, Osiris, rex amatus, regnavit, prosperitatem et iustitiam afferens. Frater eius, Seth, zelo motus, regem prodidit et occidit, ut ipse solium occuparet.

In the land of Egypt, where the waters of the Nile enrich the lands, Osiris, the beloved king, ruled, bringing prosperity and justice. His brother, Seth, driven by jealousy, betrayed and killed the king to seize the throne for himself.

"Cur frater meus tam crudele factum concepit?" Osiris in extremis suis verbis lamentabatur.

"Why did my brother conceive such a cruel deed?" Osiris lamented in his final words.

Isis, uxor Osiridis, dolore et amore mota, arte magica maritum ad vitam temporarie revocavit. "Per hanc magiam, te, Osiride, ad vitam revocabo, ut ex nobis natus Horus vindictam capiat et iustum solium reclamet," Isis sollemniter dixit.

Isis, Osiris's wife, moved by grief and love, used her magic to temporarily bring her husband back to life. "Through this magic, I will revive you, Osiris, so that our son Horus may take revenge and reclaim the rightful throne," Isis solemnly declared.

Ex eorum coniunctione Horus natus est, cui destinatum erat patrem vindicare et regnum recuperare. Horus in locis secretis educatus est, ne Seth eum inveniret et interficeret.

From their union, Horus was born, destined to avenge his father and recover the kingdom. Horus was raised in secret places, so Seth would not find and kill him.

Adultus factus, Horus paratus erat ad iustitiam restituendam. "Seth, te provoco," Horus clare pronuntiavit, "ut ius et ordinem in Aegypto restituamus."

Once grown, Horus was ready to restore justice. "Seth, I challenge you," Horus clearly declared, "to restore justice and order in Egypt."

Seth, potentia et superbia plenus, risit. "Puer, me vincere non potes. Solium Aegypti mihi pertinet," inquit arrogantia.

Seth, full of power and pride, laughed. "Boy, you cannot defeat me. The throne of Egypt belongs to me," he said arrogantly.

Sed Horus, non solum viribus sed etiam sapientia matris instructus, ad bellum paratus stetit. "Pro iustitia, pro patre, pro Aegypto pugnabo," Horus firmiter respondit.

But Horus, prepared for battle not only with strength but also with his mother's wisdom, stood ready. "I will fight for justice, for my father, for Egypt," Horus replied firmly.

Ita certamen inter deos, pro solio Aegypti, coepit. Horus, iuvenis deus, non solum pro se ipso sed etiam pro memoria patris et futuri Aegypti pugnabat. Hoc erat initium longae luctationis, quae non solum de potestate sed etiam de iustitia et legibus divinis agebat.

Thus, the struggle between the gods for the throne of Egypt began. Horus, the young god, fought not only for himself but also for the memory of his father and the future of Egypt. This was the beginning of a long struggle, which was not just about power but also about justice and divine law.

Provocatio

Postquam Horus, viribus et iustitia patris Osiridis instructus, solium Aegypti sibi vindicare constituit, Seth, potentia obscuratus, provocare non dubitavit. "Hoc regnum, quod iure mihi debetur, reclamabo," Horus apud concilium deorum pronuntiavit, oculos in Seth defigens.

After Horus, empowered by the strength and justice of his father Osiris, decided to claim the throne of Egypt for himself, Seth, overshadowed by power, did not hesitate to challenge him. "This kingdom, which rightfully belongs to me, I will reclaim," Horus declared before the council of the gods, fixing his gaze on Seth.

"Somnia," Seth contemnens inquit, "numquam regnum meum tibi cedam. Proelia decernant!" Dei Aegyptii, tumultum audiens, ad iudicium vocati sunt. Ra, deus solis, maiestatem tenens, voce tonante proposuit: "Certamina vestram virtutem, astutiam, magiamque probabunt. Quis dignus regno sit, videbimus."

"Dreams," Seth scoffed, "I will never yield my kingdom to you. Let battles decide!" The Egyptian gods, hearing the commotion, were summoned to judgment. Ra, the sun god, holding his majesty, proposed in a thunderous voice: "The trials will test your strength, cunning, and magic. We shall see who is worthy of the throne."

Ita, sub oculis immortalium, Horus et Seth in certamina varia inierunt. Vi, calliditate, artibus magicis inter se decertabant, omnia ad victoriam assequendam experiuntur. Seth, dolo et fraude non abstinens, insidias Horo struxit, sperans eum facile superare posse. "Astutia mea te superabit, Horus," Seth minitabundus dixit.

Thus, under the eyes of the immortals, Horus and Seth engaged in various contests. They fought with strength, cunning, and magic, each trying everything to achieve victory. Seth, never refraining from trickery and deceit, plotted traps for Horus, hoping to defeat him easily. "My cunning will overcome you, Horus," Seth said menacingly.

Sed Horus, non solum armis sed etiam matris sapientia munitus, insidias omnes eludebat. "Non fraude, sed virtute verus rex probatur," Horus, constantia plenus, respondebat. In una ex probis, praesertim magica, Horus aquilam magnam evocavit, super Seth volans et eum in luce solis Ra obumbrans. Populus et dei stupentes magiae Horus testes erant.

But Horus, armed not only with weapons but also with his mother's wisdom, evaded all traps. "A true king is proven not by deceit, but by virtue," Horus replied with unwavering resolve. In one of the trials, particularly one of magic, Horus summoned a great eagle, soaring above Seth and casting a shadow over him in

Ra's sunlight. The people and gods stood in awe, witnessing Horus's magic.

"In his certaminibus, non solum fortitudo corporis, sed etiam animi virtus demonstratur," Isis, filium suum spectans, susurravit. "Fili mi, iustitia et veritas semper viam inveniunt." Cum Horus in pluribus probis praestaret, Seth frustrationem et iram celare non potuit. "Hoc certamen adhuc non finitum est," Seth gravi voce promisit, sed spes eius minui coepit.

"In these trials, not only the strength of the body, but also the virtue of the spirit is demonstrated," Isis whispered, watching her son. "My son, justice and truth always find their way." As Horus excelled in several trials, Seth could no longer hide his frustration and anger. "This contest is not yet over," Seth promised in a grave voice, but his hope began to fade.

Ita, per vires, astutiam, et magiam, Horus gradatim ad victoriam propinquabat, semper matris eius sapientia et dei Aegyptiorum iudicio fretus.

Thus, through strength, cunning, and magic, Horus steadily approached victory, always relying on his mother's wisdom and the judgment of the Egyptian gods.

Deorum Iudicium

Post multas proelias acerbasque probas, consilium deorum in sacris aedibus congregatum est, ut de fato Aegypti iudicaret. Tensio in aere pendebat, omnes anhelantes quid futurum esset.

After many fierce battles and harsh trials, the council of the gods gathered in the sacred halls to judge the fate of Egypt. Tension hung in the air, with everyone holding their breath, awaiting what would come.

Isis, matre dignitate plena, ante deos stetit, filii causam defendens. "Memores estote, quaeso, virtutum Osiridis et iniustitiarum, quas Seth nobis intulit," Isis oravit, voce tremula sed firma.

Isis, full of motherly dignity, stood before the gods, defending her son's cause. "Remember, I pray, the virtues of Osiris and the injustices that Seth has inflicted upon us," Isis pleaded, her voice trembling but firm.

Seth, contra, suam causam arroganter proposuit: "Mea vis et potentia me regem legitimum demonstrant," inquit, confidentia se inflans.

Seth, on the other hand, arrogantly presented his case: "My strength and power prove me to be the rightful king," he said, swelling with confidence.

Dei, auditis ambobus partibus, in Horum virtutem et iustitiam alta impressione affecti sunt. Ra, summo deorum, graviter incepit: "Horus, tua probitas et iustitia nos admoverunt. Tu dignus es qui Aegypti solium teneas."

The gods, having heard both sides, were deeply impressed by Horus's virtue and justice. Ra, the highest of the gods, began solemnly: "Horus, your honesty and justice have moved us. You are worthy to hold the throne of Egypt."

Tum, silentio magno, deorum consilium pronuntiatum est: Horus, rex Aegypti declaratus. Laetitia et plausus inter mortales et immortales eruperunt, ordine et iustitia restitutis.

Then, in great silence, the council of the gods announced: Horus was declared king of Egypt. Joy and applause erupted among both mortals and immortals, as order and justice were restored.

Seth, licet victus, tamen in sua potentia deserti retentus est, deorum vigilentia semper subiectus. "Deserti spatia mea erunt," dixit Seth, "sed meminero huius diei."

Seth, though defeated, was still retained in his power over the desert, always under the watchful eye of the gods. "The deserts will be mine," said Seth, "but I will remember this day."

Horus, diadema capiti impositum, sollemniter pronuntiavit: "Regnum meum iustitiae et pacis erit, patris mei et Aegypti honorum custos."

Horus, with the diadem placed upon his head, solemnly declared: "My reign will be one of justice and peace, the guardian of my father's and Egypt's honour."

Ita finitur narratio de certamine pro solio Aegypti, qua Horus, virtute et iustitia praeditus, regnum assecutus est, Aegyptum in aevum novum ducens. Sed etiam meminit populus Sethi, monitionem de potentia et ambitione perennis.

Thus ends the story of the struggle for the throne of Egypt, where Horus, endowed with virtue and justice, won the kingdom and led Egypt into a new era. But the people also remembered Seth, a warning about the enduring power of ambition.

Hoc modo, deorum iudicio, Aegyptus iterum florebat, sub Horo rege sapiente et iusto, cuius regnum a deis benedictum, per saecula in memoria hominum et deorum manebat.

In this way, by the judgment of the gods, Egypt flourished once again under King Horus, wise and just, whose reign, blessed by the gods, remained in the memory of humans and gods for centuries.

Regnum Hori

Postquam consilium deorum Horum regem Aegypti fecit, magna cum solemnitate coronatus est. In magno templo, sub caelo sereno, Horus diadema regium accepit, cum populo plaudente. "Pax et ordo nunc restituuntur," Horus ad suos dixit, "iustitia et resilientia mea regna erunt."

After the council of the gods made Horus the king of Egypt, he was crowned with great solemnity. In the great temple, under a clear sky, Horus received the royal diadem as the people applauded. "Peace and order are now restored," Horus said to his people, "justice and resilience will define my reign."

Fama eius ut symboli iustitiae et fortitudinis per totam Aegyptum crescebat. Populus eum venerabatur, eius nomen laudibus celebrans. "Vide," pater filio in renovato templo Osiridis monstrans, "quomodo Horus patri suo honorem reddit. Ceremoniae nobis Osiridis virtutes memorare iubent."

His reputation as a symbol of justice and strength grew throughout Egypt. The people revered him, praising his name. "Look," a father said to his son in the newly restored temple of Osiris, "how Horus honours his father. These ceremonies remind us of Osiris's virtues."

Cum sapientia, Horus terram regebat, paternae hereditatis memor. "Sicut pater meus, Osiris, voluit, sic regnum meum sapientia et iustitia florebit," in concilio dixit.

With wisdom, Horus ruled the land, mindful of his father's legacy. "As my father, Osiris, wished, so shall my kingdom flourish with wisdom and justice," he said in council.

Frontierae securae factae sunt, commerciumque floruit, Aegyptus opulentia et prosperitate gaudebat. "Terra nostra, sub Horo rege, iterum aureum aevum invenit," mercator in foro clamabat, navibus onustis mercibus spectans.

The borders were made secure, and trade flourished, with Egypt rejoicing in wealth and prosperity. "Our land, under King Horus, has once again found a golden age," a merchant in the market shouted, watching ships laden with goods.

Dei quoque, ordine restituto, Aegyptum suis favoribus benedixerunt. "Horus, tuo regimine, Aegyptus in pace et prosperitate manebit," Isis, mater eius, benigne dixit.

The gods, too, blessed Egypt with their favour, as order was restored. "Horus, under your reign, Egypt will remain in peace and prosperity," Isis, his mother, kindly said.

Horus, regis et protectoris munere functus, non solum in Aegypto sed etiam in caelo honorem invenit. "Sub tuo auspicio, Aegyptus invicta manebit," sacerdos in templo proclamavit, ad populum orans.

Horus, fulfilling the role of king and protector, found honour not only in Egypt but also in the heavens. "Under your guidance, Egypt will remain unconquered," a priest proclaimed in the temple, praying to the people.

Ita, sub Horo rege, Aegyptus novam aetatem ingressa est, ubi iustitia, pax, et prosperitas regnaverunt. Regnum eius exemplum futuris generationibus erat, demonstrans virtutem, sapientiam, et iustitiam semper triumphare.

Thus, under King Horus, Egypt entered a new age, where justice, peace, and prosperity ruled. His reign became an example for future generations, demonstrating that virtue, wisdom, and justice always triumph.

Echo in Aeternitatem

Narratio proelii inter Horum et Sethum, memoria Aegypti indelibiliter inscripta, per saecula resonavit. Sacerdotes in templis atque aris hanc historiam ut conflictus symbolum inter bonum malumque rettulerunt. "Ecce, o fideles, quomodo Horus, bonitatis assertor, adversus Sethum, malitiae originem, stetit," sacerdos ad populum congregatum praedicabat, huius gestorum gravitatem enuntians.

The story of the battle between Horus and Seth, indelibly inscribed in Egypt's memory, echoed through the ages. Priests in temples and at altars recounted this tale as a symbol of the conflict between good and evil. "Behold, O faithful ones, how Horus, the champion of goodness, stood against Seth, the source of malice," the priest preached to the gathered people, proclaiming the significance of these deeds.

Artifices, ingenio suo utentes, Horum triumphantem depinxerunt, saepe in accipitris magnifici forma. Eius imago, per totam terram venerata, virtutem et iustitiam symbolizabat.

Artists, using their skill, depicted Horus in triumph, often in the form of a magnificent falcon. His image, venerated throughout the land, symbolised virtue and justice.

Festivitates annuae, Horis victoriam celebrantes, gaudio et spiritualitate replebantur. "Hodie, Horus victoriam suam super Seth commemoramus," civitas in festo clamabat, cum laetitia et musica per vias effluerent.

Annual festivals celebrating Horus's victory were filled with joy and spirituality. "Today, we commemorate Horus's victory over Seth," the city cried out during the festivities, as joy and music flowed through the streets.

Pueri puellaeque, auditis fabulis de audaci Horo et callido Seth, exempla fortitudinis et iustitiae ediscebant. "Sicut Horus adversus Sethum stetit, ita et nos adversus difficultates stare debemus," magister ad discipulos suos narrabat.

Boys and girls, hearing stories of the brave Horus and the cunning Seth, learned examples of strength and justice. "Just as Horus stood against Seth, so too must we stand against difficulties," a teacher told his students.

Templa Horo dicata, loca sacra peregrinationis facta sunt, ubi homines mulieresque deorum auxilium et protectionem quaerebant. Peregrini longis itineribus veniebant, ut ante simulacra Horis preces suas offerrent.

Temples dedicated to Horus became sacred pilgrimage sites, where men and women sought the gods' help and protection. Pilgrims travelled long distances to offer their prayers before the images of Horus.

Amuleta, Horis effigie ornata, ab multis gestabantur, divinam protectionem quaerentes. "Hoc amuleto, Horus nos custodiat," mater filio suo donans, signum spei et securitatis dabat.

Amulets adorned with the image of Horus were worn by many, seeking divine protection. "With this amulet, may Horus protect us," a mother said, giving it to her son, as a symbol of hope and security.

Leges et iudicia Aegypti, iustitia Horis inspirata, aequitate et veritate fundatae sunt. "In iudiciis nostris, Horis exemplar nobis sit," iudex, ante causam dicendam, meditabatur.

The laws and judgments of Egypt, inspired by the justice of Horus, were founded on fairness and truth. "In our judgments, may Horus be our example," a judge reflected before delivering a verdict.

Scribae, diligenter, magni certaminis narrationes in papyris et parietibus tomborum regalium conservaverunt, memoria gestorum ne umquam evanesceret. "Haec gesta in aeternum servemus," scriba, calamo laborans, susurrabat.

Scribes carefully preserved the stories of the great battle on papyrus and the walls of royal tombs, ensuring that the memory of these deeds would never fade. "Let us preserve these deeds for eternity," a scribe whispered as he worked with his quill.

Hoc modo, cultus Horis per Aegyptum et regiones transmarinas diffusus est, eius nomen ut dei protectoris magis magisque veneratum. Mythes de Horo et Setho, spirituales Aegypti thesauros aluerunt, profundas vitae veritates docentes.

In this way, the worship of Horus spread throughout Egypt and across distant lands, with his name increasingly revered as that of a protector god. Myths of Horus and Seth nourished Egypt's spiritual treasures, teaching deep truths about life.

Conflictus inter Horum et Sethum, naturae et vitae cyclos aeternos repraesentans, in philosophiam Aegyptiam imbutus est. "Per Horum et Sethum, vitae mortisque mysteria contemplamur," philosophus in schola explicabat.

The conflict between Horus and Seth, representing the eternal cycles of nature and life, was deeply embedded in Egyptian philosophy. "Through Horus and Seth, we contemplate the mysteries of life and death," a philosopher explained in a school.

Sic victoria Horis non solum dynastiae divinae continuatio sed etiam fundamentum mythologiae Aegyptiae facta est, aequilibrii et harmoniae in mundo significans. Haec fabula, per aetates narrata, aeternam veritatem de virtute, sapientia, et iustitia generatim docet.

Thus, Horus's victory became not only a continuation of the divine dynasty but also the foundation of Egyptian mythology, symbolising balance and harmony in the world. This story, told through the ages, teaches an eternal truth about virtue, wisdom, and justice.

Mythus de Dea Maât

Origo Maât

In principio mundi, cum chaos et tenebrae rerum dominabantur, Maât, dea veritatis, iustitiae, et harmoniae, orta est. Ex cogitatione Atoum, dei creatoris, nata, Maât destinata erat ut universum ordine et iustitia impleret. "Ex mea mente, Maât, tu nata es, ut mundum ordine et lege nostra regas," Atoum, in aetheris luminibus sedens, dixit.

In the beginning of the world, when chaos and darkness ruled, Maât, the goddess of truth, justice, and harmony, was born. From the thought of Atum, the creator god, Maât was destined to fill the universe with order and justice. "From my mind, Maât, you were born to rule the world with our order and law," Atum, seated in the lights of the ether, said.

In capite suo Maât pluma struthionis portabat, quae symbolum universae veritatis erat. Hoc insigne omnes deos mortalesque ad veritatem semper loquendam admonuit. "Mea pluma non solum ornatui est, sed etiam magni ponderis symbolo," Maât, caelum intuens, affirmavit. "Meo munere, chaos in creationem, inordinatio in ordinem convertitur."

On her head, Maât wore an ostrich feather, which was the symbol of universal truth. This insignia reminded all gods and mortals to always speak the truth. "My feather is not merely for adornment but is also a symbol of great importance," Maât, gazing at the sky, affirmed. "Through my role, chaos is transformed into creation, and disorder into order."

Ex alto caelo, Maât mundum deorum hominumque observabat, curans ut omnia secundum principia sua procederent. Aegyptii crediderunt sine Maât universum in pristinum chaos recidere posse. "Maât fundamentum vitae nostrae est," sacerdos in templo dixit, "sine ea, neque veritas neque iustitia exsistere possunt."

From the high heavens, Maât watched over the world of gods and humans, ensuring that everything proceeded according to her principles. The Egyptians believed that without Maât, the universe could fall back into primordial chaos. "Maât is the foundation of our life," a priest in the temple said, "without her, neither truth nor justice can exist."

In Maât erat virtus quaedam, non solum chaos moderans sed etiam creationem ipsam fovente. "Per me, ordo universi conservatur," Maât suaviter pronuntiavit, "et per me, cursus vitae sine impedimento fluit."

In Maât was a certain power, not only moderating chaos but also nurturing creation itself. "Through me, the order of the universe is maintained," Maât softly declared, "and through me, the flow of life proceeds without hindrance."

Ita Maât non solum dea sed etiam principium erat, quod mundum regit, et sine quo nec dei nec homines in pace et harmonia vivere possunt. Aegyptii eius principia in corde societatis suae collocaverunt, credentes Maât in aeternum mundum sustinere.

Thus, Maât was not only a goddess but also a principle that governs the world, without which neither gods nor humans could live in peace and harmony. The Egyptians placed her principles at the heart of their society, believing that Maât would eternally sustain the world.

Munus Maât

Cotidie, Ra, deus solis, per caelum iter faciebat, Maât, deam veritatis, secum ferens. Maât, quasi nauta divina, Ra in itinere suo dirigebat, curans ut eius navis solaria tutum per aetherem navigaret. "Maât, tu lux mea in tenebris es," Ra, solis currum regens, dixit, "tua praesentia meum iter dirigit."

Every day, Ra, the sun god, journeyed across the sky, bringing Maât, the goddess of truth, with him. Maât, like a divine navigator, guided Ra on his journey, ensuring that his solar boat sailed safely through the heavens. "Maât, you are my light in the darkness," said Ra, steering the sun chariot, "your presence guides my journey."

In regno mortuorum, Maât iudicium animarum adiuvabat. Cor uniuscuiusque defuncti contra plumam veritatis eius pensabatur.

Si cor leve erat, anima ad aeternitatem admittebatur; si gravius, monstrum terribile illud devorabat. "Videamus," Maât, cor et plumam in statera tenens, susurravit, "an anima tua digna est lucis aeternae an tenebris damnata."

In the realm of the dead, Maât helped in the judgment of souls. The heart of each deceased person was weighed against her feather of truth. If the heart was light, the soul was admitted to eternity; if heavier, a terrible monster would devour it. "Let us see," Maât whispered, holding the heart and feather on the scales, "whether your soul is worthy of eternal light or condemned to darkness."

Reges Aegypti, Maât legibus obsequentes, regnum in prosperitate et pace conservabant. "Per Maât principia, regnum nostrum florebit," pharao, sceptro in manu, consiliariis suis affirmavit.

The kings of Egypt, adhering to Maât's laws, maintained the kingdom in prosperity and peace. "Through the principles of Maât, our kingdom will flourish," the pharaoh, holding his sceptre, declared to his advisors.

Iudices, Maât effigies portantes, iustitiam in omnibus iudiciis suis quaerebant. "Haec dea nobis testis est," iudex, figurinam elevans, dixit, "ut veritas in iudicio nostro semper praevaleat."

Judges, carrying images of Maât, sought justice in all their rulings. "This goddess is our witness," said the judge, raising the figurine, "so that truth may always prevail in our judgment."

Ita Maât non solum dea sed etiam norma vitae quotidiane erat, cuius principia et in caelo et in terra observabantur. Aegyptii, eius leges sequentes, in societate ordine et iustitia fundamentis positis, vivebant. "Maât nos in omni actione nostra ducit," civis, in templum procedens, oravit, "ut in vita nostra harmonia et iustitia regnet."

Thus, Maât was not only a goddess but also the standard of daily life, whose principles were observed both in heaven and on earth. The Egyptians, following her laws, lived in a society founded on order and justice. "Maât guides us in all our actions," prayed a citizen entering the temple, "so that harmony and justice may reign in our lives."

Per hanc deam, Aegyptus antiqua exemplar societatis, ubi veritas et iustitia supremum locum tenebant, praebebat. Maât, in corde et animo omnium Aegyptiorum profunde insita, tam in vita cotidiana quam in aeternitate spiritus eorum ducebat.

Through this goddess, ancient Egypt provided an example of a society where truth and justice held the highest place. Maât, deeply rooted in the hearts and minds of all Egyptians, guided their spirits both in daily life and in eternity.

Cultus Maât

Per totam Aegyptum, templa magnifica in honorem Maât, deae veritatis iustitiaeque, exstructa sunt. In his sacris locis, sacerdotes cotidie ritus sollemnes agebant, ut deae gratiam principiaque venerarentur.

Throughout Egypt, magnificent temples were built in honour of Maât, the goddess of truth and justice. In these sacred places, priests performed solemn rituals daily to venerate the goddess's grace and principles.

"In hoc templo, Maât colimus," sacerdos, ante altare stans, populo congregato explicavit, "ut eius benedictiones in vita nostra semper maneant."

"In this temple, we worship Maât," the priest, standing before the altar, explained to the gathered people, "so that her blessings may always remain in our lives."

Offertae Maât variabantur a statuis pulchris ad amuleta sacra et inscriptiones laudum. "Haec dona Maât dedicamus," fidelis, donum in aram ponens, oravit, "ut nos in iustitia veritateque ducat."

Offerings to Maât ranged from beautiful statues to sacred amulets and inscriptions of praise. "We dedicate these gifts to

Maât," a devotee prayed, placing the offering on the altar, "so that she may guide us in justice and truth."

Fideles, iustitiae et veritatis semitas quaerentes, ad Maât preces fuderunt, eius in omni aspectu vitae eorum ductum petentes. "O Maât, nos in decisionibus nostris duce," orans in templo susurravit, "ut semper verum et iustum agamus."

The faithful, seeking the paths of justice and truth, poured out prayers to Maât, asking for her guidance in every aspect of their lives. "O Maât, guide us in our decisions," one prayed softly in the temple, "so that we always act truthfully and justly."

Scribae, divina inspiratione ducti, hymnos et preces ad Maât dedicabant. "Per haec verba, Maât honorem damus," scriba, calamo laborans, dixit, "ut eius principia in corde populi Aegypti resonent."

Scribes, led by divine inspiration, dedicated hymns and prayers to Maât. "Through these words, we give honour to Maât," a scribe said, working with his pen, "so that her principles may resonate in the hearts of the people of Egypt."

Educatio iuvenum Aegyptiorum Maât principiis imbuta erat, docentes eos de importantia veritatis, iustitiae, et harmoniae in vita cotidiana. "Discite et vivite secundum Maât," magister, discipulos suos adhortans, praecipiebat, "quia in eius principiis vera vita est."

The education of young Egyptians was steeped in Maât's principles, teaching them the importance of truth, justice, and harmony in daily life. "Learn and live according to Maât," a teacher instructed his students, "for in her principles lies true life."

Ita, cultus Maât non solum in templa et ritus publicos sed etiam in vita privata et educatione iuventutis profunde infuditur, demonstrans quam centralis et pervasiva deae praesentia in societate Aegyptia esset. Per hoc divinum cultum, Aegyptii sperabant se ad maiorem harmoniam universalem contribuere, Maât principiis in omnibus suis actionibus sequentes.

Thus, the worship of Maât permeated not only temples and public rituals but also private life and the education of the youth, demonstrating how central and pervasive the goddess's presence was in Egyptian society. Through this divine worship, Egyptians hoped to contribute to a greater universal harmony, following Maât's principles in all their actions.

Influentia Maât

In societatis Aegyptiae corde, iustitia et aequitas, Maât gratia, fundamentales erant. "Per Maât, iustitia et pax in regno nostro dominatur," pharao, ad suum populum loquens, pronuntiavit, terrae suae patronam celebrans.

At the heart of Egyptian society, justice and equity, thanks to Maât, were fundamental. "Through Maât, justice and peace reign in our kingdom," the pharaoh proclaimed to his people, celebrating the patroness of their land.

Pharaones ipsi ut Maât legati in terra considerabantur, eius principia in omni administratione sua reflectentes. "Nos Maât servimus," pharao in concilio dixit, "ut eius ordo et harmonia per Aegyptum perseverent."

The pharaohs themselves were considered as Maât's representatives on Earth, reflecting her principles in all their governance. "We serve Maât," the pharaoh said in council, "so that her order and harmony may persist throughout Egypt."

Festivitates et celebrationes Maât memoriam saepe tenebant, eius doctrinam in culturae Aegyptiae corde inserentes. "Hodie Maât laudamus," populus in festivitate clamabat, cantibus et orationibus deam honorantes.

Festivals and celebrations often kept Maât's memory alive, embedding her doctrine in the heart of Egyptian culture. "Today we praise Maât," the people cried at the festival, honouring the goddess with songs and prayers.

Artifices, Maât inspiratione moti, eam in operibus suis depictam relinquebant, ut in templorum parietibus et in monumentis. "Per artem nostram, Maât ad aeternitatem pervenit," pictor, imaginem deae pingens, susurravit.

Artists, inspired by Maât, depicted her in their works, as seen on the walls of temples and monuments. "Through our art, Maât reaches eternity," a painter whispered, as he painted the image of the goddess.

Mores et ethica Aegyptiorum profunde in Maât principiis radicabantur, omnes ad vitam secundum eius normas vivendam hortantes. "Maât nos ad meliorem vitam ducit," civis, in colloquio familiaris, explicavit.

Egyptian morals and ethics were deeply rooted in Maât's principles, encouraging everyone to live according to her standards. "Maât leads us to a better life," a citizen explained during a family conversation.

In tractatibus et in accordis, Maât invocabatur, ut fides et iustitia in omnibus negotiis assecurarentur. "Per Maât, pax et honestas in hoc foedere regnant," legatus, pactum signans, dixit.

In treaties and agreements, Maât was invoked to ensure faithfulness and justice in all dealings. "Through Maât, peace and honesty reign in this pact," said the envoy, signing the agreement.

Societas Aegyptia, Maât ordine et harmonia mota, in omnibus vitae aspectibus hanc reflectionem quaerebat. "In omnibus quae agimus, Maât principia sequimur," sacerdos, ad altare stans, populum docebat, "ut ordo divinus in mundum nostrum influat."

Egyptian society, driven by Maât's order and harmony, sought to reflect this in every aspect of life. "In all we do, we follow Maât's principles," a priest, standing at the altar, taught the people, "so that divine order may flow into our world."

Ita Maât non solum in templis et in sacris ritibus sed etiam in quotidiana vita et in societatis structura profundam influentiam habebat, demonstrans quam essentialis eius doctrina ad vitam Aegyptiorum erat. Per hanc divinam praesentiam, Aegyptii ad maiorem societatis harmoniam aspirabant, Maât principiis in omnibus suis actionibus ducti.

Thus, Maât held deep influence not only in temples and sacred rites but also in daily life and the structure of society, demonstrating how essential her doctrine was to the lives of Egyptians. Through this divine presence, Egyptians aspired to greater societal harmony, guided by Maât's principles in all their actions.

Haereditas Aeterna Maât

Conceptus Maât culturam religionemque Aegyptiam altius affecit. "Per Maât nos ad maiorem cognitionem veritatis iustitiaeque venimus," magister in schola antiquitatis explicabat, discipulis suis praecepta deae tradens.

The concept of Maât profoundly influenced Egyptian culture and religion. "Through Maât, we come to a greater understanding of truth and justice," the teacher in the school of antiquity explained, passing on the goddess's teachings to his students.

Generatio post generationem, Maât veneratio perseveravit, eius principia perenniter in vita Aegyptiorum insita. "Maât in corde nostro et in actionibus nostris vivit," pater, filio suo narrans, de immortalitate eius doctrinae loquebatur.

From generation to generation, the veneration of Maât persisted, her principles permanently rooted in the lives of the Egyptians. "Maât lives in our hearts and actions," a father, speaking to his son, talked about the immortality of her teachings.

Fabulae de Maât, saeculorum decursu traditae, iustitiam et veritatem in animis audientium inspirabant. "Haec historia, quam de Maât narrant, nos ad meliores nos ipsos efficiendos hortatur," avus, ad focum sedens, nepotibus suis fabulam veterem referebat.

Stories of Maât, passed down through the centuries, inspired justice and truth in the minds of listeners. "This story they tell of Maât encourages us to become better versions of ourselves," a grandfather, sitting by the hearth, recounted an old tale to his grandchildren.

Aegyptologi, vestigia cultus eius in textibus antiquis artefactisque reperientes, magnitudinem eius influentiae revelaverunt. "In hoc documento Maât principia clare videntur," aegyptologus, in museo studens, collegis suis ostendebat.

Egyptologists, finding traces of her worship in ancient texts and artefacts, revealed the magnitude of her influence. "In this document, Maât's principles are clearly visible," an Egyptologist, studying in the museum, showed his colleagues.

Maât, ut potentissimum ordinis cosmici ethicaeque symbolum, perseveravit, eius imago in arte et literatura Aegyptia saepe repraesentata. "Maât nos ad universalem harmoniam spectare docet," artifex, deam in opere suo delineans, meditabatur.

Maât, as the most powerful symbol of cosmic order and ethics, endured, her image often represented in Egyptian art and literature. "Maât teaches us to strive for universal harmony," an artist, sketching the goddess in his work, reflected.

Philosophiae legesque orbis terrarum in Maât doctrinis resonantiam inveniebant, eius principia transcendentia culturas et temporum limites. "In hac philosophia Maât echo videmus," philosophus, in concilio loquens, argumentabat.

The philosophies and laws of the world found resonance in Maât's teachings, her principles transcending cultures and the limits of time. "In this philosophy, we see an echo of Maât," a philosopher, speaking at a council, argued.

Ita Maât dea eiusque praecepta testificationem aeternam humanitatis in aequilibrio iustitiaque quaerendi offerunt. "Maât non solum Aegyptiis sed etiam nobis omnibus exemplar est," orator, ad auditorium dicens, "ut in vita nostra quotidiana eius vias sequamur."

Thus, the goddess Maât and her teachings offer an eternal testament to humanity's search for balance and justice. "Maât is an example not just for the Egyptians but for all of us," an orator said to the audience, "so that we may follow her ways in our daily lives."

Per haec omnia, Maât non modo antiquitatis reliquiae sed etiam vivens haereditas est, quae adhuc hodie nos ad iustitiam, veritatem, harmoniamque aspirare docet, eius spiritus per aetates immutatus manens.

Through all of this, Maât is not merely a relic of antiquity but a living heritage, still today teaching us to aspire to justice, truth, and harmony, her spirit unchanged through the ages.

Iter Solis per Caelum

Ortus Solis

Quoque mane, Ra, deus solis, in oriente oriebatur, mundum suo lumine illustrans. Navi sua solari vehens, diem novum inchoabat, caelum coloribus vividis imbuens.

Every morning, Ra, the sun god, would rise in the east, illuminating the world with his light. Sailing in his solar barque, he began a new day, filling the sky with vibrant colours.

"In hac navigatione, vos, Maât et Horus, mecum estote," Ra, solis cursum dirigens, dixit, "ut ordo et tutela in nostro itinere praesint."

"On this journey, Maât and Horus, be with me," Ra, guiding the course of the sun, said, "so that order and protection may be present on our path."

Creaturae mythicae, eius ascensionem salutantes, hymnos laudis canebant, lumina caeli novo splendore fulgentia.

Mythical creatures, greeting his ascent, sang hymns of praise as the lights of the sky shone with new brilliance.

"Ra, te celebramus," chorus angelorum et daemonum, ad aetheris limites congregatus, intonabat.

"Ra, we celebrate you," a chorus of angels and demons, gathered at the edges of the sky, intoned.

Homines, lumine novo fruentes, preces matutinas offerebant, diem benedictione divina implorantes.

Humans, enjoying the new light, offered morning prayers, asking for divine blessing on the day.

"Da nobis, Ra, lucem et prosperitatem," sacerdos in templo orabat, incenso sacro ad altare accenso.

"Grant us light and prosperity, Ra," a priest in the temple prayed, lighting sacred incense at the altar.

Ros scintillans mane, donum Ra putabatur, terrae fertilitatem afferens.

The morning dew, sparkling, was considered a gift from Ra, bringing fertility to the land.

"Hoc rore, vita nova in agris nostris oritur," agricola, in campo laborans, murmurabat.

"With this dew, new life arises in our fields," a farmer, working in the field, murmured.

Aves, lumine ductae, caelum replebant, novi diei initium annuntiantes. Similiter, lilia in Nilo fluminis se aperiebant, primis radiis solis salutandis.

Birds, guided by the light, filled the sky, announcing the start of a new day. Similarly, the lilies in the Nile opened, greeting the first rays of the sun.

In templis, sacerdotes incensa ad honorem Ra accendebant, eius viam per caelum sanctificantes.

In the temples, priests lit incense in honour of Ra, sanctifying his path across the sky.

"Per haec sacra, te, Ra, honoramus," sacerdos, ante simulacrum dei stans, proclamavit.

"Through these sacred rites, we honour you, Ra," the priest proclaimed, standing before the god's image.

Artifices, inspiratione solis moti, opus suum incipiebant, eius calore ac luce animati.

Artisans, moved by the inspiration of the sun, began their work, animated by its warmth and light.

"Sub tuo numine, opera magna creabimus," faber, in officina sua laborans, sperabat.

"Under your guidance, we will create great works," a craftsman, working in his workshop, hoped.

Pueri, fabulis de Ra auditis, de eius itineribus caelestibus somniabant, imaginantes se inter sidera navigantes.

Children, having heard tales of Ra, dreamed of his celestial journeys, imagining themselves sailing among the stars.

"Quam mirabile est iter Ra!" puer, ad caelum aspiciens, exclamavit.

"How marvellous is Ra's journey!" a boy, looking up at the sky, exclaimed.

Calor solis, nebulae dissipatae, magnitudinem Aegypti revelabat, eius flumina et pyramides in luce nova splendentes.

The sun's warmth, dissipating the mist, revealed the grandeur of Egypt, its rivers and pyramids gleaming in the new light.

"Solis gratia, terra nostra viget," civis, in via ambulans, admirabatur.

"By the grace of the sun, our land thrives," a citizen, walking down the street, marvelled.

Ita, ortu solis, dies sub signo potentiae et munificentiae Ra incepit, symbolo renascentis spei et novi principii.

Thus, with the sunrise, the day began under the sign of Ra's power and generosity, symbolising renewed hope and a new beginning.

Aegyptii, in eius lumine viventes, diem novum cum gratitudine et spe accipiebant, semper memores donorum, quae solis deus eis attulit.

The Egyptians, living in his light, received each new day with gratitude and hope, always mindful of the gifts the sun god brought them.

Traversus Caeli

Cum zenithum attingeret, Ra, luminis vitaeque fons, caelum imperabat. Navi sua aurea per azureum caeli mare vehebatur, deorum custodia circumdatus.

When Ra reached his zenith, the source of light and life, he ruled the sky. He sailed through the blue sea of the heavens in his golden barque, surrounded by the guardians of the gods.

"Ecce, universum sub meo lumine floret," Ra, per aetheris spatia navigans, dixit, deserto aureo sub se mirante.

"Behold, the universe flourishes under my light," Ra said, as he sailed through the vast skies, with the golden desert beneath him in awe.

Agricolae in campis laborabant, solis virtute vivificante fruentes. "Ra nos alit," unus ex eis, sudore frontem detergens, exclamavit, fruges in terram feracem seminans.

Farmers worked in the fields, enjoying the life-giving power of the sun. "Ra nourishes us," one of them exclaimed, wiping sweat from his brow as he sowed crops into the fertile earth.

Mercatores, diei clari ductu, suas vias pergebant, negotia longinqua gerentes. "Solis luce, iter nostrum dirigitur," mercator, camelum per vias pulvereas agens, confidebat.

Merchants, guided by the clear light of day, continued their journeys, conducting distant business. "By the sun's light, our path is guided," a merchant confidently said, leading his camel along dusty roads.

Animalia, solis ardore lassi, umbras quaerebant, in quibus requiescerent. Interim, flores in hortis et agris colores vividos expandebant, caeli claritatem celebrantes.

Animals, weary from the heat of the sun, sought shade to rest. Meanwhile, flowers in gardens and fields spread their vibrant colours, celebrating the clarity of the sky.

Flumina lacusque, solis cursu illustrati, quasi specula caelestia lucebant. "Aqua et lux, vita mundi," poeta, ad ripam sedens, scribebat, naturae pulchritudinem admirans.

Rivers and lakes, illuminated by the sun's path, gleamed like celestial mirrors. "Water and light, the life of the world," a poet wrote, sitting by the riverbank, admiring the beauty of nature.

Daily life, regulated by the sun's position in the sky, followed its course. At midday, when Ra was most powerful, the priests performed sacred rites. "In this moment, Ra is most present," a priest, standing before the altar, taught the people.

Artists, observing the changes in light, created works that captured the essence of eternity. "Through art, we make the sunlight eternal," a painter mused, infusing colour into his canvas.

Scribes, recording the day's events under Ra's watchful gaze, wrote history. "These deeds, done under the sun, will nourish future memory," a scribe affirmed as he inscribed a scroll.

Shadows, lengthened by the sun's course, announced the approach of evening. Ra, casting his light over everything, offered warmth and protection. "Under my patronage, all are safe," Ra promised, ruling over the sky.

Thus, the sun's passage across the sky not only illuminated the day but also governed the course of life throughout the universe, showing that Ra was not only a god but also the guardian of all life.

Per hoc quotidium iter, Ra suam maiestatem et triumphum super mundum demonstrabat, omnes sub sua luce viventes ad meliorem crastinum ducens.

Through this daily journey, Ra demonstrated his majesty and triumph over the world, leading all who lived under his light towards a better tomorrow.

Occasus Solis

Vesperascente caelo, Ra ad occidentem vergens, descensum suum parabat. Caelum rubro aureoque colore tingebatur, mirabile spectaculum praebens.

As the sky darkened, Ra, moving towards the west, prepared for his descent. The sky was tinged with red and gold, providing a marvellous spectacle.

"Tandem, finis itineris mei appropinquat," Ra, ad fines caeli spectans, dixit, "sed eius pulchritudo semper in corde manebit."

"At last, the end of my journey approaches," Ra said, gazing at the edge of the sky, "but its beauty will remain forever in my heart."

Cum sol se inclinaret, vita quotidiana paulatim ad quietem redibat, animi ad vesperum conversi. Familiae, sub lumine candelarum, convocabantur, epulas fabulasque inter se communicantes.

As the sun set, daily life gradually returned to rest, with minds turning towards evening. Families gathered by candlelight, sharing meals and stories.

"Ecce, stellae caelum nocturnum implebunt," pater, caelum nocturnum indicans, filiis narravit, "nos in tenebris custodientes."

"Look, the stars will fill the night sky," the father, pointing to the sky, told his children, "watching over us in the darkness."

Ra, in horizontem demergens, diem finiebat, eius lux paulatim evanescens. "Gratias tibi, Ra, pro lumine tuo," plebs, ad occidentem spectans, in precatione dixit.

Ra, sinking into the horizon, ended the day, his light gradually fading. "Thank you, Ra, for your light," the people said in prayer, looking towards the west.

Sacerdotes, sacra vespertina perficientes, templa clausura erant, diurnos ritus concludentes. "Per haec sacra, tibi, Ra, valedicimus," sacerdos, antequam fores sacrae aedis clauderet, oravit.

The priests, completing the evening rites, were closing the temples, concluding the day's rituals. "Through these rites, we bid you farewell, Ra," the priest prayed before closing the sacred temple doors.

Cantus orationesque in aere resonabant, gratitudinem pro benignitate Ra exprimentes. "Tua praesentia nos hodie sustinuit," chorus fidelium, in templi atrio congregatus, cecinit.

Songs and prayers echoed in the air, expressing gratitude for Ra's kindness. "Your presence sustained us today," sang the choir of the faithful, gathered in the temple courtyard.

Serotina aura, post calores diurnos, refrigerium et pacem afferebat. "Haec vespertina frigus nos reficit," mater, liberos ad lectum parans, susurravit.

The evening breeze, after the day's heat, brought refreshment and peace. "This evening coolness refreshes us," the mother whispered, preparing her children for bed.

Custodes, taedas accendentes, nocturnam custodiam parabant, tenebras illuminantes. "Per hanc lucem, noctem secure transigemus," vigil, taedam in manu tenens, dixit.

The guards, lighting torches, prepared for the night watch, illuminating the darkness. "With this light, we will safely pass through the night," the watchman said, holding a torch.

Narratores, ad ignem congregati, fabulas incipiebant, audientium imaginationem excitantes. "Audite, o liberi, fabulas deorum," narrator, ante ignem sedens, coepit, stellas super caput scintillantes.

Storytellers, gathered around the fire, began telling tales, stirring the listeners' imaginations. "Listen, children, to the stories of the gods," the storyteller began, seated by the fire, with stars twinkling above.

In somniis, homines divinam inspirationem capiebant, a numinibus caelestibus missam. "In nocte, deis ducimur," puella, oculis clausis, in lecto susurravit.

In their dreams, people received divine inspiration, sent by the heavenly deities. "In the night, we are guided by the gods," the girl whispered, her eyes closed in bed.

Luna, Ra absente, caeli custodiam assumebat, noctis silentium sua luce mitigans. "Nunc, soror mea Luna, vos custodit," Ra, ultimo lumine emisso, murmuravit.

The moon, in Ra's absence, took over the guardianship of the sky, softening the silence of the night with its light. "Now, my sister Moon will guard you," Ra murmured, as he cast his final light.

Natura, in silentium lapsa, solis et lunae aeterno ritu se committerebat, pacem nocturnam amplectens. "In hoc tranquillo, vita pausat," poeta, sub lumine lunae scribens, contemplabat.

Nature, falling into silence, entrusted itself to the eternal ritual of the sun and moon, embracing the peace of the night. "In this stillness, life rests," the poet mused, writing under the moonlight.

Speratio novi diei, cum Ra rediret, in cordibus omnium vigebat, promissionem novae lucis et novi initii portans. "Cum aurora venit, iterum Ra nos salutabit," senex, ad caelum stellatum spectans, finivit.

The hope of a new day, when Ra would return, flourished in the hearts of all, carrying the promise of new light and a new beginning. "When dawn comes, Ra will greet us again," the old man concluded, gazing at the starry sky.

Ita finitur dies sub Ra tutela, cuius occasus non finis sed promissio novae aurorae et perpetui vitae cycli est.

Thus, the day ends under Ra's guardianship, whose setting is not the end but the promise of a new dawn and the eternal cycle of life.

Mythus Anubidis et Librationis Cordium

Missio Anubidis

Anubis, deus embalamationis et rituum funerum, capite canis praeditus, mortis dominus habebatur. Eius sacra munera erant defunctos in Orcum ducere et corpora eorum ad vitam aeternam conservare.

Anubis, the god of embalming and funerary rites, with the head of a dog, was considered the lord of death. His sacred duties were to guide the dead to the underworld and preserve their bodies for eternal life.

"In hac terra inter vivos et mortuos, ego sum dux," Anubis, umbris in crypta loquens, affirmabat, *"mea arte, animas ad aeternitatem praeparo."*

"In this land between the living and the dead, I am the guide," Anubis, speaking to the shadows in the crypt, declared, "with my skill, I prepare souls for eternity."

Doctrinam mumificationis Aegyptiis tradidit, ut mortui in futurum sine fine manerent. "Per meam scientiam," Anubis discipulis suis in templi sacris aedibus docens explicabat, *"mortales immortalitatem tangere possunt."*

He taught the Egyptians the doctrine of mummification so that the dead could remain for an endless future. "Through my knowledge," Anubis, teaching his disciples in the sacred halls of the temple, explained, "mortals can touch immortality."

Sepulcra sacra faciebat, animas a malis spiritibus protegens. "Hoc sepulcrum, meis benedictionibus, inviolabile erit," Anubis, sepulcrum consecrans, pronuntiabat.*

He made sacred tombs, protecting souls from evil spirits. "This tomb, by my blessings, will remain inviolate," Anubis, consecrating the tomb, declared.

Custos coemeteriorum, quietem mortuorum vigilabat, ne quid eos turbaret. "Sub mea custodia, pacem invenietis," Anubis, per noctem coemeterium perambulans, susurrabat.*

As the guardian of cemeteries, he watched over the peace of the dead, ensuring nothing disturbed them. "Under my protection, you will find peace," Anubis whispered, walking through the cemetery at night.

*Aequitate et misericordia corda iudicabat, veritatem in omni anima quaerens. "Iustitia mea omnes tangit," Anubis, ante stateram stans, dicebat, cor et plumam Maât parans.**

With fairness and compassion, he judged hearts, seeking the truth in every soul. "My justice touches all," Anubis, standing before the scales, said, preparing the heart and Maât's feather.

*Eius praesentia vivis consolationem praebebat, sperantes amatos in pace esse. "Anubis, custos carorum nostrorum, te invocamus," familia, ante aram orans, rogabat.**

His presence brought comfort to the living, hoping their loved ones were in peace. "Anubis, guardian of our dear ones, we invoke you," a family, praying before the altar, pleaded.

*Ritibus funebribus, Anubis invocabatur, ut transitus tutus esset. "Per haec sacra, animam ad aeternam domum ducimus," sacerdos, masca Anubidis indutus, officiabat.**

During funeral rites, Anubis was invoked to ensure a safe passage. "Through these sacred rites, we lead the soul to the eternal home," a priest, wearing the mask of Anubis, officiated.

*Familiae, dona et preces Anubidi offerebant, eius favorem implorantes. "Accipe munera nostra, o Anubis," mater, ante imaginem dei dona ponens, orabat.**

Families offered gifts and prayers to Anubis, seeking his favour. "Accept our offerings, O Anubis," a mother, placing gifts before the god's image, prayed.

*Amuleta eius effigie contra daemonia tutabantur, portatores suos defendentes. "Hoc amuleto, ab omni malo custodiar," vir, amuletum collo suspendens, confidebat.**

Amulets bearing his image protected against demons, defending their wearers. "With this amulet, I will be guarded against all evil," a man, hanging the amulet around his neck, trusted.

*Hymnis, Anubidis iustitia et benignitas celebrabantur, eius nomen per aetatem laudatum. "O Anubis, tua iustitia nos regat," chorus in templo canebat.**

With hymns, Anubis' justice and kindness were celebrated, his name praised through the ages. "O Anubis, let your justice guide us," a choir in the temple sang.

*Per fidem in protectione Anubidis, Aegyptii spem et fortitudinem inveniebant, in futurum cum fiducia spectantes. "In tua custodia, Anubis, securi sumus," puer, ad caelum nocturnum aspiciens, somniabat.**

Through faith in Anubis' protection, the Egyptians found hope and strength, looking to the future with confidence. "In your care, Anubis, we are safe," a boy, gazing at the night sky, dreamed.

Ita, Anubis, per sua officia sacra et munera divina, non solum in morte sed etiam in vita Aegyptiorum profunde insederat, dux et protector in via ad aeternitatem.

Thus, Anubis, through his sacred duties and divine gifts, was deeply rooted not only in death but also in the lives of the Egyptians, as a guide and protector on the path to eternity.

Cordium Libratio

In secreto Orci loco, aula cordium librationis posita erat, ubi Anubis animas ad ultimum iudicium ducebat.

In a secret place of the Underworld, the Hall of the Weighing of Hearts was situated, where Anubis guided souls to their final judgment.

"Hic, veritas uniuscuiusque revelabitur," Anubis, ad limen aulae stans, animas introducens, pronuntiabat.*

"Here, the truth of each will be revealed," Anubis, standing at the threshold of the hall, leading the souls, proclaimed.

Cordis defuncti ponderatio adversus plumam Maât fiebat, iustitiae veritatisque signum.

The weighing of the deceased's heart was performed against the feather of Maât, the symbol of justice and truth.

"Tuae vitae momenta nunc examinabuntur," Anubis, stateram tenens, solemniter dicebat.*

"The moments of your life will now be examined," Anubis, holding the scales, solemnly said.

Si cor leve esset, anima digna iudicabatur ad aeterna prata transire. "Levitas cordis tui te ad aeternitatem ducit," Anubis, cor leve deprehendens, annuntiabat.*

If the heart was light, the soul was judged worthy to pass into the eternal fields. "The lightness of your heart leads you to eternity," Anubis, finding the heart light, announced.

Contra, si cor peccatis gravatum esset, Ammit, devoratrix, illud consumebat. "Gravitas iniquitatis tuae te ad Ammit tradit," Anubis, cor grave ostendens, tristis sed iustus, pronuntiabat.*

On the other hand, if the heart was weighed down by sins, Ammit, the devourer, would consume it. "The weight of your wrongdoings delivers you to Ammit," Anubis, showing the heavy heart, pronounced, sad but just.

Cum summa aequitate, Anubis libram gubernabat, ne ullum praeiudicium iudicium inflecteret. "Mea lance, nulla anima sine vera aestimatione iudicabitur," Anubis, lanceae aequilibrium scrutans, affirmabat.*

With the highest fairness, Anubis controlled the scale, ensuring no bias influenced the judgment. "By my scales, no soul shall be judged without true evaluation," Anubis, scrutinizing the balance, affirmed.

Thoth, sapientiae deus, iudicium in aeternis libris scribebat, ne ullum factum oblivione deleretur. "Tua fata hic in aeternum conservabuntur," Thoth, calamo scribens, animabus explicabat.*

Thoth, the god of wisdom, recorded the judgment in eternal books, ensuring that no deed would be erased by forgetfulness. "Your fate will be preserved here forever," Thoth, writing with his pen, explained to the souls.

*Animae purae ad Osiridis campos invitabantur, ubi aeternam pacem fruebantur. "In his pratis, requies aeterna te manet," Osiris, novas animas excipiens, promittebat.**

Pure souls were invited to the fields of Osiris, where they enjoyed eternal peace. "In these fields, eternal rest awaits you," Osiris, welcoming new souls, promised.

*Ritualis huius gravitas vitam virtutemque praedicabat, exhortans Aegyptios ad Maât concordiam persequendam. "Per acta nostra, ad Maât harmoniam aspiramus," civis, in templum orans, meditabatur.**

The solemnity of this ritual preached life and virtue, urging Egyptians to strive for harmony with Maât. "Through our deeds, we aspire to Maât's harmony," a citizen, praying in the temple, meditated.

*Fabulae Anubidis moralitatem et divinarum legum reverentiam docebant, Aegyptios ad iustitiam hortantes. "Ex Anubidis legendis, iustitiae semitam discimus," magister, discipulis narrans, docebat.**

The stories of Anubis taught morality and reverence for divine laws, encouraging Egyptians towards justice. "From the legends of Anubis, we learn the path of justice," a teacher, narrating to his students, instructed.

*In tumulis, picturae cordium librationem illustrabant, iudicii memoriam visualem praebentes. "Haec imagines nos ad iustam vitam vivendam admonent," visitator, per cryptam ambulans, contemplabatur.**

In the tombs, paintings depicted the weighing of hearts, providing a visual reminder of judgment. "These images remind us to live a just life," a visitor, walking through the crypt, reflected.

Preces Anubidi, eius misericordiam directionemque petebant, animas ad iustitiam ducere sperantes. "O Anubis, tua clementia nos duce," fidelis, ante altare supplicans, orabat.*

Prayers to Anubis sought his mercy and guidance, hoping he would lead souls to justice. "O Anubis, guide us with your mercy," a worshipper, kneeling before the altar, prayed.

Ritus funebres, iustitiae post mortem credentiam reflectebant, perpetuam animarum aestimationem demonstrantes. "Per haec sacra, ad aeternam iustitiam pervenimus," sacerdos, funus celebrans, affirmabat.*

Funeral rites reflected the belief in justice after death, demonstrating the perpetual assessment of souls. "Through these sacred rites, we reach eternal justice," a priest, conducting a funeral, affirmed.

Cordium libratio, in conceptione Aegyptiaca de orco centralis, vitam ultra mortem regendam esse docebat. "Per hoc iudicium, vitae nostrae verum pondus cognoscimus," philosophus, ad auditorium loquens, explicabat.*

The weighing of hearts, central to the Egyptian conception of the underworld, taught that life beyond death would be ruled. "Through this judgment, we learn the true weight of our lives," a philosopher, speaking to an audience, explained.

Ita, Anubidis et cordium libratio, non solum mortuos sed etiam vivos ad vitam meliorem instabant, iustitiam, veritatem, et moralitatem in corde Aegyptiorum culturae infixum relinquentes.

Thus, Anubis and the weighing of hearts urged not only the dead but also the living towards a better life, leaving justice, truth, and morality deeply embedded in the heart of Egyptian culture.

Hereditas Anubidis

Per totam Aegyptum, Anubis pro sua sapientia et iustitia venerabatur.

Throughout all of Egypt, Anubis was venerated for his wisdom and justice.

"O Anubis, tua iustitia nos ad meliorem vitam ducit," populus in templum congregatus, deo laudes cantabat.*

"O Anubis, your justice leads us to a better life," the people, gathered in the temple, sang praises to the god.

Templa magnifica in honorem Anubidis exstructa erant, sacrae orationis loca.

Magnificent temples were built in honour of Anubis, places of sacred prayer.

"In his sacris aedibus, Anubis colimus," sacerdos, ante aram stans, fidelibus explicabat.*

"In these sacred buildings, we worship Anubis," the priest, standing before the altar, explained to the faithful.

Sacerdotes eius, magna cum pietate ac cura, ritus funebres exercebant.

His priests, with great devotion and care, performed funeral rites.

"Per haec sacra, Anubidi servimus," sacerdos, ritum peragens, susurrabat.*

"Through these sacred rites, we serve Anubis," the priest, conducting the ceremony, whispered.

Festivitates Anubidis, aeternae vitae celebrantes, per totam terram fiebant.

Festivals in honour of Anubis, celebrating eternal life, were held throughout the land.

"Hodie Anubis honoramus," civitas, in viis festum celebrans, clamabat.*

"Today we honour Anubis," the city, celebrating the festival in the streets, shouted.

Fabulae de Anubis, aequitatis mortuorumque respectus valores tradentes, per generationes narrabantur.

Stories of Anubis, imparting values of justice and respect for the dead, were passed down through generations.

"Ex his narrationibus, virtutem discimus," magister, ad pueros circumsedentes, fabulam incipiebat.*

"From these stories, we learn virtue," the teacher, beginning a story to the children seated around, began.

Infantes, eius historiae moralis ductu edocti, ad virtutem aspirabant.

Children, educated under the moral guidance of his stories, aspired to virtue.

"Anubis nobis exemplar est," puer, in schola discens, meditabatur.*

"Anubis is our example," a boy, studying in school, reflected.

Iudicia Anubidis, aequitatem in societate Aegyptia inspirantes, omnibus nota erant.

The judgments of Anubis, inspiring fairness in Egyptian society, were known to all.

"Iustitia Anubidis nos regit," iudex, in foro loquens, affirmabat.*

"The justice of Anubis governs us," a judge, speaking in the court, affirmed.

Pharaones, Anubis ut protectoris aeternitatis suae recognoscentes, eum magni pendebant.

The Pharaohs, recognising Anubis as the protector of their eternity, held him in high regard.

"Anubis, aeternitatis meae custos," pharao, in solio sedens, orabat.*

"Anubis, guardian of my eternity," the Pharaoh, seated on his throne, prayed.

Investigationes archaeologicae magnitudinem Anubidis in arte funeraria revelaverunt.

Archaeological investigations revealed the importance of Anubis in funerary art.

"Hae repertae, Anubidis in cultura nostra pondus demonstrant," archaeologus, in excavatione laborans, collegis narrabat.*

"These discoveries demonstrate the significance of Anubis in our culture," an archaeologist, working on an excavation, told his colleagues.

Amuleta Anubidis, inter res funerarias vulgata, contra mala spiritus tutabantur.

Amulets of Anubis, commonly found among funerary items, protected against evil spirits.

"Hoc amuleto, Anubis nos in orco proteget," civis, amuletum emens, sperabat.*

"With this amulet, Anubis will protect us in the underworld," a citizen, buying the amulet, hoped.

Imago eius, aeternae tutelae symbolo, in vita post mortem praesidium offerebat.

His image, a symbol of eternal protection, offered safety in the afterlife.

"Sub imagine Anubidis, securi sumus," familia, ante statuam orans, confidebat.*

"Under the image of Anubis, we are safe," a family, praying before the statue, believed.

Scriptores eius laudes in sacris voluminibus conservabant, aeternam eius memoriam tenentes.

Writers preserved his praises in sacred scrolls, keeping his memory eternal.

"Per haec verba, Anubis in aeternum vivet," scriba, scripturam exarans, dicebat.*

"Through these words, Anubis will live forever," a scribe, inscribing the writing, said.

Anubis, vitae mortisque nexum significans, transformationis viam praebuit.

Anubis, representing the link between life and death, provided the path of transformation.

"Anubis, vita ad mortem, morte ad vitam ducit," philosophus, in academia docens, explicabat.*

"Anubis leads from life to death, and from death to life," a philosopher, teaching in the academy, explained.

Legenda eius, Aegypto transgressa, culturas alias afficiebat, eius sapientiam diffundens.

His legend, extending beyond Egypt, affected other cultures, spreading his wisdom.

"Anubis, ultra fines nostros notus," mercator, terras longinquas petens, narrabat.*

"Anubis is known beyond our borders," a merchant, travelling to distant lands, told.

Mythus Anubidis, iustitiae immortalitatisque quaestionem tractans, potentem humanitatis aspirationis symbolum manet.

The myth of Anubis, addressing the question of justice and immortality, remains a powerful symbol of humanity's aspirations.

"In Anubide, aeternam iustitiae immortalitatisque spem invenimus," sacerdos, ad coetum loquens, conclamabat.*

"In Anubis, we find the eternal hope of justice and immortality," a priest, speaking to the gathering, proclaimed.

Ita, Anubidis hereditas, per saecula manens, non tantum in Aegypto sed etiam per orbem terrarum, iustitiae, sapientiae, et aeternae vitae significationem portat, animas ad meliorem futurum ducens.

Thus, the legacy of Anubis, lasting through the centuries, carries the meaning of justice, wisdom, and eternal life, not only in Egypt but across the world, leading souls to a better future.

Mythus de Dea Sekhmet

Nativitas Sekhmet

In antiquis Aegypti temporibus, Sekhmet, dea belli, vastationis et sanitatis, in mundo apparuit. Leonis capite ornata, potestatem mortiferam simul et curativam gerebat.

In ancient Egyptian times, Sekhmet, the goddess of war, devastation, and health, appeared in the world. Adorned with the head of a lion, she wielded both deadly and healing powers.

"Ex ira mea, Sekhmet nata est," Ra, deus solis, caelestibus potestatibus narravit, "ut hominum insolentiam puniret."

"From my wrath, Sekhmet was born," Ra, the sun god, told the celestial powers, "to punish the arrogance of humans."

Cum ira solis in terram descendit, Sekhmet, eius furoris instrumentum, creata est. Illa, igne solari armata, terram adiit, ubi eius spiritus ardentes deserta inflammarunt et flumina in fervorem verterunt.

When the wrath of the sun descended to the earth, Sekhmet, the instrument of his fury, was created. Armed with solar fire, she came to the earth, where her burning spirit set deserts ablaze and turned rivers into boiling streams.

"Nihil meae vi resistere potest," Sekhmet, per deserta gradiens, magna voce exclamabat, omnia in suo itinere consumens.

"Nothing can resist my power," Sekhmet declared in a loud voice, walking through the deserts, consuming everything in her path.

Hominum corda, eius mentione, metu tremebant, potentiam eius vastatricem agnoscentes. "Quis nos ab hac ira liberabit?" plebs, timore capti, inter se susurrabant.

The hearts of men trembled with fear at her mention, recognising her destructive power. "Who will deliver us from this wrath?" the people, seized by fear, whispered among themselves.

Etiam Ra, eius creator, potentia Sekhmet perturbatus est, miratus quantum vastitatis illa afferre posset. "Fortasse nimium longe processi," Ra, in solio suo sedens, secum cogitavit.

Even Ra, her creator, was disturbed by Sekhmet's power, amazed at how much devastation she could bring. "Perhaps I have gone too far," Ra, sitting on his throne, thought to himself.

Sekhmet non solum perniciei sed etiam tutelae dea erat, pharaones in proeliis ducebat. "Tua virtute, victoria nostra est," pharao, ante proelium orans, Sekhmet invocabat.

Sekhmet was not only a goddess of destruction but also of protection, leading pharaohs into battles. "By your strength, our victory is assured," the pharaoh prayed before the battle, invoking Sekhmet.

Sacerdotes, eius iram placare cupientes, sacrificia ei offerebant. "Accipe haec dona, o Sekhmet, et iram tuam a nobis averte," sacerdos, altari stans, deprecabatur.

Priests, wishing to appease her wrath, offered sacrifices to her. "Accept these gifts, O Sekhmet, and turn your anger away from us," the priest, standing at the altar, prayed.

In honorem eius, templa magnifica aedificabantur, ubi fideles eius cultum exercebant. "In his sacris aedibus, tua magnitudo celebratur," architectus, templum inspiciens, laudabat.

In her honour, magnificent temples were built, where her faithful worshipped her. "In these sacred halls, your greatness is celebrated," the architect praised, inspecting the temple.

Hymni et preces Sekhmet invocabant, eius tutelam et curas petentes. "O Sekhmet, nos ab omni malo protege," fidelis in templo orans, supplicabat.

Hymns and prayers invoked Sekhmet, seeking her protection and care. "O Sekhmet, protect us from all harm," a faithful person prayed in the temple.

Medici et sanatores, eius auxilium in sanatione quaerebant, morbos curare sperantes. "Per nomen Sekhmet, sanitatem hanc impetremus," medicus, herbas medicinales miscens, optabat.

Doctors and healers sought her assistance in healing, hoping to cure diseases. "By the name of Sekhmet, we grant this healing," the doctor, mixing medicinal herbs, wished.

Ita, Sekhmet, inter mortem et vitam dominans, in Aegypti cultura profunde radicata erat, monstrans vim vitae mortisque aequilibrium, inter destructionem et sanationem pendens.

Thus, Sekhmet, ruling over both death and life, was deeply rooted in Egyptian culture, demonstrating the power of life's balance, hanging between destruction and healing.

Furor Sekhmet

Vastatio, quam Sekhmet efferebat, in dies crescebat, Aegypti terras sanguine et desolatione implebat. "Quis nos ab hac ira liberare potest?" homines, ad caelum manus tendentes, clamabant, Ra auxilium petentes.

The devastation that Sekhmet unleashed grew day by day, filling the lands of Egypt with blood and desolation. "Who can deliver us from this wrath?" people, raising their hands to the sky, cried out, seeking help from Ra.

Ra, destructionis magnitudinem considerans, Sekhmet furiam sistere statuit. "Opus est consilio, quo furor eius mitigetur," Ra, cum consiliariis suis collocutus, decrevit.

Ra, considering the extent of the destruction, decided to stop Sekhmet's fury. "A plan is needed to calm her rage," Ra, after speaking with his advisors, declared.

Imperavit ut cerevisia cum rubro pigmento mixta pararetur, sanguinem imitans. "Hoc consilio, Sekhmet decipiemus," Ra, potionis parationem iubens, dixit.

He ordered beer to be prepared, mixed with red pigment to resemble blood. "With this plan, we will deceive Sekhmet," Ra said, commanding the preparation of the drink.

Cerevisia in campis proeliis aspersa est, Sekhmet in errorem inducens. "En, sanguis hostium meorum," Sekhmet, potionem pro sanguine habens, exclamavit et exhausit.

The beer was scattered across the battlefields, tricking Sekhmet. "Behold, the blood of my enemies," Sekhmet, mistaking the drink for blood, exclaimed and drank it all.

Eius ebrietas sanguinis sitim sedavit, furiamque eius placavit. "Quid hoc loco accidit?" Sekhmet, mente turbata, se interrogavit, pacis sensum experiens.

Her intoxication quenched her thirst for blood and calmed her fury. "What has happened here?" Sekhmet, her mind confused, asked herself, feeling a sense of peace.

Ra, occasione capta, Sekhmet in Hathor, amorem gaudiumque ferentem deam, transformavit. "Nunc, nova forma tibi datur," Ra, mutationem efficiens, pronuntiavit.

Ra, seizing the opportunity, transformed Sekhmet into Hathor, a goddess who brings love and joy. "Now, a new form is given to you," Ra proclaimed, carrying out the transformation.

Hathor, divinitate mutata, harmoniam et sanationem per Aegyptum diffudit. "Per me, nunc amor et laetitia florebunt," Hathor, inter homines ambulans, affirmabat.

Hathor, now changed in her divinity, spread harmony and healing throughout Egypt. "Through me, love and joy will now flourish," Hathor, walking among the people, affirmed.

Humani, miraculo facto, Sekhmet conversionem in Hathor laetantes celebraverunt. "Gratias tibi, Ra, pro misericordia tua," populus, novo deae aspectu gaudentes, canebant.

The people, witnessing the miracle, joyfully celebrated Sekhmet's transformation into Hathor. "Thank you, Ra, for your mercy," the people sang, rejoicing in the new form of the goddess.

Ex hoc gesto, aequilibrii et reverentiae momenti docebantur. "In hac historia, naturae divinae dualitatem videmus," sacerdos, ad congregatos narrans, docebat.

From this act, they were taught the importance of balance and reverence. "In this story, we see the duality of divine nature," the priest taught, speaking to the gathered people.

Festivitates Sekhmet et Hathor honorem tribuebant, eorum transformationem memorantes. "Hodie, deae nostrae magnitudinem celebramus," civitas, in festo conveniens, exsultabat.

Festivals honoured both Sekhmet and Hathor, remembering their transformation. "Today, we celebrate the greatness of our goddess," the city, gathering for the festival, rejoiced.

Ita, Sekhmet furoris legenda et in Hathor transformationis narratio, per saecula tradita, iustitiae et immortalitatis symbolum mansit, populo Aegyptio constantem virtutis et moderationis admonitionem praebens.

Thus, the legend of Sekhmet's fury and the story of her transformation into Hathor, passed down through the ages, remained a symbol of justice and immortality, providing the Egyptian people with a constant reminder of virtue and moderation.

Hereditas Sekhmetis

In mythologia Aegyptiaca, Sekhmet, etiam post multa saecula, potens dea manebat. "Sekhmet, vis et tutela nostra," artifex, imaginem eius in templo pingens, murmuravit.

In Egyptian mythology, Sekhmet, even after many centuries, remained a powerful goddess. "Sekhmet, our strength and protection," the artist murmured, painting her image in the temple.

Eius effigies, in templorum parietibus sculptae vel pictae, magnitudinem et potentiam eius demonstrabant. "Haec imago nos proteget," sacerdos, ad statuam deae in sanctuario stans, adorabat.

Her effigies, carved or painted on the walls of temples, displayed her greatness and power. "This image will protect us," the priest, standing before the goddess's statue in the sanctuary, worshipped.

Talismanis eius imagine signatis uti solebant Aegyptii, ut vires et protectionem haberent. "Per hanc amuletam, Sekhmetis praesidio fruamur," vir, talismanum collo suspendens, sperabat.

The Egyptians used talismans marked with her image to gain strength and protection. "Through this amulet, may we enjoy Sekhmet's protection," the man, hanging the talisman around his neck, hoped.

Medici sanatoresque Sekhmetem invocabant, ut aegrotis salutem et sanationem ferret. "O Sekhmet, da nobis sanitatem," medicus, herbam medicinalem praeparans, precabatur.

Doctors and healers invoked Sekhmet to bring health and healing to the sick. "O Sekhmet, grant us health," the doctor prayed, preparing a medicinal herb.

Ritualibus in eius honorem factis, cum saltationibus et cerevisiae libationibus, colentes eius iram placare studebant. "Per haec sacrificia, iram tuam a nobis avertere speramus," populus in festo, ad altare stans, cantabat.

Through rituals in her honour, with dances and beer offerings, her followers sought to appease her anger. "Through these sacrifices, we hope to turn away your wrath," the people sang, standing at the altar during the festival.

Fabulae de Sekhmet viribusque eius et irae periculis narrabantur ut monitiones et doctrinae. "Audite, o liberi, fabulas de Sekhmet, quae nos docent irae dominari," magister, ad circulum discipulorum sedens, incipiebat.

Stories about Sekhmet's power and the dangers of her anger were told as warnings and lessons. "Listen, children, to the tales of Sekhmet, which teach us how to control anger," the teacher, sitting in a circle of students, began.

Pharaones se cum Sekhmet, dea belligera, identificabant, ut suam auctoritatem confirmarent. "Sub Sekhmetis protectione, in proelium eamus," pharao, ante pugnam loquens, exhortabatur.

Pharaohs identified themselves with Sekhmet, the warrior goddess, to assert their authority. "Under Sekhmet's protection, let us go into battle," the pharaoh urged, speaking before the fight.

Festivitates Sekhmet dedicatae purificationis et tutelae ritus includebant. "Hoc festo, purificationem et Sekhmetis protectionem petimus," sacerdos, populum ad ceremoniam ducens, pronuntiabat.

Festivals dedicated to Sekhmet included purification and protection rituals. "In this festival, we seek purification and Sekhmet's protection," the priest proclaimed, leading the people to the ceremony.

Orationibus Sekhmet adhibitis, fideles vires in adversis petebant. "In his difficultatibus, Sekhmet, tua fortitudine indigemus," mulier, in templo genuflectens, oravit.

In prayers to Sekhmet, the faithful sought strength in adversity. "In these difficulties, Sekhmet, we need your strength," the woman prayed, kneeling in the temple.

Doctrina Sekhmetis de sui dominio magni momenti erat. "Per Sekhmet, discimus quomodo nosmet ipsos regere debemus," philosophus, in foro disputans, docebat.

Sekhmet's teaching on self-control was of great importance. "Through Sekhmet, we learn how we must govern ourselves," the philosopher taught, debating in the forum.

Templa Sekhmetis, non solum adorationis sed etiam sanationis et sapientiae loci erant. "In his sacris aedibus, et curam et sapientiam invenimus," peregrinus, templum ingressus, admirabatur.

Sekhmet's temples were places not only of worship but also of healing and wisdom. "In these sacred halls, we find both care and wisdom," the traveller marvelled, entering the temple.

Peregrini ex longinquis terris venerunt ut deae honores redderent eiusque benedictionem quaererent. "Longum iter fecimus ut Sekhmet honoremus," peregrinus, ante deae simulacrum stans, confitebatur.

Travellers from distant lands came to pay homage to the goddess and seek her blessing. "We have travelled a long way to honour Sekhmet," the traveller confessed, standing before the goddess's statue.

Contationes de Sekhmet naturae divinitatumque viribus reverentiam inspirabant. "Ex his fabulis, divinarum rerum magnitudinem discimus," senex, ad focum narrans, explicabat.

Tales of Sekhmet and the powers of nature and divinity inspired reverence. "From these stories, we learn the greatness of divine things," the old man explained, telling the story by the fire.

Dualitas Sekhmetis et Hathoris vitae et mortis, belli pacisque, interitus et creationis aequilibrium docebat. "In Sekhmet et Hathor, vitae mysteria contemplamur," sacerdos, ad populum docendum, explicabat.

The duality of Sekhmet and Hathor taught the balance of life and death, war and peace, destruction and creation. "In Sekhmet and Hathor, we contemplate the mysteries of life," the priest explained, teaching the people.

Cultus Sekhmetis, per saecula durans, eius in Aegypti civilisationem immutabilem impressionem testabatur. "Sekhmet, etiam nunc, in cordibus nostris vivit," fidelis, in caerimonia participans, affirmabat.

The cult of Sekhmet, enduring for centuries, bore witness to her unchanging impression on Egyptian civilisation. "Sekhmet, even now, lives in our hearts," a faithful worshipper, participating in the ceremony, affirmed.

Ita Sekhmetis hereditas, eius cultus perpetuitate, Aegyptiorum in historia profundam vestigium reliquit, potentiam, sapientiam, et divinitatis aequilibrium semper commemorans.

Thus, Sekhmet's legacy, through the continuity of her cult, left a profound mark on Egyptian history, always commemorating power, wisdom, and the balance of divinity.

Deae Sorores Aegypti

Sorores Divinae

In mythologia Aegyptiaca, Sekhmet, etiam post multa saecula, potens dea manebat. "Sekhmet, vis et tutela nostra," artifex, imaginem eius in templo pingens, murmuravit.

In Egyptian mythology, Sekhmet, even after many centuries, remained a powerful goddess. "Sekhmet, our strength and protection," the artist murmured, painting her image in the temple.

Eius effigies, in templorum parietibus sculptae vel pictae, magnitudinem et potentiam eius demonstrabant. "Haec imago nos proteget," sacerdos, ad statuam deae in sanctuario stans, adorabat.

Her effigies, carved or painted on the walls of temples, displayed her greatness and power. "This image will protect us," the priest, standing before the goddess's statue in the sanctuary, worshipped.

Talismanis eius imagine signatis uti solebant Aegyptii, ut vires et protectionem haberent. "Per hanc amuletam, Sekhmetis praesidio fruamur," vir, talismanum collo suspendens, sperabat.

The Egyptians used talismans marked with her image to gain strength and protection. "Through this amulet, may we enjoy Sekhmet's protection," the man, hanging the talisman around his neck, hoped.

Medici sanatoresque Sekhmetem invocabant, ut aegrotis salutem et sanationem ferret. "O Sekhmet, da nobis sanitatem," medicus, herbam medicinalem praeparans, precabatur.

Doctors and healers invoked Sekhmet to bring health and healing to the sick. "O Sekhmet, grant us health," the doctor prayed, preparing a medicinal herb.

Ritualibus in eius honorem factis, cum saltationibus et cerevisiae libationibus, colentes eius iram placare studebant. "Per haec sacrificia, iram tuam a nobis avertere speramus," populus in festo, ad altare stans, cantabat.

Through rituals in her honour, with dances and beer offerings, her followers sought to appease her anger. "Through these sacrifices, we hope to turn away your wrath," the people sang, standing at the altar during the festival.

Fabulae de Sekhmet viribusque eius et irae periculis narrabantur ut monitiones et doctrinae. "Audite, o liberi, fabulas de Sekhmet, quae nos docent irae dominari," magister, ad circulum discipulorum sedens, incipiebat.

Stories about Sekhmet's power and the dangers of her anger were told as warnings and lessons. "Listen, children, to the tales of Sekhmet, which teach us how to control anger," the teacher, sitting in a circle of students, began.

Pharaones se cum Sekhmet, dea belligera, identificabant, ut suam auctoritatem confirmarent. "Sub Sekhmetis protectione, in proelium eamus," pharao, ante pugnam loquens, exhortabatur.

Pharaohs identified themselves with Sekhmet, the warrior goddess, to assert their authority. "Under Sekhmet's protection, let us go into battle," the pharaoh urged, speaking before the fight.

Festivitates Sekhmet dedicatae purificationis et tutelae ritus includebant. "Hoc festo, purificationem et Sekhmetis protectionem petimus," sacerdos, populum ad ceremoniam ducens, pronuntiabat.

Festivals dedicated to Sekhmet included purification and protection rituals. "In this festival, we seek purification and Sekhmet's protection," the priest proclaimed, leading the people to the ceremony.

Orationibus Sekhmet adhibitis, fideles vires in adversis petebant. "In his difficultatibus, Sekhmet, tua fortitudine indigemus," mulier, in templo genuflectens, oravit.

In prayers to Sekhmet, the faithful sought strength in adversity. "In these difficulties, Sekhmet, we need your strength," the woman prayed, kneeling in the temple.

Doctrina Sekhmetis de sui dominio magni momenti erat. "Per Sekhmet, discimus quomodo nosmet ipsos regere debemus," philosophus, in foro disputans, docebat.

Sekhmet's teaching on self-control was of great importance. "Through Sekhmet, we learn how we must govern ourselves," the philosopher taught, debating in the forum.

Templa Sekhmetis, non solum adorationis sed etiam sanationis et sapientiae loci erant. "In his sacris aedibus, et curam et sapientiam invenimus," peregrinus, templum ingressus, admirabatur.

Sekhmet's temples were places not only of worship but also of healing and wisdom. "In these sacred halls, we find both care and wisdom," the traveller marvelled, entering the temple.

Peregrini ex longinquis terris venerunt ut deae honores redderent eiusque benedictionem quaererent. "Longum iter fecimus ut Sekhmet honoremus," peregrinus, ante deae simulacrum stans, confitebatur.

Travellers from distant lands came to pay homage to the goddess and seek her blessing. "We have travelled a long way to honour Sekhmet," the traveller confessed, standing before the goddess's statue.

Contationes de Sekhmet naturae divinitatumque viribus reverentiam inspirabant. "Ex his fabulis, divinarum rerum magnitudinem discimus," senex, ad focum narrans, explicabat.

Tales of Sekhmet and the powers of nature and divinity inspired reverence. "From these stories, we learn the greatness of divine things," the old man explained, telling the story by the fire.

Dualitas Sekhmetis et Hathoris vitae et mortis, belli pacisque, interitus et creationis aequilibrium docebat. "In Sekhmet et Hathor, vitae mysteria contemplamur," sacerdos, ad populum docendum, explicabat.

The duality of Sekhmet and Hathor taught the balance of life and death, war and peace, destruction and creation. "In Sekhmet and Hathor, we contemplate the mysteries of life," the priest explained, teaching the people.

Cultus Sekhmetis, per saecula durans, eius in Aegypti civilisationem immutabilem impressionem testabatur. "Sekhmet, etiam nunc, in cordibus nostris vivit," fidelis, in caerimonia participans, affirmabat.

The cult of Sekhmet, enduring for centuries, bore witness to her unchanging impression on Egyptian civilisation. "Sekhmet, even now, lives in our hearts," a faithful worshipper, participating in the ceremony, affirmed.

Ita Sekhmetis hereditas, eius cultus perpetuitate, Aegyptiorum in historia profundam vestigium reliquit, potentiam, sapientiam, et divinitatis aequilibrium semper commemorans.

Thus, Sekhmet's legacy, through the continuity of her cult, left a profound mark on Egyptian history, always commemorating power, wisdom, and the balance of divinity.

Tutela et Magia

In Aegypti finibus, ubi Nili fluminis undae terras feraces alluunt, Isis et Nephtys, deae venerandae, vitam mortemque regunt. Isis, magiae perita, Horum filium suumque protegebat, hominibusque viam praebebat, ut recte viverent. Nephtys, altera parte, mortuorum custos, eorum animas in aeternum iter ad astra comitabatur.

In the lands of Egypt, where the waves of the Nile wash over the fertile grounds, Isis and Nephthys, revered goddesses, ruled over life and death. Isis, skilled in magic, protected Horus, her son, and showed humans the way to live rightly. Nephthys, on the other hand, was the guardian of the dead, accompanying their souls on the eternal journey to the stars.

Hae deae, orationibus invocatae, curas sanabant et tutelam praebebant. Potestates earum, diversae sed complementariae, mundi harmoniam conservabant. Ritus sacri, deabus dicati, dona et carmina magica includebant.

These goddesses, invoked in prayers, healed worries and provided protection. Their powers, different but complementary, maintained the harmony of the world. Sacred rites dedicated to the goddesses included offerings and magical chants.

Isis, praecipue, feminarum doctrix erat, artem sanandi per herbas cantusque edocens. Nephtys, contraria, luctum solabatur, eis qui suos amiserant confortationem ferens.

Isis, in particular, was the teacher of women, instructing them in the art of healing through herbs and songs. Nephthys, in contrast, consoled grief, bringing comfort to those who had lost loved ones.

Una, per Nili vada navigabant, aquas terramque Aegypti benedicentes. Eorum numen, mortis portis praesidens, maxime sentiebatur.

Together, they sailed through the shallows of the Nile, blessing the waters and the land of Egypt. Their divine presence, presiding over the gates of death, was deeply felt.

Sacerdotes sacerdotaeque, eorum imagines amuletis gestantes, deorum vim canaliculabant. Templum utriusque deae, scientiae spiritualitatisque foci, erant.

Priests and priestesses, wearing amulets with their images, channelled the power of the gods. The temples of both goddesses were centres of knowledge and spirituality.

Mythi narrabant, quomodo earum coniunctio tenebras chaosque superaret.

Myths told of how their union overcame darkness and chaos.

Isis et Nephtys, animas ad iudicium Osiridis in aeternum ducendo, viam mortuorum lucebant. Festi, earum honore instituti, vitae, mortis, renascentisque cyclum significabant.

Isis and Nephthys, leading souls to the judgement of Osiris for eternity, illuminated the path of the dead. Festivals in their honour symbolised the cycle of life, death, and rebirth.

Cultus earum, fraternae caritatis et auxilii necessitatem sublineabat.

Their worship emphasised the need for fraternal charity and assistance.

Conversatio Inter Isis et Nephtys:

In lumine lunae, Isis et Nephtys ad Nili ripam conveniunt, consilium capientes.

In the light of the moon, Isis and Nephthys meet at the bank of the Nile, making plans.

Isis: "Nephtys, soror, nostrum munus gravissimum est, mortales et immortales iuvandi."

Isis: "Nephthys, sister, our duty is most important, helping both mortals and immortals."

Nephtys: "Verum dicis, Isis. Mea opera, mortuorum animae pacem inveniunt."

Nephthys: "You speak the truth, Isis. Through my work, the souls of the dead find peace."

Isis: "Egoque, vivis viam rectam monstrando, vitam meliorem facio. Magia nostra, coniunctim adhibita, mundum tuetur."

Isis: "And I, by showing the living the right path, improve their lives. Our magic, used together, protects the world."

Nephtys: "Fiat. Per nostra ritus et carmina, tenebras repellamus, lucemque adferamus."

Nephthys: "So be it. Through our rituals and chants, let us drive away the darkness and bring forth the light."

Sub lunae splendore, magicae vires earum confluunt, aquas Nilique terrasque benedicentes. Deae, munere suo fideliter fungentes, Aegypti populum in vita et morte ducunt, perpetuo amorem fraternum et auxilium celebrantes.

Under the splendour of the moon, their magical powers merge, blessing the waters and lands of the Nile. The goddesses, faithfully carrying out their duty, guide the people of Egypt in life and death, always celebrating fraternal love and assistance.

Sic finit capitulum de Tutela et Magia, ubi Isis et Nephtys, per magiam et devotionem, Aegypti fines sacros custodiunt, mortalesque ad meliorem vitam ducunt.

Thus ends the chapter of Protection and Magic, where Isis and Nephthys, through magic and devotion, guard the sacred lands of Egypt and lead mortals to a better life.

Hereditas Aeterna

Per Aegyptum amplam et ultra fines eius, Isis et Nephtys, deae praeclarae, magna veneratione colebantur. Artifices, poetae, musicaeque magistri ab eorum fabulis inspirationem hauriebant, quae per saecula et generationes traducebantur. Reges sapientesque earum consilia et sapientiam quaerebant, communitates in festis earum in honorem congregabantur.

Throughout vast Egypt and beyond its borders, Isis and Nephthys, renowned goddesses, were worshipped with great reverence. Artists, poets, and musicians drew inspiration from their stories, which were passed down through the ages and generations. Kings and wise men sought their counsel and wisdom, and communities gathered at festivals in their honour.

Templorum parietes et sepulcrorum maenia earum imaginibus exornabantur, vivos mortuosque tutandos esse in precationibus petebant. Culturae vicinae etiam earum influentiam senserunt, mysteriaque earum doctos fascinabant.

The walls of temples and the enclosures of tombs were adorned with their images, as prayers were made for the protection of the living and the dead. Nearby cultures also felt their influence, and their mysteries fascinated scholars.

Cultus earum, etiam post antiquae Aegypti civilitatis occlusum, perduravit, novaeque archaeologicae inventiones earum momenti indicia praebebant.

Their worship endured even after the fall of ancient Egyptian civilisation, and new archaeological discoveries continued to provide evidence of their significance.

Amor earum, protectio, et resilientia, universalia nuntia manebant, deae ipsae unionis in adversitate superandae symbola efficiebantur. Isis et Nephtys, in mythologia Aegypti insignes, spiritualem et culturalem profunditatem Aegypti antiquae testabantur.

Their love, protection, and resilience remained universal messages, and the goddesses themselves became symbols of overcoming adversity through unity. Isis and Nephthys, prominent in Egyptian mythology, bore witness to the spiritual and cultural depth of ancient Egypt.

In Templo Aeterno:

Isis et Nephtys, in sancto templo convenientes, de aeternitate suae hereditatis cogitabant.

Isis and Nephthys, meeting in the sacred temple, thought about the eternity of their legacy.

Isis: "Soror, videsne quam longe nostra fabula pervenit? Per Aegyptum et ultra, nostri memores manent."

Isis: "Sister, do you see how far our story has travelled? Throughout Egypt and beyond, they still remember us."

Nephtys: "Ita vero, Isis. Nostri cultus et amor, etiam in temporum fluxu, constant. Quam magnificum est videre nostros nuntios adhuc valere."

Nephthys: "Indeed, Isis. Our worship and love remain constant, even through the passage of time. How magnificent it is to see that our messages still hold strong."

Isis: "Docuimus homines amare, protegere, et resilire. Haec dona nostra sunt, quae semper in mundo resonabunt."

Isis: "We have taught humans to love, protect, and endure. These are our gifts, which will always resonate in the world."

Nephtys: "Per omnes has aetates, nostrae imagines in templis et sepulcris manent, nostrae voces in precationibus et carminibus audiantur."

Nephthys: "Throughout all these ages, our images remain in temples and tombs, and our voices are heard in prayers and songs."

Isis: "Eamus, soror, flumina nostra benedicamus. Nostri spiritus per Nili undas fluant, terramque Aegypti semper fovent."

Isis: "Come, sister, let us bless our rivers. May our spirits flow through the waters of the Nile and always nurture the land of Egypt."

Nephtys: "Fiat. Per nostram unionem, mundus semper in lumine et amore manebit."

Nephthys: "So be it. Through our union, the world will always remain in light and love."

Et sic, deae, manu in manu, ad Nilum descendebant, eorum benedictiones in aquas effundentes, perpetuam terrae fertilitatem promittentes. Eorum hereditas, per saecula lata, amoris, protectionis, et resilientiae nuntium ad futuras generationes portat, demonstrans quomodo divinitas et humanitas in perpetuo dialogo manent.

And so, the goddesses, hand in hand, descended to the Nile, pouring their blessings into the waters, promising the land's perpetual fertility. Their legacy, spread across the centuries, carries a message of love, protection, and resilience to future generations, showing how divinity and humanity remain in perpetual dialogue.

Hoc modo, capitulum de hereditate aeterna clauditur, Isis et Nephtys, mythologiae Aegyptiae lumina, in cordibus hominum per aeternitatem vivent.

In this way, the chapter on eternal legacy closes, with Isis and Nephthys, the lights of Egyptian mythology, living forever in the hearts of humanity.

Mythus Inundationis Nili

Nili Benedictio

In antiqua Aegypti terra, Nilus, fluvius magnus, vitae fons erat, aquam ad vitam necessariam ferens. Anno quolibet, fluvius ripas suas excedebat, terras inundans easque fertilizans. Aegyptii credebant hanc inundationem deorum donum esse. Hâpy, deus inundationis aquarumque fertilitatis dominus, erat. Homo cum ubere et ventre, alimentorum et abundantiae symbolis, repraesentabatur.

In the ancient land of Egypt, the Nile, a great river, was the source of life, bringing the water necessary for survival. Every year, the river would overflow its banks, flooding and fertilising the lands. The Egyptians believed this flood was a gift from the gods. Hâpy, the god of the flood and lord of the waters' fertility, was represented as a man with a breast and belly, symbols of nourishment and abundance.

Sacerdotes stellas observabant ut inundationis tempus praedicerent. Ritibus Hâpy honorabatur ut inundatio salutaris assecuraretur. Offertae fructus, flores, et tus includebant. Cantus et saltationes aquae adventum laudabant.

Priests observed the stars to predict the time of the flood. Hâpy was honoured with rituals to ensure a beneficial flood. Offerings included fruit, flowers, and incense. Songs and dances praised the arrival of the water.

Agricolae agros suos parabant, messis ubertatem sperantes. Liberi in aquis crescentibus ludebant, inundationem cum gaudio excipientes. Artifices amuleta Hâpy repraesentantia pro tutela creabant. Scribae aquae altitudinem annuatim scribebant.

Farmers prepared their fields, hoping for an abundant harvest. Children played in the rising waters, joyfully welcoming the flood. Craftsmen created amulets representing Hâpy for protection. Scribes recorded the annual water level.

Templa Hâpy dicata celebrationis et orationis centra erant. Nili inundatio tempus renovationis et spei pro toto regno erat.

Temples dedicated to Hâpy were centres of celebration and prayer. The flooding of the Nile was a time of renewal and hope for the entire kingdom.

In Templo Hâpy:

Sacerdos et agricola ante aram stant, preces et offertae parantes.

In the Temple of Hâpy:

The priest and farmer stand before the altar, preparing prayers and offerings.

Sacerdos: "Hâpy, aquarum dominus, te colimus ut terras nostras benedicas. Fructus, flores, tusque tibi offerimus."

Priest: "Hâpy, lord of the waters, we worship you so that you may bless our lands. We offer you fruits, flowers, and incense."

Agricola: "Te precor, Hâpy, ut agros nostros fertilem facias, messim ubertatemque nobis des."

Farmer: "I pray to you, Hâpy, to make our fields fertile and grant us an abundant harvest."

Sacerdos: "Stellae nobis signa dant, tempus adventus tui annuntiant. Omnia parata sunt ad tuam celebrationem."

Priest: "The stars give us signs, announcing the time of your arrival. Everything is ready for your celebration."

Agricola: "Inundationis tuae dono laetamur. Terra nostra te exspectat, vita plena sperans."

Farmer: "We rejoice in the gift of your flood. Our land awaits you, hoping for abundant life."

Cum ritibus perfectis, sacerdos aquam in aram fundit, symbolo benedictionis Hâpy. Agricolae, sacerdotes, liberi, omnes communitatis membra in una celebratione coniunguntur, spem et gratitudinem exprimentes.

With the rituals completed, the priest pours water on the altar, a symbol of Hâpy's blessing. Farmers, priests, children, all members of the community join in one celebration, expressing hope and gratitude.

Amuleta Hâpy gestant, se et agros suos protegendo. Scribae, sollemnia et aquae altitudinem in tabulis aeternis notant, futuris generationibus narraturi.

They wear Hâpy amulets, protecting themselves and their fields. Scribes record the ceremonies and the water's height on eternal tablets, to tell future generations.

Hoc modo, capitulo primo de Nili benedictione finito, mythus profundae connectionis inter Aegyptios et eorum vitalem fluvium, Nilum, demonstratur. Hâpy, non solum deus inundationis sed etiam symbolum vitae et renovationis, in corde Aegyptiae cultus manet.

Thus, with the first chapter on the blessing of the Nile concluded, the myth of the deep connection between the Egyptians and their vital river, the Nile, is demonstrated. Hâpy, not only the god of the flood but also a symbol of life and renewal, remains at the heart of Egyptian worship.

Provocationes Inundationis

Inundatio Nili, licet ad vitam Aegyptiorum necessaria esset, interdum vastationem et desolationem afferre poterat. Anni, in quibus inundatio parva erat, ad famem et siccitatem ducebant. Contra, inundationes nimis magnae domos frugesque destruere valebant. Aegyptii itaque modum invenire debuerunt, ut cum Nili variabilitate pacterentur.

The flooding of the Nile, although essential for the life of the Egyptians, could at times bring devastation and desolation. Years when the flood was too small led to famine and drought. Conversely, floods that were too large could destroy homes and crops. The Egyptians therefore had to find a way to cope with the variability of the Nile.

Ad aquas regendas, systemata irrigationis aedificata sunt. Aggeres et canales aquam ad agros sitientes ducebant. Ingeniarii operariique indefesse laborabant, ut terras protegerent.

Sacerdotes divinam consulere orabant, ut Nili voluntates intellegere possent.

To control the waters, irrigation systems were built. Dykes and canals directed water to thirsty fields. Engineers and workers laboured tirelessly to protect the land. Priests prayed to consult the divine, hoping to understand the will of the Nile.

Communitates post inundationes ad damna reparanda congregabantur. Mercatores occasionem ad mercaturam fluvio vehendam capiebant. Piscatores in aquis fertilibus piscium copiam inveniebant. Aves migratoriae in multitudine adventabant, a Nili vita abundante allectae.

Communities gathered after the floods to repair the damage. Merchants seized the opportunity to transport goods by river. Fishermen found an abundance of fish in the fertile waters. Migratory birds arrived in great numbers, attracted by the abundant life of the Nile.

Fabulae de superatione et ingenio de generatione in generationem traditae sunt. Deae fertilitatis invocabantur, ut Hâpy benedictionem complerent. Non obstantibus difficultatibus, Nili inundatio cor Aegypti palpitans manebat.

Stories of overcoming and ingenuity were passed down from generation to generation. Fertility goddesses were invoked to complete Hâpy's blessing. Despite the difficulties, the flood of the Nile remained the beating heart of Egypt.

In Agro ad Nilum:

Agricola et sacerdos, post recentem inundationem, de futuro agri colloquuntur.

In the Fields by the Nile:

The farmer and the priest, after the recent flood, discuss the future of the land.

Agricola: "Vidisti inundationem huius anni? Nimis fuit; agri mei paene deleti sunt."

Farmer: "Did you see this year's flood? It was too much; my fields were almost destroyed."

Sacerdos: "Ita, sed scis, Nilus et dator et destructor est. Nunc ad deos orandum est, ut proxima inundatio sit moderata."

Priest: "Yes, but you know, the Nile is both a giver and a destroyer. Now we must pray to the gods that the next flood will be moderate."

Agricola: "Quid facere possumus? Annum alterum vastationis ferre non possum."

Farmer: "What can we do? I can't endure another year of destruction."

Sacerdos: "Aedificabimus aggeres meliores et canales, aquam dirigentes. Et orationes ad Hâpy et deas fertilitatis offeremus, ut nos adiuvant."

Priest: "We will build better dykes and canals to direct the water. And we will offer prayers to Hâpy and the fertility goddesses, so they help us."

Agricola: "Spero deorum auxilio nos protegere. Labor nostri, spero, non erit frustra."

Farmer: "I hope the gods will protect us. I hope our work will not be in vain."

Sacerdos: "Dei semper Aegyptum fovissent. Cum labore tuo et fide nostra, superabimus."

Priest: "The gods have always favoured Egypt. With your labour and our faith, we will overcome."

Cum hoc colloquio finito, agricola et sacerdos ad laborem revertuntur, spem renovatam habentes. Communitas, coniuncta, ad futuras provocationes parata erat, scientes se non solum esse, sed cum divina benevolentia et ingenio suo adversus Nili caprices stare.

With this conversation finished, the farmer and the priest return to their work, with renewed hope. The community, united, was ready for future challenges, knowing they were not alone but stood with divine goodwill and their own ingenuity against the whims of the Nile.

Sic finitur caput secundum de Nili inundationis provocationibus, demonstrans Aegyptiorum resilientiam, ingenium, et profundam cum naturalibus suis vinculum, quae eos per saecula sustentavit.

Thus ends the second chapter on the challenges of the Nile's flood, demonstrating the resilience, ingenuity, and profound connection of the Egyptians with their natural environment, which sustained them through the ages.

Aeternus Nili Cyclus

Inundatio Nili, mortis et renascentiae aeternum cyclus symbolizabat. Aegyptii in hac annua inundatione vitam aeternam promissam videbant. Mythi narrabant quomodo dii Nilo uterentur ad communicandum cum hominibus. Templa ad fluminis ripas, astra spectantia, alignata erant, crurum initium notantia.

The flooding of the Nile symbolised the eternal cycle of death and rebirth. The Egyptians saw the promise of eternal life in this annual flood. Myths told how the gods used the Nile to communicate with humans. Temples along the river's banks were aligned with the stars, marking the beginning of the seasons.

Festa Nili erant tempora communionis et gratitudinis erga divinitates. Pharaones Hâpy, pro eius liberalitate, honorabant. Nobilium sepulcra inundationis scenis ornabantur, in altera vita abundantiam assecurantes. Carmina et cantus Nili pulchritudinem potentiamque laudabant.

The festivals of the Nile were times of communion and gratitude towards the gods. Pharaohs honoured Hâpy for his generosity. The tombs of nobles were decorated with scenes of the flood, ensuring abundance in the afterlife. Poems and songs praised the beauty and power of the Nile.

Docti flumen investigabant, eius mysteria solvendi cupidi. Exploratores Nili cursu sequebantur, eius fontes secretos sperantes invenire. Per commercium fluvii, regionum Aegypti inter se relationes firmabantur. Nuptiae et natales secundum inundationis calendarium saepe ordinabantur.

Scholars studied the river, eager to solve its mysteries. Explorers followed the course of the Nile, hoping to discover its hidden sources. Through river trade, the regions of Egypt strengthened their connections. Marriages and births were often planned according to the flood calendar.

Antiqui Aegyptii credebant fatum suum Nili destino coniunctum esse. Nili legenda per aetates transibat, respectum et admirationem inspirans. Mythus Nili inundationis in corde identitatis Aegyptiae manebat, nexum indissolubilem inter homines et naturam demonstrans.

The ancient Egyptians believed their fate was tied to the destiny of the Nile. The legend of the Nile passed through the ages, inspiring respect and admiration. The myth of the Nile's flood remained at the heart of Egyptian identity, demonstrating the unbreakable bond between humans and nature.

In Litore Nili:

Doctus et pharaon, ad fluminis margines, de Nili significatu colloquuntur.

On the Banks of the Nile:

A scholar and a pharaoh, standing by the river's edge, discuss the significance of the Nile.

Doctus: "Videsne, o rex, quam magnus Nilus non solum aquam sed etiam vitam et sapientiam nobis fert?"

Scholar: "Do you see, O king, how the great Nile brings us not only water but also life and wisdom?"

Pharaon: "Ita, docte. Nili inundatio, ut Hâpy nobis benedicit, vitam aeternam nobis promittit. Eius dona semper in corde et animo meo sunt."

Pharaoh: "Yes, scholar. The flood of the Nile, as Hâpy blesses us, promises us eternal life. His gifts are always in my heart and mind."

Doctus: "Dii per Nilum loquuntur, nobis viam vitae, mortis, renascentiaeque monstrantes. Eius cursus, sicut astra, fata nostra ducit."

Scholar: "The gods speak through the Nile, showing us the path of life, death, and rebirth. Its course, like the stars, guides our fate."

Pharaon: "In templis quae ad eius ripas stant, deorum voluntatem quaerimus, crurum tempus celebrantes. Nili festa nos ad maiorem gratitudinem divinitatibus ducunt."

Pharaoh: "In the temples that stand by its banks, we seek the will of the gods, celebrating the time of the seasons. The Nile's festivals lead us to greater gratitude towards the deities."

Doctus: "Nonne mirabile est quomodo Nilus non tantum Aegyptum corporaliter sed etiam spiritualiter nutrit?"

Scholar: "Isn't it marvellous how the Nile nourishes not only Egypt physically but also spiritually?"

Pharaon: "Maxime. Eius legenda, aeternum cyclus mortis et vitae, fundamentum nostrae culturae et identitatis est."

Pharaoh: "Absolutely. Its legend, the eternal cycle of death and life, is the foundation of our culture and identity."

Cum sermone finito, ambos, doctus et pharaon, ad templum proximum pergunt, Hâpy et aliis deis pro benedictionibus suis gratias agentes. Sic, Nili inundatio, aeternus vitae et mortis cyclus, in Aegypti anima perpetuo vivit, nexum sempiternum inter divinum et humanum, naturam et culturam celebrans.

With the conversation finished, both the scholar and the pharaoh proceed to the nearby temple, giving thanks to Hâpy and the other gods for their blessings. Thus, the flooding of the Nile, the eternal cycle of life and death, continues to live in the soul of Egypt, celebrating the eternal bond between the divine and the human, nature and culture.

Hoc capitulo concluso, Nili mythus tamquam vitalis Aegypti spiritus permanet, eius aquae non solum terram sed etiam Aegyptiorum cor et animam feracem facientes.

With this chapter concluded, the myth of the Nile remains as the vital spirit of Egypt, its waters making not only the land but also the hearts and souls of the Egyptians fertile.

Mythus Pyramidum

Divina Conceptio

Pyramides Aegypti, divinae creationis opera habebantur. Diis ipsi Aegyptiis artem monumentorum talium exstruendi revelaverant. Thoth, sapientiae scientiaeque deus, ipsos planos dedisse dicebatur. Quaeque pyramis tamquam nexum inter Terram caelumque erat, scala deorum.

The pyramids of Egypt were considered works of divine creation. The gods themselves had revealed to the Egyptians the art of building such monuments. Thoth, the god of wisdom and knowledge, was said to have given them the plans. Each pyramid was seen as a link between Earth and the heavens, a stairway to the gods.

Loca constructionis secundum caelestia signa sacra electa erant. Lapidibus adhibitum erat inscriptiones benedictionum sortilegiorumque ferentibus. Opifices hymnos cantabant dum laborabant, divinam protectionem invocantes.

The construction sites were chosen according to sacred celestial signs. The stones were inscribed with blessings and spells. The workers sang hymns as they laboured, invoking divine protection.

In Campo Constructionis:

Architectus et sacerdos, de plano pyramidis colloquuntur, sub caelo stellato.

On the Construction Site:

The architect and the priest discuss the pyramid's plan under the starry sky.

Architectus: "Videsne, sacerdos, quomodo stellae nos ad perfectum locum ducunt? Thoth ipse nos adiuvat."

Architect: "Do you see, priest, how the stars guide us to the perfect location? Thoth himself is helping us."

Sacerdos: "Ita, architecte. Omnia divinitus ordinata sunt. Hymnos canamus ut deorum benedictionem in opere nostro habeamus."

Priest: "Yes, architect. Everything is divinely arranged. Let us sing hymns so that we may have the gods' blessing on our work."

Architectus: "Thoth nobis sapientiam dedit, ut hanc pyramiden, pontem ad aeternitatem, aedificemus. Quamvis arduum sit opus, divinum auxilium sentimus."

Architect: "Thoth has given us the wisdom to build this pyramid, a bridge to eternity. Though the work is difficult, we feel divine assistance."

Sacerdos: "Lapidum inscriptiones, benedictiones et sortilegia portantes, nostrum iter ad deos confirmant. Caelum ipsum in terra reflectimus."

Priest: "The inscriptions on the stones, carrying blessings and spells, confirm our journey to the gods. We reflect the heavens themselves on Earth."

Opifices, adstantes et audientes, hymnum incipiunt, voces suas in unum concordantes. Sacerdos aquam sanctificatam super fundamenta aspergit, locum purificans et sanctificans. Architectus, planum in manibus tenens, caelum respicit, divinam inspirationem quaerens.

The workers, standing and listening, begin a hymn, their voices harmonising as one. The priest sprinkles holy water over the foundations, purifying and sanctifying the site. The architect, holding the plan in his hands, looks to the sky, seeking divine inspiration.

Dialogus Inter Opifices:

Opifex 1: "Sentisne magnitudinem operis nostri? Quasi cum deis ipsi laboramus."

Opifex 2: "Ita, frater. Quotidie, cum sol oritur, divinam praesentiam in labore nostro sentio. Thoth nos non deserit."

Dialogue Between the Workers:

Worker 1: "Do you feel the greatness of our work? It is as if we are working with the gods themselves."

Worker 2: "Yes, brother. Every day, when the sun rises, I feel the divine presence in our labour. Thoth does not abandon us."

Cum opere diei finito, omnes in silentio caelum stellatum contemplantur, sensum profundi mysterii et connectionis cum divino sentientes. Pyramis, non solum monumentum, sed etiam via ad immortalitatem, gradatim ad caelum ascendit.

When the day's work is finished, everyone silently contemplates the starry sky, feeling a profound sense of mystery and connection with the divine. The pyramid, not only a monument but also a path to immortality, gradually rises toward the heavens.

Sic finitur caput primum de divina conceptione pyramidum, mirabilem nexum inter humanam industriam et divinam inspirationem demonstrans, monumentum aeternitatis in terra Aegypti fundans.

Thus ends the first chapter on the divine conception of the pyramids, demonstrating the marvellous link between human industry and divine inspiration, founding a monument of eternity in the land of Egypt.

Pharaonis Tumulus

Pyramides in Aegypto non solum magnificae structurae erant sed etiam tumuli pharaonum, deorum regumque terrae. Credebatur pyramidem pharaonem in itinere ad alteram vitam adiuvare. Cor pyramidis, camera funeraria, quasi palatium caeleste designabatur.

The pyramids in Egypt were not only magnificent structures but also the tombs of pharaohs, gods, and kings of the land. It was believed that the pyramid aided the pharaoh on his journey to the afterlife. The heart of the pyramid, the burial chamber, was designed like a heavenly palace.

Thesauri et dona cum pharaone collocabantur ut in mundo altero adiuvarentur. Paries textibus sacris decorabatur, quae animam pharaonis ducerent. Rituali nomine "oris apertio" adhibito, statua pharaonis animabatur. Sacerdotes ceremonias agebant ut pyramidem purificarent sanctificarentque.

Treasures and gifts were placed with the pharaoh to assist him in the afterlife. The walls were decorated with sacred texts to guide the pharaoh's soul. A ritual called the "Opening of the Mouth" was performed to animate the pharaoh's statue. Priests conducted ceremonies to purify and sanctify the pyramid.

In Camera Funeraria:

Sacerdos et architectus, ante statuam pharaonis stantes, de ritu et pyramidis significatione loquuntur.

In the Burial Chamber:

The priest and the architect, standing before the statue of the pharaoh, discuss the ritual and the significance of the pyramid.

Sacerdos: "Hic, in hoc sacro loco, pharaonis animam ad aeternitatem ducimus. 'Oris apertio', statuam nostram regis animabit."

Priest: "Here, in this sacred place, we lead the pharaoh's soul to eternity. The 'Opening of the Mouth' will animate the statue of our king."

Architectus: "Miror quomodo omnia, a stellis ad textus in parietibus, ad perfectum iter pharaonis ad aeternitatem dirigantur."

Architect: "I marvel at how everything, from the stars to the texts on the walls, directs the pharaoh's perfect journey to eternity."

Sacerdos: "Omnis thesaurus hic positus, omnis oratio dicta, pharaonis animae in altera vita viam facit. Aegyptus non solum terram sed etiam caelum in monumentis suis reflectit."

Priest: "Every treasure placed here, every prayer spoken, creates the path for the pharaoh's soul in the afterlife. Egypt reflects not only the earth but also the heavens in its monuments."

Architectus: "Quam magnum est opus nostrum, quam sanctum. Pyramis haec, tumulus regis, etiam nobis viam ad immortales contemplationes aperit."

Architect: "How great and sacred is our work. This pyramid, the tomb of the king, also opens for us the path to eternal reflections."

Sacerdos, statuam pharaonis adiens, ritum 'oris apertionis' incipit, precationes et incantationes susurrans. Architectus, assistens, tacite orationem offert, divinam praesentiam in opere eorum sentiens.

The priest approaches the statue of the pharaoh and begins the 'Opening of the Mouth' ritual, whispering prayers and incantations. The architect, assisting, offers a silent prayer, sensing the divine presence in their work.

Dialogus Post Ritualem:

Sacerdos: "Sentisne, architecte, quam sanctificata sit haec pyramis nunc, post ceremonias nostras?"

Architectus: "Ita, sacerdos. Quasi aura divina totum locum implevit. Pharaonis anima, credo, nunc tutum iter habet."

Dialogue After the Ritual:

Priest: "Do you feel, architect, how sanctified this pyramid is now, after our ceremonies?"

Architect: "Yes, priest. It's as if a divine aura has filled the whole place. I believe the pharaoh's soul now has a safe journey."

Cum sol occidit, et caelum stellis plenissimum est, ambos, sacerdotem et architectum, profunda cum reverentia pyramidis magnitudinem et sacrum eius propositum contemplari. Pyramis, pharaonis ad aeternitatem vehiculum, in Aegypti terra, quasi stella ipsa, lucet.

As the sun sets and the sky is full of stars, both the priest and the architect, with deep reverence, contemplate the magnitude and sacred purpose of the pyramid. The pyramid, a vehicle for the pharaoh's journey to eternity, shines like a star itself in the land of Egypt.

Sic finitur caput secundum, pharaonis tumulum et pyramidis sacra mysteria revelans, aeternitatis quaerentium animos et corda tangens.

Thus ends the second chapter, revealing the pharaoh's tomb and the sacred mysteries of the pyramid, touching the hearts and minds of those who seek eternity.

Aeternitatis Custodes

Pyramides Aegypti a statuis sphingum, mythicis custodibus, protegebantur. Sphinges, corporibus leonum et capitibus pharaonum, vires sapientiamque significabant. Aditus incantationibus muniebantur ne fures spiritusve maligni appropinquarent. Anubis, embalsamationis deus, invocabatur ut super defunctos vigilaret. Sacerdotes prope pyramides manebant, animas placandas precationes recitantes.

The pyramids of Egypt were protected by statues of sphinxes, mythical guardians. The sphinxes, with the bodies of lions and the heads of pharaohs, symbolised strength and wisdom. The entrances were guarded by incantations to prevent thieves or evil spirits from approaching. Anubis, the god of embalming, was invoked to watch over the deceased. Priests remained near the pyramids, reciting prayers to appease the souls.

In Sphingis Umbraculo:

Sacerdos et custos, sphingis magnae ad pedes stantes, de eorum munere et pyramidum sacralitate colloquuntur.

The priest and the guardian, standing at the feet of the great sphinx, discuss their duty and the sacredness of the pyramids.

Sacerdos: "Vide, custos, quomodo sphinx nostra, robore et sapientia pharaonis insignita, hanc sanctam sedem custodit. Nulla mala spiritus huc accedere possunt."

Priest: "Look, guardian, how our sphinx, marked with the strength and wisdom of the pharaoh, guards this sacred place. No evil spirits can approach here."

Custos: "Sentio, sacerdos, tamquam Anubis ipse nos adspiciat, defunctorum quietem assecurans. Sphinx haec non solum custos est, sed etiam signum aeternitatis."

Guardian: "I feel, priest, as though Anubis himself watches over us, ensuring the rest of the dead. This sphinx is not just a guardian but also a symbol of eternity."

Sacerdos: "Incantationes ad portas posuimus, ut malum procul teneamus. Anubis precationibus nostris adiuvatur, ut mortuorum somnus numquam turbetur."

Priest: "We have placed incantations at the gates to keep evil at bay. Anubis is aided by our prayers to ensure that the sleep of the dead is never disturbed."

Custos: "Quam mirabilis est nostra cultura, quae talia monumenta aeternitati erigit! Sphinx haec, Anubisque veneratio, mortuorum pacem aeternam promittunt."

Guardian: "How marvellous is our culture, which raises such monuments to eternity! This sphinx, and the reverence for Anubis, promise eternal peace for the dead."

Sacerdos, ad sphingem respiciens, incipit precari, Anubis auxilium implorans, ut pyramidis sanctitatem perpetuo conservet. Custos, circumspiciens, sollemnitatem momenti sentit, communem eorum causam, mortuorum animarum pacem, agnoscens.

The priest, looking at the sphinx, begins to pray, invoking the help of Anubis to preserve the sanctity of the pyramid forever. The guardian, looking around, feels the solemnity of the moment, recognising their shared purpose: the peace of the souls of the dead.

Dialogus Post Precationem:

Custos: "Sacerdos, tua verba, ad deos directa, me profunde movent. Sentio hoc locum, nostras pyramides, vera aeternitatis signa esse."

Sacerdos: "Ita est, custos. In his sollemnibus actis, in sphingum nostrorum praesentia, tangimus quod mortalibus raro conceditur: aeternitatis sensum."

Dialogue After the Prayer:

Guardian: "Priest, your words, directed to the gods, move me deeply. I feel that this place, our pyramids, are true symbols of eternity."

Priest: "That is so, guardian. In these solemn acts, in the presence of our sphinxes, we touch something rarely granted to mortals: the sense of eternity."

Cum nocte descendente, et stellis supra pyramidem micantibus, ambo, sacerdos et custos, in silentio stant, magnitudinem aeternitatis, quam pyramides sphingesque custodiunt, contemplantes. Hic locus, tempore et historia saturatus, aeternitatis custodes, tam vivos quam mortuos, in memoria Aegypti tenet.

As night falls, and the stars twinkle above the pyramid, both the priest and the guardian stand in silence, contemplating the magnitude of eternity that the pyramids and sphinxes guard. This place, rich in time and history, holds the keepers of eternity, both the living and the dead, in the memory of Egypt.

Sic finitur caput tertium, aeternitatis custodum mysterium et sanctitatem revelans, pyramidumque et sphingum in Aegypti cultura immortalem locum demonstrans.

Thus ends the third chapter, revealing the mystery and sanctity of the keepers of eternity, and demonstrating the immortal place of the pyramids and sphinxes in Egyptian culture.

Architectonica Miracula

Constructio pyramidis ingenii et determinationis proelium erat. Lapides, cum maxima diligentia caesi, per multos passus transportabantur. Rampae levesque ad lapides tollendos adhibebantur. Architecti Aegyptii, geometriae astronomiaeque peritissimi, ad mirabilia creanda operam dabant. Magna Pyramis, cum incredibili accuratia ad cardinales puncta directa, testimonium peritiae eorum erat.

The construction of the pyramid was a battle of skill and determination. Stones, cut with the greatest care, were transported over many steps. Ramps and levers were used to lift the stones. Egyptian architects, highly skilled in geometry and astronomy, worked to create wonders. The Great Pyramid, aligned with incredible precision to the cardinal points, was a testament to their expertise.

Operarii ex omni Aegypto conveniebant, sacrum commune propositum participantes. Communitates circa pyramides, in communi labore unitae, florebant.

Workers gathered from all over Egypt, participating in a shared sacred purpose. Communities around the pyramids flourished, united in common labour.

In Lapidicinis Prope Pyramidem:

Architectus et operarius, lapidem magnum considerantes, de constructionis artificio colloquuntur.

In the Quarries Near the Pyramid:

The architect and a worker, considering a large stone, discuss the craftsmanship of the construction.

Architectus: "Videsne, operarie, quantam curam in unumquemque lapidem infigimus? Geometriae nostrae scientia, caelum ipsum in terra replicamus."

Architect: "Do you see, worker, how much care we put into each stone? With our knowledge of geometry, we replicate the heavens on earth."

Operarius: "Miror, architecte, quomodo nos, humiles operarios, ad astra per pyramides ascendere possimus. Quisquis hanc structuram aspiciet, Aegyptiorum ingenium agnoscet."

Worker: "I marvel, architect, at how we, humble workers, can ascend to the stars through the pyramids. Whoever sees this structure will recognise the genius of the Egyptians."

Architectus: "Etiam, omnis lapis hic positus non solum terram sed etiam caelum tangit. Magna Pyramis, quasi solida oratio ad deos, statuitur."

Architect: "Indeed, every stone placed here touches not only the earth but also the sky. The Great Pyramid stands as a solid prayer to the gods."

Operarius, ad rampam spectans: "Labor hic non solum corporis est sed etiam animi. Sentio nos parte alicuius maioris esse."

Worker, looking at the ramp: "This labour is not only of the body but also of the spirit. I feel we are part of something greater."

Architectus: "Communitates nostrae, in hoc opere coniunctae, testamentum sunt quod homines, ad commune bonum laborantes, incredibilia efficiant."

Architect: "Our communities, united in this work, are proof that when people labour for the common good, they can achieve incredible things."

Dialogus Post Laboris Diem:

Operarius: "Quotidie, cum ad pyramidem redeo, non solum operis nostri magnitudinem sed etiam communitatis nostrae unitatem sentio."

Architectus: "Ita est, amice. Pyramis haec non tantum regis tumulus est, sed etiam monumentum humanitatis, quae ad aeternitatem tendit."

Dialogue After the Day's Work:

Worker: "Every day, when I return to the pyramid, I feel not only the greatness of our work but also the unity of our community."

Architect: "That's right, my friend. This pyramid is not just the tomb of a king, but also a monument to humanity, which reaches for eternity."

Cum sol occidit, pyramis sub caelo purpureo eminet, symbolo aeterni Aegyptii spiritus. Architectus et operarius, una cum ceteris, in silentio stant, opus suum contemplantes, conscii se historiae paginam scribere.

As the sun sets, the pyramid rises beneath a purple sky, a symbol of the eternal Egyptian spirit. The architect and the worker, along with others, stand in silence, contemplating their work, aware that they are writing a page of history.

Ita finitur caput quartum, architectonica mirabilia et humani spiritus magnitudinem celebrans, pyramidum constructionem non solum technicae peritiae sed etiam humanae cooperationis et aspirationis monumentum demonstrans.

Thus ends the fourth chapter, celebrating the architectural wonders and the greatness of the human spirit, demonstrating that the construction of the pyramids is not only a monument to technical skill but also to human cooperation and aspiration.

Pyramidorum Hereditas

Pyramides, Aegypti antiquae magnitudinis symbola, hodieque admirationem et mysterium incitant. Investigatores secreta eorum revelare pergunt, et mythi de eorum constructione popularis imaginationem pascunt. Pyramides humanitatis immortalem quaestionem memorant, et futurae generationes antiquorum Aegyptiorum scientiam ac mysteria hereditabunt.

The pyramids, symbols of ancient Egypt's greatness, continue to inspire admiration and mystery today. Researchers keep uncovering their secrets, and myths about their construction feed the popular imagination. The pyramids remind us of humanity's eternal questions, and future generations will inherit the knowledge and mysteries of the ancient Egyptians.

Pyramidorum historia, fidei, artis, scientiaeque coniunctionem testatur, praeteritum custodit, pharaonum secreta servans. Mundus totus ad eorum maiestatem visendam adhuc convenit, cum historia pyramidum in Aegypti corde insculpta, splendoris et spiritualitatis legatum.

The history of the pyramids bears witness to the union of faith, art, and science, preserving the past and guarding the secrets of the pharaohs. The whole world still gathers to witness their majesty, as the story of the pyramids, engraved in the heart of Egypt, remains a legacy of splendour and spirituality.

In Museo Aegypti:

Doctus et visitator, pyramidorum imagines spectantes, de eorum significatu colloquuntur.

In the Museum of Egypt:

A scholar and a visitor, looking at images of the pyramids, discuss their significance.

Doctus: "Videsne, visitator, quomodo hae structurae, millenniis post, nos adhuc tangunt? Non solum arte et scientia sed etiam spiritu humano."

Scholar: "Do you see, visitor, how these structures, even after millennia, still move us? Not only with their art and science but also with the human spirit."

Visitator: "Miror, quanta diligentia antiqui Aegyptii ad aeternitatem aspiraverint. Pyramides, ut videtur, non solum sunt tumuli sed etiam immortalitatis symbola."

Visitor: "I marvel at the great care the ancient Egyptians took to aspire to eternity. The pyramids, it seems, are not just tombs but also symbols of immortality."

Doctus: "Ita est. Quisque lapis, quaeque inscriptio nobis narrat de fide, de hominum conatu ad superos perveniendi. Hereditas, quam nobis reliquerunt, pretiosa est, scientiae arcanisque plena."

Scholar: "That's right. Every stone, every inscription tells us of their faith and their effort to reach the heavens. The heritage they left us is precious, full of knowledge and mystery."

Visitator: "Et hodie, nos, ex toto orbe terrarum venientes, hanc sapientiam admiramur, mysteriis capti. Quomodo, puto, nostrae aetatis opera futuras generationes inspirabunt?"

Visitor: "And today, we come from all over the world, admiring this wisdom, captivated by its mysteries. I wonder how the works of our age will inspire future generations?"

Doctus: "Bona quaestio. Sicut pyramides, opera nostra quoque tempus superare debent, humanitatis quaestiones aeternas tractantes. Ars, scientia, spiritualitas - omnia in unum confluunt, futurum formantes."

Scholar: "Good question. Like the pyramids, our works must also withstand time, addressing the eternal questions of humanity. Art, science, spirituality – all converge to shape the future."

Dialogus Post Visitationem:

Visitator: "Gratias tibi ago, docte. Haec visitatio non solum educatio sed etiam spiritualis peregrinatio fuit."

Doctus: "Laetor te fructum cepisse. Pyramides non solum Aegypti sed totius humanitatis thesauri sunt, nos ad maiora semper aspirare monentes."

Dialogue After the Visit:

Visitor: "Thank you, scholar. This visit was not just educational but also a spiritual journey."

Scholar: "I'm glad you found it rewarding. The pyramids are treasures not just of Egypt but of all humanity, always reminding us to aspire to greater things."

Cum crepusculum advenit, et stellae supra musei atrium micare incipiunt, visitator et doctus in silentio stant, pyramidorum et humanitatis immensitatem contemplantes, certi has magnificas structuras aeternitatem, ut stellae in caelo, illustrare.

As twilight descends, and the stars begin to twinkle above the museum's atrium, the visitor and scholar stand in silence, contemplating the immensity of the pyramids and humanity, certain that these magnificent structures, like the stars in the sky, illuminate eternity.

Ita finitur caput quintum, pyramidorum hereditatem et eorum aeternam humanitatis cum divino nexum celebrans, testamentum antiquae Aegypti magnitudinis et humani spiritus inquisitionis.

Thus ends the fifth chapter, celebrating the legacy of the pyramids and their eternal connection between humanity and the divine, a testament to the greatness of ancient Egypt and the questing spirit of humankind.

Certamina Hori et Sethi

Conflictus Origo

Horus, Osiridis Isisque filius, ad Aegypti regnum destinatus erat. Seth, Osiridis frater, thronum appetebat et Horus legitimitatem contendebat. Magnum deorum consilium convocatum est ad controversiam solvendam. Horus et Seth coram deis causas suas dixerunt, uterque thronum sibi vindicans. Seth vi et astutia uti conatus est ut suam superioritatem demonstraret. Horus, Isis sapientia et magia sustentatus, probationibus restitit. Dei varia certamina proposuerunt ut contendentes experirentur.

Horus, the son of Osiris and Isis, was destined for the throne of Egypt. Seth, the brother of Osiris, sought the throne and contested Horus's legitimacy. A great council of the gods was called to resolve the dispute. Horus and Seth presented their cases before the gods, each claiming the throne. Seth attempted to use force and cunning to demonstrate his superiority. Horus, supported by the wisdom and magic of Isis, withstood the trials. The gods proposed various challenges to test the contenders.

In Consilio Deorum:

Osiris, ad consilium deorum spectans, Horum filium suum et Seth fratrem suum observat, cum Isis colloquitur.

In the Council of the Gods:

Osiris, watching the council of the gods, observes his son Horus and his brother Seth, speaking with Isis.

Osiris: "Videsne, Isis, quam acriter frater et filius noster pro throno contendunt? Quis, putas, victor erit?"

Osiris: "Do you see, Isis, how fiercely our brother and our son contend for the throne? Who do you think will be the victor?"

Isis: "Filius noster Horus iure thronum meretur. Sapientia mea et magia eius latus firmabunt."

Isis: "Our son Horus rightfully deserves the throne. My wisdom and magic will strengthen his side."

Seth, interea, confidenter ad deos loquitur: "Ego, Seth, sum qui Aegyptum regere debet. Vi mea et astutia, regnum ad maiorem gloriam ducam."

Meanwhile, Seth confidently speaks to the gods: "I am Seth, and I am the one who should rule Egypt. With my strength and cunning, I will lead the kingdom to greater glory."

Horus, serenus sed certus, respondet: "Non vi sed iustitia et legitima successione regnum gubernandum est. Ego, Horus, Osiridis filius, iustus heres sum."

Horus, calm but resolute, replies: "The kingdom must be governed not by force, but by justice and rightful succession. I, Horus, son of Osiris, am the rightful heir."

Dei, auditis utriusque partis argumentis, inter se consilium capiunt, modos probandi utrumque contendentes deliberantes.

The gods, having heard both sides of the argument, deliberate amongst themselves, considering ways to test both contenders.

Ra, solis deus, ad ceteros deos vertit: "Debemus sapienter iudicare. Non solum de throno est res sed de Aegypti futuro."

Ra, the god of the sun, turns to the other gods: "We must judge wisely. This matter is not just about the throne but about the future of Egypt."

Post Consilium:

Isis ad Horum: "Fili, quamvis Seth tuum ius regni petat, tua virtus et iustitia te verum regem demonstrabunt. Deorum iudicio confide."

After the Council:

Isis to Horus: "Son, although Seth challenges your right to the throne, your virtue and justice will prove you to be the true king. Trust in the judgement of the gods."

Horus, matris verba audiens, firmo animo respondet: "Matris sapientia et patris virtus me sustentant. Pro iusto et legitimo regno pugnabo."

Horus, hearing his mother's words, replies with determination: "My mother's wisdom and my father's strength sustain me. I will fight for a just and rightful kingdom."

Sic incipit narratio de certaminibus Horus et Sethi, historia plena magiae, sapientiae, et divinae iustitiae, Aegypti fata decernentium.

Thus begins the story of the contests between Horus and Seth, a tale full of magic, wisdom, and divine justice, determining the fate of Egypt.

Divinae Probationes

In divinis probationibus, Horus et Seth in potentissimas creaturas se transformare debuerunt ut inter se confligerent. Horus in accipitrem, Seth in hippopotamum mutatus est, violentia magna dimicantes. Alia probatio eos in naves lapideas navigare iussit, suum in elementa imperium demonstrantes. Isis, arte sua utendo, Seth fefellit ut Horis moralis fortitudinem ostenderet. Seth, suam superioritatem demonstrare cupiens, Horum ad certamen navale in Nilo provocavit. Horus, ingenio suo utendo, navem construxit quae lapidea videri poterat, sed lignea erat, Seth sic superans.

In the divine trials, Horus and Seth had to transform into powerful creatures to battle each other. Horus became a falcon, while Seth turned into a hippopotamus, fighting fiercely. Another trial required them to sail stone boats, demonstrating their command over the elements. Isis, using her skills, tricked Seth to reveal Horus's moral strength. Seth, eager to show his superiority, challenged Horus to a naval contest on the Nile. Horus, using his ingenuity, built a ship that appeared to be made of stone but was actually wooden, thus defeating Seth.

Ad Nili Rivos:

Seth, provocans, ad Horum dicit: "Videamus, frater, quis nostrum vere dignus regno sit. Hac in nave lapidea, tua vires et astutia proba."

At the Banks of the Nile:

Seth, issuing a challenge, says to Horus: "Let us see, brother, who is truly worthy of the throne. In this stone boat, prove your strength and cunning."

Horus, confidenter respondens: "Non fallaciis, Seth, sed vera virtute et ingenio regnum defendetur. Accipe hunc ictum!"

Horus, responding confidently: "The kingdom will not be defended by deception, Seth, but by true virtue and ingenuity. Take this blow!"

Post Navalem Pugnam:

Isis, ad Horum accedens, consilium dat: "Fili mi, non solum in viribus corporis sed etiam in mentis acumen regnum nostrum stat. Tuam sapientiam ostendisti."

After the Naval Battle:

Isis approaches Horus and gives advice: "My son, our kingdom stands not only on physical strength but also on sharpness of mind. You have shown your wisdom."

Horus, victoriae suae conscio, respondet: "Matris consilio et dei auxilio, quidquid artes Sethi sunt, superabo. Aequitas et iustitia semper praevalebunt."

Horus, conscious of his victory, replies: "With my mother's counsel and the gods' help, I will overcome whatever tricks Seth may use. Justice and fairness will always prevail."

In Deorum Concilio:

Ra, deorum concilium advocans, de probatio resultatis loquitur: "Horum et Sethi, vestrae virtutes et defectus in his probationibus manifesti facti sunt. Horus, ingenio et virtute, Seth, viribus et astutia, uterque suam causam demonstravistis."

In the Council of the Gods:

Ra, calling the council of the gods, speaks about the results of the trials: "Horus and Seth, your strengths and weaknesses have been revealed in these trials. Horus, with ingenuity and virtue, and Seth, with strength and cunning, you have both made your case."

Osiris, addit: "Filius meus, Horus, non solum fortitudine sed etiam iustitia et sapientia regnare demonstravit. Haec sunt vera regis insignia."

Osiris adds: "My son, Horus, has shown that he will rule not only with strength but also with justice and wisdom. These are the true marks of a king."

Sic finitur caput secundum, divinae probationes ostendentes, non solum vi et potentia, sed etiam ingenio et iustitia in regni gubernatione esse praestantia. Horus et Seth, per has arduas probationes, suum ad thronum ius demonstrare conati sunt, deorum iudicio semper subiecti.

Thus ends the second chapter, showing through divine trials that not only strength and power, but also ingenuity and justice, are paramount in ruling a kingdom. Horus and Seth, through these difficult tests, attempted to prove their right to the throne, always subject to the judgement of the gods.

Deorum Sententia

Post multas probationes, dei in consilio congregati sunt ut de vero herede throni deliberarent. Ra, solis deus, Horo determinatione permotus est. Osiris, ex ulteriore vita, pro filio suo Horo advocavit. Iustitia Maât, ordinis dea, ad iudicium clarificandum invocata est. Denique, dei Horum ut legitimum Aegypti regem proclamaverunt.

After many trials, the gods gathered in council to deliberate on the true heir to the throne. Ra, the sun god, was moved by Horus's determination. Osiris, from the afterlife, advocated for his son Horus. Maât, the goddess of order, was invoked to bring clarity to the judgement. Finally, the gods proclaimed Horus as the legitimate king of Egypt.

In Consilio Deorum:

Ra, ad coetum deorum praesidens, initium facit: "Vidimus Horum et Sethi virtutes atque ingenia. Nunc decidere debemus quis Aegypti regnare dignus sit."

In the Council of the Gods:

Ra, presiding over the assembly of the gods, begins: "We have seen the virtues and talents of Horus and Seth. Now we must decide who is worthy to rule Egypt."

Osiris, spiritus eius inter deos adstans, orat: "Filius meus, Horus, iustus et legitimus heres est. Per mea et Isis virtutes educatus est, regere paratus."

Osiris, his spirit standing among the gods, prays: "My son, Horus, is the just and rightful heir. He has been raised by the virtues of Isis and me, ready to rule."

Maât, serenitate sua omnes adiens, addit: "Ordinem et iustitiam in nostra sententia conservare debemus. Horus non solum vi sed etiam iustitia demonstravit se dignum esse."

Maât, approaching all with her calm presence, adds: "We must preserve order and justice in our judgement. Horus has shown himself worthy not only by strength but also by justice."

Post Deliberationem:

Ra, omnibus deis consensum nuntians, pronuntiat: "Consilio nostro perfecto, Horum, Osiridis filium, legitimum Aegypti regem declaravimus. Eius regnum iustitia et pace florebit."

After Deliberation:

Ra, announcing the gods' consensus, declares: "With our council complete, we have declared Horus, son of Osiris, as the legitimate king of Egypt. His reign will flourish with justice and peace."

Horus, gratia plenus, deos alloquitur: "Gratias vobis ago, o dei immortales. Regnum meum in iustitia, pace, et prosperitate fundabo, populi Aegyptii beneficio."

Horus, full of gratitude, speaks to the gods: "I thank you, immortal gods. I will found my kingdom on justice, peace, and prosperity, for the benefit of the Egyptian people."

Seth, licet victus, sententiam accipit, dicens: "Licet certamine non superavi, Horum regem agnosco. Exsilium meum in deserto patiar."

Seth, though defeated, accepts the decision, saying: "Though I did not win the contest, I acknowledge Horus as king. I will endure my exile in the desert."

Conclusio:

Horus, nunc legitime coronatus, ad Aegyptum regendam se praeparat, populum in aetatem novam prosperitatis ducens. Deorum iudicio, iustitia et ordine victoriae, Horus non solum Aegypti sed etiam divinae voluntatis minister factus est.

Conclusion:

Horus, now legitimately crowned, prepares to rule Egypt, leading the people into a new era of prosperity. With the gods' judgement, the victory of justice and order, Horus becomes not only the ruler of Egypt but also the servant of divine will.

Sic finitur caput tertium, deorum sententia non solum Aegypti fatum sed etiam aeternum ordinis et chaos certamen definiens. Horus regnum suum incepit, promittens Aegyptum ad maiorem gloriam et stabilitatem ducere, divinae iustitiae et humani consilii exemplum aeternum praebens.

Thus ends the third chapter, with the judgement of the gods defining not only Egypt's fate but also the eternal struggle between order and chaos. Horus began his reign, promising to lead Egypt to greater glory and stability, providing an eternal example of divine justice and human wisdom.

Regnum Hori

Horus, in regem Aegypti sollemni ritu coronatus, novae prosperitatis aetatem inchoavit. Seth, Horum legitimitatem agnoscens, in desertum exsulatum est. Horus Aegyptum unificavit, pacem stabilitatemque regno attulit. Templa renovata sunt et deorum honores celebritatesque renovatae. Populus Aegyptius Horum ut protectorem ducemque coluit. Victoria Horus super Seth annuatim celebrata est, unitatem nationalem corroborans.

The Reign of Horus

Horus, crowned as king of Egypt in a solemn ritual, began a new era of prosperity. Seth, acknowledging Horus's legitimacy, was exiled to the desert. Horus unified Egypt, bringing peace and stability to the kingdom. Temples were restored, and the honours and celebrations of the gods were renewed. The Egyptian people worshipped Horus as their protector and leader. Horus's victory over Seth was celebrated annually, strengthening national unity.

In Templo Magni Dei Solis:

Horus, adstante populo et deis, de suo regno loquitur: "Hodie, nova aetate pro Aegypto incepta, pacem et prosperitatem vobis polliceor. Uniti, maiora assequemur."

In the Temple of the Great Sun God:

Horus, with the people and gods present, speaks of his reign: "Today, with a new era for Egypt beginning, I promise you peace and prosperity. United, we will achieve greater things."

Sacerdos, ad Horum conversus, orationem facit: "O Horus, divinitus electe rex, tua sub ditione, Aegyptus florebit. Dei tecum sunt."

The priest, turning to Horus, delivers a speech: "O Horus, divinely chosen king, under your rule, Egypt will flourish. The gods are with you."

Apud Desertum Limites:

Seth, solus in exsilium iturus, secum cogitat: "Licet hodie victus sim, Horum regem agnosco. Fortasse olim reconciliatio fieri poterit."

Seth, going into exile alone, thinks to himself: "Though I am defeated today, I acknowledge Horus as king. Perhaps one day, reconciliation may be possible."

Inter Populum Aegyptium:

Civis 1: "Videsne quam Horus nos ad meliorem futurum ducat? Pax et stabilitas nobis sunt."

Among the People of Egypt:

Citizen 1: "Do you see how Horus is leading us toward a better future? We now have peace and stability."

Civis 2: "Ita, Horus non solum victor in certamine est, sed etiam in cordibus nostris. Eius regno, Aegyptus renascitur."

Citizen 2: "Yes, Horus is not only victorious in battle but also in our hearts. Under his reign, Egypt is being reborn."

In Sollemni Victoriae Celebratione:

Horus, ante populum congregatum, victoriam suam celebrat: "Hac in victoria, non solum de Seth triumphavi, sed etiam ostendi quid vere significat esse regem Aegypti. Uniti stamus, divisi cadimus."

At the Solemn Victory Celebration:

Horus, before the assembled people, celebrates his victory: "In this victory, I have not only triumphed over Seth but have also shown what it truly means to be the king of Egypt. United we stand, divided we fall."

Populus, Horum laudibus plenus, unitatem et novam spem in corde ferens, in futurum spectat, confidens in ducatu Horus regis. Templorum lumina, deorum honori accensa, novam aetatem illuminant, ubi pax, prosperitas, et divina gratia regnant.

The people, full of praise for Horus, carry unity and new hope in their hearts, looking to the future with confidence in the leadership of King Horus. The lights of the temples, lit in honour of the gods, illuminate a new era, where peace, prosperity, and divine grace reign.

Sic finitur caput quartum, Horus regem non solum belli victorem sed etiam pacis unitatisque artificem demonstrans. Aegyptus sub eius imperio ad novam gloriam surgit, historiae paginas novis triumphis et speratis implet.

Thus ends the fourth chapter, showing King Horus not only as a victor in war but also as a creator of peace and unity. Under his rule, Egypt rises to new glory, filling the pages of history with new triumphs and hopes.

Hereditas Aeterna

Historia conflictus inter Horum et Seth per generationes transmissa est, ordinis et chaos, boni atque mali luctam significans. Sacerdotes Certamina ut exemplar iustitiae divinae narrabant. Artifices Horum triumphalem super Seth in multis operibus pictis sculptisque repraesentabant. Pharaones se cum Horo, celesti accipitre, identificabant, eius hereditatem amplectentes. Templa Horo dicata peregrinationis loca facta sunt. Narratio Horus et Sethi resilientiae et legitimae necessitatis docebat.

The Eternal Legacy

The story of the conflict between Horus and Seth was passed down through generations, symbolising the struggle between order and chaos, good and evil. Priests told of the trials as an example of divine justice. Artists depicted Horus's triumph over Seth in many paintings and sculptures. Pharaohs identified themselves with Horus, the celestial falcon, embracing his legacy. Temples dedicated to Horus became places of pilgrimage. The story of Horus and Seth taught resilience and the importance of rightful rule.

In Templo Horo Dedicato:

Sacerdos, ad turmam peregrinatorum loquens: "Hic, in hoc sacro loco, Horus et Sethi historia non tantum antiquitatis fabula est, sed etiam nostrae vitae moralis. Ordo ex chaos, bonum ex malo emergit."

The priest, speaking to a group of pilgrims: "Here, in this sacred place, the story of Horus and Seth is not just an ancient tale but also a moral lesson for our lives. Order emerges from chaos, good from evil."

Peregrinator: "Mirabile est quomodo haec antiqua fabula adhuc nostris in cordibus resonat. Quae vis, quae sapientia in ea!"

Pilgrim: "It is amazing how this ancient story still resonates in our hearts. What power, what wisdom it holds!"

In Artificis Studio:

Artifex, imaginem Horus triumphantis pingens, discipulo suo explicat: "In hac imagine, Horus non solum Seth superat, sed etiam nos docet quamvis arduae luctae, iustitia et bonitas semper praevalebunt."

In the Artist's Studio:

The artist, painting an image of triumphant Horus, explains to his student: "In this image, Horus not only defeats Seth but also teaches us that, despite difficult struggles, justice and goodness will always prevail."

Discipulus: "O magister, opera tua nos ad meliora aspirare docent. Horus et Sethi historia quasi lux in tenebris est."

Student: "Oh master, your work teaches us to aspire to greater things. The story of Horus and Seth is like a light in the darkness."

Apud Regiam Aulam:

Pharaon, consilium habens, dicit: "Sicut Horus, et nos adversus difficultates luctamur, regnum iustitia et pace gubernantes. Eius exemplum nobis viam monstrat."

In the Royal Court:

The pharaoh, holding council, says: "Like Horus, we too struggle against difficulties, ruling the kingdom with justice and peace. His example shows us the way."

Consiliarius: "Rex sapientissime, tua verba veritatem ferunt. In Horo exemplar, in Seth monitum invenimus."

Counselor: "Wisest king, your words bear truth. In Horus, we find the example, in Seth, we find the warning."

Conclusio:

Historia Horus et Sethi, per aetates narrata, non solum Aegypti sed etiam humanitatis universae hereditas facta est. Docet nos adversus adversa resilire, ordinem in chaos, lucem in tenebris quaerere. Haec narratio, aeternum Aegypti spiritum testans, adhuc vias nostras illuminat, docet, inspirat.

Conclusion:

The story of Horus and Seth, told through the ages, has become the heritage not only of Egypt but of all humanity. It teaches us to persevere through adversity, to seek order in chaos, and light in darkness. This tale, bearing witness to the eternal spirit of Egypt, still illuminates, teaches, and inspires us today.

Sic finitur quintum caput, Horus et Sethi fabulae hereditatem aeternam celebrans, monstrans quam historiae antiquae adhuc hodie nos formare, docere, inspirare queant.

Thus ends the fifth chapter, celebrating the eternal legacy of the story of Horus and Seth, showing how ancient histories can still shape, teach, and inspire us today.

Mythus Iter Solis Nocturnum

Occasus Solis

In omni vespera, Ra, deus solis, nocturnum iter suum incepit. Ad occidentem horizontem descendebat, diem finiens. Ra in navicula millionum annorum vehebatur, per infernum mundum navigans. Coeli obscurabantur, lunae et stellis locum dantes. Aegyptii credebant noctem esse transitum periculosum pro Ra.

Every evening, Ra, the sun god, began his nocturnal journey. He descended towards the western horizon, ending the day. Ra travelled in his boat of millions of years, navigating through the underworld. The skies darkened, giving way to the moon and stars. The Egyptians believed the night was a dangerous passage for Ra.

Dum sol ad occasum vergit, Ra solus in sua navicula stetit, paratus ad iter periculosum. "Ecce iterum," Ra dixit, "nox venit et mea via per tenebras incipit."

As the sun set, Ra stood alone in his boat, ready for the perilous journey. "Here we go again," Ra said, "the night comes, and my path through the darkness begins."

Subito, Aegyptius quidam, ad ripam Nili stans, Ra videntem exclamavit, "O Ra, lumen nostrum, te custodimus et in tua redeunte speramus!"

Suddenly, an Egyptian, standing on the bank of the Nile, shouted as he saw Ra, "O Ra, our light, we watch over you and hope for your return!"

Ra, voce gravi et calida, respondit, "Nolite timere, fideles mei. Etsi pericula magna sunt, semper ad vos revertar."

Ra, with a deep and warm voice, replied, "Do not fear, my faithful. Though the dangers are great, I will always return to you."

Navigatio coepit. Tenebrae circumfusae sunt, sed Ra, fidenter et fortiter, naviculam suam per noctem duxit. Conversatio inter Ra et Aegyptium ostendit fidem populi in deum suum et spem quae in corde cuiusque vivebat.

The journey began. Darkness surrounded them, but Ra, confident and brave, steered his boat through the night. The conversation between Ra and the Egyptian showed the people's faith in their god and the hope that lived in each heart.

Sic primus dies mythi solis iter per noctem finitur, promittens multas narrationes de periculis, deis auxiliantibus, et magica protegente quae in capitulis sequentibus explorabuntur.

Thus, the first day of the sun god's journey through the night ends, promising many stories of dangers, gods providing help, and protective magic to be explored in the following chapters.

Mundus Subterraneus

Inferus mundus, plenus creaturis mythicis daemonibusque, Ra noctu peragrabat. Apep, serpens ingens, inimicus mortalis Ra, semper paratus erat ad naviculam solarem devorandam, mundum in tenebras aeternas mergere conans.

The underworld, full of mythical creatures and demons, was traversed by Ra during the night. Apep, a giant serpent, Ra's mortal enemy, was always ready to devour the solar boat, attempting to plunge the world into eternal darkness.

Dum Ra in tenebris navigat, Apep subito apparet, minans. "Hodie," Apep sibilat, "tenebrae regnabunt et sol numquam rursus orietur!"

As Ra navigates through the darkness, Apep suddenly appears, threatening. "Today," Apep hisses, "the darkness will reign, and the sun will never rise again!"

Ra, non territus, respondet: "Numquam desistam, Apep. Lux vincit tenebras, et ego semper tuam malitiam superabo."

Ra, undeterred, responds: "I will never give up, Apep. Light conquers darkness, and I will always overcome your evil."

Interim, Set, deus chaos, advenit, gladium suum fulgente. "Frater," Set Ra adiuvare vocat, "una Apep superemus. Eius malitia finem habebit!"

Meanwhile, Set, the god of chaos, arrives with his gleaming sword. "Brother," Set calls out to help Ra, "together we shall defeat Apep. His evil will come to an end!"

Cum deis auxiliantibus, Ra et Set contra Apep pugnant. Pugna ardua est, sed una stant, potestatem tenebrarum repugnantes.

With the gods' help, Ra and Set fight against Apep. The battle is fierce, but together they stand, resisting the power of the darkness.

"Hoc iter," Ra Set dicit, "periculum magnum nobis affert, sed simul, nihil nos superare potest."

"This journey," Ra says to Set, "brings great danger to us, but together, nothing can defeat us."

Creaturae subterraneae, testes pugnae, circumstant, mirantes. Aliae Ra favebant, aliae silentio terrae obscurae fruebantur.

Subterranean creatures, witnesses to the battle, stand around in awe. Some supported Ra, while others enjoyed the silence of the dark earth.

Post multum certamen, Apep repulsus est, et Ra iter suum pergere potest. "Gratias tibi, Set," Ra dicit, "sine tua virtute, hodie victoria difficilior fuisset."

After much struggle, Apep is driven back, and Ra can continue his journey. "Thank you, Set," Ra says, "without your strength, today's victory would have been more difficult."

Set, oculos in caelum levans, respondet: "Solis lumen est quod chaos meum temperat. Semper pro lumine pugnabo."

Set, lifting his eyes to the sky, replies: "The light of the sun is what tempers my chaos. I will always fight for the light."

Sic, Ra et Set, licet interdum adversarii, in hoc itinere coniuncti sunt, monstrantes etiam in mythologia, unitatem in adversitate magnam fortitudinem afferre.

Thus, Ra and Set, although sometimes adversaries, are united on this journey, showing that even in mythology, unity in adversity brings great strength.

Hoc capitulum finit, promittens magis de magia et de ritibus quae Ra per noctem tuebantur in capitulis sequentibus narrari.

This chapter ends, promising more about the magic and rituals that protected Ra through the night, to be told in the following chapters.

Tutela Naviculae

Magica erat navicula solis, quae per aquas et caelos navigare poterat. Sortilegiis incantationibusque, Ra et navicula eius protegebantur. Sacerdotes ritus agebant ut securitas Ra per noctem assecuraretur. Aegyptii in Ra fidem collocabant, eiusque reditum matutinum precabantur. Amuleta talismanaque adhibebantur ut tenebris obsisterent.

The solar boat was magical, capable of navigating through waters and skies. With spells and incantations, Ra and his boat were protected. Priests performed rituals to ensure Ra's safety during the night. The Egyptians placed their faith in Ra and prayed for his morning return. Amulets and talismans were used to ward off the darkness.

In sacra Aegypti templa, sacerdos maior, stola alba indutus, ad altare accessit, incipiens ritum. "O Ra," inquit, "tutare te ipsum et naviculam tuam periculis nocturnis."

In the sacred temples of Egypt, the high priest, dressed in a white robe, approached the altar, beginning the ritual. "O Ra," he said, "protect yourself and your boat from the dangers of the night."

Alibi, in domo parva prope Nilum, familia parva simul stetit, manus iunctas, orantes. "Ra, rede ad nos luce cum nova," mater susurravit, amuletum solis figuram tenens.

Elsewhere, in a small house near the Nile, a small family stood together, holding hands, praying. "Ra, return to us with new light," the mother whispered, holding a sun-shaped amulet.

Subito, in profundo caeli nocturni, Ra voce magica incantationem pronuntiat. "Per hanc naviculam, per vires solis, ab omni periculo me defende."

Suddenly, in the depths of the night sky, Ra uttered a magical incantation with his voice. "Through this boat, through the power of the sun, protect me from all danger."

Tunc, sacerdos, amuletum elevans, clarum lumen emittit, naviculam circumdans, signum protectionis divinae creans. "Hoc lumine, Ra tutus erit," sacerdos exclamat, fiduciam populi confirmans.

Then, the priest, raising an amulet, emitted a bright light, surrounding the boat, creating a sign of divine protection. "With this light, Ra will be safe," the priest exclaimed, reassuring the people's faith.

Interim, Ra, pericula sentiens, amuletum suum tangit, sentiens vim protectionis ex Aegypto venientem. "Gratias vobis, sacerdotes et fideles. Vestra fides et magia me custodiunt."

Meanwhile, sensing danger, Ra touched his amulet, feeling the power of protection coming from Egypt. "Thank you, priests and faithful ones. Your faith and magic guard me."

Cum prima lux oriri coepit, Aegyptii ad templa festinabant, gratias agentes pro tutela Ra et solis reditu. "O Ra, gratias tibi agimus," omnes una voce dicunt, "quia tenebras superasti et ad nos rediisti."

As the first light began to rise, the Egyptians hurried to the temples, giving thanks for Ra's protection and the return of the sun. "O Ra, we thank you," they all said in unison, "for overcoming the darkness and returning to us."

Hoc capitulum ostendit quamvis pericula magna sint, fides et magia coniunctae Ra per noctem tutum reddere possunt, et quomodo Aegyptii, deos suos venerantes, in cotidianis vitis suis spem et securitatem inveniunt.

This chapter shows that, although the dangers are great, faith and magic together can keep Ra safe through the night, and how the Egyptians, in worshipping their gods, find hope and security in their daily lives.

Renovatio Aurorae

Postquam pericula noctis superavit, Ra ad orientem horizontem apparebat. Reditus eius initium novi diei, cycli renascentiae, significabat. Victoria Ra super Apep ut triumphus lucis super tenebras celebrabatur. Aegyptii auroram cum gaudio et levamine excipiebant. Templa aperiebantur pro primis precationibus et donis Ra dedicatis.

After overcoming the dangers of the night, Ra appeared at the eastern horizon. His return marked the beginning of a new day, a cycle of rebirth. Ra's victory over Apep was celebrated as the triumph of light over darkness. The Egyptians welcomed the dawn with joy and relief. Temples were opened for the first prayers and offerings dedicated to Ra.

Cum primum lumen aurorae caelum tingebat, Ra, renovatus, in caelo splendidus refulsit. "Ecce iterum," inquit Ra, "tenebras superavi et novum diem vobis afferre possum."

As the first light of dawn tinged the sky, Ra, renewed, shone brilliantly in the heavens. "Here I am again," Ra said, "I have overcome the darkness and can bring you a new day."

In templo magno, sacerdos ad altare stetit, Ra gratias agens. "O Ra, tua virtute, iterum tenebrae repulsae sunt. Tibi gratias agimus," sacerdos, fumigationem sacram faciens, pronuntiavit.

In the great temple, the priest stood at the altar, giving thanks to Ra. "O Ra, by your strength, the darkness has been driven back once again. We give thanks to you," the priest proclaimed while performing a sacred incense offering.

Civitas, templum circumdans, sollemnia celebrabat. Familiae, flores et dona portantes, ad templa properabant, laetitiam et gratitudinem exprimentes. "Ra, vita nostra," populus in unisono clamabat, "gratias tibi pro nova luce!"

The city surrounding the temple celebrated the solemn occasion. Families, carrying flowers and offerings, hurried to the temples, expressing joy and gratitude. "Ra, our life," the people shouted in unison, "thank you for the new light!"

Inter haec sollemnia, iuvenis Aegyptius, oculis in auroram fixis, quiete dixit, "Quam pulchra est renovatio, quae nos docet nunquam in adversitate desperare."

During these celebrations, a young Egyptian, his eyes fixed on the dawn, quietly said, "How beautiful is renewal, which teaches us never to despair in adversity."

Subito, Ra, voce plena amoris, ad omnes loquitur, "Fideles mei, vestra devotio et preces vires mihi praebent. Simul, nullum malum superare non possumus."

Suddenly, Ra, with a voice full of love, spoke to everyone, "My faithful ones, your devotion and prayers give me strength. Together, we can overcome any evil."

Sol, altius in caelo ascendens, diem novum et promissiones infinitas afferens, universum illuminat. "Hodie," omnes dicunt, "novam spem et fortitudinem invenimus."

The sun, rising higher in the sky, illuminated the universe, bringing a new day and infinite promises. "Today," everyone said, "we have found new hope and strength."

Hoc capitulum finit, monstrans quomodo Ra et Aegyptii in perpetuo cyclo mortis et renascentiae, tenebrarum et lucis, participent. Narratio non solum de deo solis est, sed etiam de humani spiritus resilentia et perpetua spe.

This chapter ends, showing how Ra and the Egyptians partake in the perpetual cycle of death and rebirth, darkness and light. The story is not only about the sun god but also about the resilience of the human spirit and eternal hope.

Significatio Mythi

Nocturnum iter Ra symbolum erat cycli mortis et renascentiae. Docuit perseverantiam adversus adversitates et fidem in boni victoriam. Mythos in arte, litteratura, et architectura Aegyptiorum integrabatur. Narrationes de Ra homines ad vivendum cum audacia et spe inspirabant. Mythos de nocturno itinere Ra columnam centralem religionis et cosmologiae Aegyptiae manebat.

Ra's nocturnal journey was a symbol of the cycle of death and rebirth. It taught perseverance in the face of adversity and faith in the victory of good. The myth was integrated into Egyptian art, literature, and architecture. Stories of Ra inspired people to live with courage and hope. The myth of Ra's nocturnal journey remained a central pillar of Egyptian religion and cosmology.

In magna bibliotheca Aegypti, sapiens scriptor, volumen de Ra scribens, cogitavit. "Hic mythos," inquit, "non solum antiquae narrationis memoria est, sed etiam hodiernae vitae doctrina."

In the great library of Egypt, a wise scribe, writing a volume about Ra, reflected. "This myth," he said, "is not only a memory of an ancient story but also a lesson for modern life."

Discipulus iuvenis, audiendo, interrogavit, "Quomodo potest antiquus deus solis nos hodie docere, magister?"

A young student, listening, asked, "How can an ancient sun god teach us today, master?"

Sapiens, pausans, respondit, "Ra nos docet, quamvis nox longa et plena periculorum sit, semper est aurora nova. Docet nos nunquam desperare."

The wise man, pausing, replied, "Ra teaches us that although the night is long and full of dangers, there is always a new dawn. He teaches us never to despair."

In taberna artificis, pictor magnam picturam de Ra creabat. "Per hoc opus," artifex dixit, "volo homines sentire potentiam lucis et spei, quae tenebras superat."

In an artist's workshop, a painter was creating a great picture of Ra. "Through this work," the artist said, "I want people to feel the power of light and hope, which overcomes the darkness."

Per vias Aegypti, populus ad magnas pyramides et templos spectabat, monumenta mythi viventis. "Haec structurae," pater filio suo narravit, "testamentum sunt ad nostram historiam et deorum nostrorum virtutem."

Through the streets of Egypt, people gazed at the great pyramids and temples, monuments of the living myth. "These structures," a father told his son, "are a testament to our history and the power of our gods."

Nocte, sub stellis, familia congregata, historias de Ra et eius iter nocturnum narrabant. "Vide," mater dixit, "sicut Ra tenebras superavit, ita nos adversitatibus in vita nostra superare possumus."

At night, under the stars, a family gathered, telling stories of Ra and his nocturnal journey. "Look," the mother said, "just as Ra overcame the darkness, so we too can overcome the adversities in our lives."

Hoc capitulum finit, ostendens quomodo mythus Ra non solum antiquitatis reliquiae sed etiam aeternae sapientiae et inspirationis fons sit. Narrat de connexione inter deos et homines, et quomodo antiquae fabulae adhuc hodiernam vitam informare et illuminare possunt.

This chapter ends, showing how the myth of Ra is not only a relic of the past but also a source of eternal wisdom and inspiration. It tells of the connection between gods and humans and how ancient stories can still inform and illuminate modern life.

Legenda Nutis Deae Caeli

Nativitas Nutis

Nut, in mythologia Aegyptia, dea caeli vocabatur. Fuit filia Shu, dei aeris, et Tefnut, deae humidi. Nut figurabatur ut mulier caelum tegens, corpus eius stellis ornatum. Solis, lunae, siderumque custos erat, ea in itinere suo ducens.

Nut, in Egyptian mythology, was called the goddess of the sky. She was the daughter of Shu, the god of air, and Tefnut, the goddess of moisture. Nut was depicted as a woman covering the sky, her body adorned with stars. She was the guardian of the sun, moon, and stars, guiding them on their journeys.

In altis caelis, ubi aether ipse vivit, Nut primum suos oculos aperuit. "Quis sum?" Nut suaviter in aerem susurravit, stellas circum se mirans.

In the high heavens, where the very ether lives, Nut opened her eyes for the first time. "Who am I?" Nut softly whispered into the air, marvelling at the stars around her.

Shu, pater eius, ad eam vento leni respondit, "Tu es Nut, nostra caeli domina, qui omnia lumina noctis tenes."

Shu, her father, answered her in a gentle breeze, "You are Nut, our lady of the sky, who holds all the lights of the night."

Tefnut, mater eius, rosam dulcem addens, inquit, "Et tu nostrae mundi custos es, filia. Tua est potestas omnia sidera ducendi."

Tefnut, her mother, adding a sweet dew, said, "And you are the guardian of our world, daughter. It is your power to guide all the stars."

Nut, caput elevans, vastitatem caeli supra se vidit. "Promitto," dixit, "me curaturam esse ut sol, luna, et omnia sidera in suo cursu maneant. Noctis et dierum custos ero."

Nut, lifting her head, saw the vastness of the sky above her. "I promise," she said, "I will ensure that the sun, moon, and all the stars remain on their course. I will be the guardian of night and day."

Sed Nut non solum sidera custodiebat; etiam cor habebat plenum amoris. Geb, deus terrae, mox eius animam complevit. Inter caelum et terram, amor eorum floruit, universum in mirum spectaculum transformans.

But Nut did not only guard the stars; she also had a heart full of love. Geb, the god of the earth, soon filled her soul. Between the sky and the earth, their love blossomed, transforming the universe into a wondrous spectacle.

Tamen, Ra, solis deus, eorum unionem vidit et turbatus est. "Hoc amor," Ra decrevit, "mundi ordinem perturbare potest. Non licet!"

However, Ra, the sun god, saw their union and was troubled. "This love," Ra decreed, "could disturb the order of the world. It is not allowed!"

Nut, corde fracto, sed fortis, inquit ad Geb, "Amor noster fortasse prohibitus est, sed numquam desinet. Modum inveniemus."

Nut, heartbroken but strong, said to Geb, "Our love may be forbidden, but it will never end. We will find a way."

Et sic, in caelo alto et terra vasta, Nut et Geb suum amorem secretum coluerunt, promittentes se invicem nunquam deserere, etiamsi omnes dei contra eos starent.

And so, in the high sky and the vast earth, Nut and Geb nurtured their secret love, promising never to abandon each other, even if all the gods stood against them.

Hoc capitulum finit, promissionem amoris aeternum, divinae custodiae, et siderum perpetui motus introducens, fundamenta ponens pro legendis et mysteriis quae sequerentur.

This chapter ends, introducing the promise of eternal love, divine guardianship, and the perpetual motion of the stars, laying the foundations for the legends and mysteries that would follow.

Amor Prohibitus

Nut, caeli dea, Gebum, deum terrae, amore ardebat. Amor eorum tam magnus erat ut caelum et terram coniungere minaretur. Ra, solis deus, eorum coniunctionem vetuit, timens ne amor eorum mundum ex aequilibrio duceret. Tamen, Thoth, sapientiae deus, intervenit ut amantes adiuvaret.

Nut, the goddess of the sky, was passionately in love with Geb, the god of the earth. Their love was so great that it threatened to unite the sky and the earth. Ra, the sun god, forbade their union, fearing that their love would throw the world out of balance. However, Thoth, the god of wisdom, intervened to help the lovers.

In secretis mundi angulis, Nut Gebum convenit. "Cur," Nut flebiliter dixit, "noster amor tam formidatus est? Numquam volui quemquam nisi te."

In the hidden corners of the world, Nut met with Geb. "Why," Nut said tearfully, "is our love so feared? I never wanted anyone but you."

Geb, terram suaviter tangens, respondit, "Amor noster naturae ipsius potentia est. Sed Ra timet quid possit fieri."

Geb, gently touching the earth, replied, "Our love is the power of nature itself. But Ra fears what might happen."

Subito, lumine aureo fulgens, Ra apparuit. "Nut, Geb," voce tonitruante dixit, "vestrum amor mundi ordinem minatur. Prohibitus est!"

Suddenly, glowing with golden light, Ra appeared. "Nut, Geb," he said in a thunderous voice, "your love threatens the order of the world. It is forbidden!"

Nut, lacrimis in oculis, supplicavit, "Sed amor noster, quid possumus facere si cor nostrum alter in altero est?"

Nut, with tears in her eyes, pleaded, "But our love, what can we do if our hearts are in each other?"

Tunc, Thoth, ales magnus, advenit, "Est via," suaviter dixit. "Sapientia mea vos adiuvare potest. Audite consilium meum."

Then, Thoth, the great bird, arrived and gently said, "There is a way. My wisdom can help you. Listen to my counsel."

Ra, ira commotus sed curiosus, inquit, "Loquere, Thoth. Quam rem proponis?"

Ra, stirred by anger but curious, said, "Speak, Thoth. What do you propose?"

Thoth, calmus et certus, "Propono ludum," inquit. "Ludus qui tempus ipsum extendere potest, dando Nuti et Gebo spem."

Thoth, calm and certain, said, "I propose a game. A game that can extend time itself, giving Nut and Geb hope."

Nut et Geb, spe refecti, Thoth adtenderunt. "Quid facere debemus?" Nut rogavit.

Nut and Geb, their hope restored, listened intently to Thoth. "What must we do?" Nut asked.

"Me cum luna ludere oportet," Thoth explicavit. "Si vincam, dies extra calendarii ordinem creabuntur. Dies in quibus Nut libera erit a maledictione Ra."

"I must play a game with the moon," Thoth explained. "If I win, days outside the regular calendar will be created. Days during which Nut will be free from Ra's curse."

Ra, considerans, tandem consensit. "Fiat," dixit, "sed scitote, hoc magnum experimentum est. Consequentiis parati estote."

Ra, considering it, finally agreed. "So be it," he said, "but know that this is a great experiment. Be prepared for the consequences."

Et sic, Thoth ad lunam ivit, paratus ingenio suo uti ad amorem Nut et Gebi salvandum. Nut et Geb, manibus iunctis, sperabant contra spem, amorem eorum fortasse futurum esse liberum.

And so, Thoth went to the moon, ready to use his wit to save the love of Nut and Geb. Nut and Geb, holding hands, hoped against hope that their love might one day be free.

Hoc capitulum finit, historia amoris interditi profundiora mysteria et consilia deorum explorans, praesertim Thothis ingenium et audaciam in facie decretorum divinorum.

This chapter ends, exploring the deeper mysteries and the plans of the gods, especially Thoth's ingenuity and daring in the face of divine decrees.

Maledictio Ra

Ra, iratus quod Nut eius praeceptum neglexisset, decrevit eam non posse in trecentis sexaginta diebus anni parere. Nut, desperata, ad Thothem conversa est, solutionem quaerens. Thoth, sua astutia, tempus additum lucratus est ludens tesseras cum luna. Quinque dies extra ordinem a Ra statutum creavit.

Ra, angry that Nut had ignored his command, decreed that she could not give birth in the 360 days of the year. Desperate, Nut turned to Thoth, seeking a solution. Thoth, with his cunning, gained extra time by playing dice with the moon. He created five days beyond the order established by Ra.

Nut ad Thothem accessit, lacrimis in oculis. "Thoth, o Thoth," inquit, "Ra maledictionem terribilem mihi imposuit. Num auxilium tuum sperare audeo?"

Nut approached Thoth, tears in her eyes. "Thoth, oh Thoth," she said, "Ra has placed a terrible curse upon me. Dare I hope for your help?"

Thoth, in luna sedens, serenum vultum prae se ferens, respondit, "Nut, amica mea, ne desperes. Ingenium et sapientia saepe viam ubi minime expectatur inveniunt."

Thoth, sitting on the moon, with a calm expression, replied, "Nut, my friend, do not despair. Cunning and wisdom often find a way where it is least expected."

Sub luna plena, Thoth tesseras vibravit. "Ecce," inquit, "cum luna hac nocte ludam. Si vincam, tempus nobis dabitur, maledictionem Ra eludendi."

Under the full moon, Thoth shook the dice. "Look," he said, "I will play with the moon tonight. If I win, we will be given time to evade Ra's curse."

Nut, sperans sed dubitans, rogavit, "Quomodo hoc fieri potest? Ra potens et iratus est."

Nut, hopeful but doubtful, asked, "How can this be done? Ra is powerful and angry."

"Ah," Thoth subridens dixit, "luna mecum pactum faciet. Si eius cursum paulum retardare possum, dies extra ordinem creabuntur. Hi dies tui erunt, libera a vinculo Ra."

"Ah," Thoth said with a smile, "the moon will make a pact with me. If I can slow its course a little, extra days will be created. These days will be yours, free from Ra's bond."

Ludo finito, Thoth triumphavit. "Nut," exclamavit, "victoria nostra est! Quinque dies extra annum creavi. In his diebus, liber eris parere."

When the game ended, Thoth triumphed. "Nut," he exclaimed, "the victory is ours! I have created five extra days in the year. During these days, you will be free to give birth."

Nut, cor plenum gratitudine, inquit, "Thoth, quomodo tibi gratias agere possum? Tu mihi spem dedisti ubi nulla videbatur."

Nut, her heart full of gratitude, said, "Thoth, how can I thank you? You gave me hope where there seemed to be none."

"Nil debes," Thoth respondit, "Amor et iustitia semper viam inveniunt. Nunc, praepara te ad futurum tuum, liberum a maledictione."

"You owe nothing," Thoth replied, "Love and justice always find a way. Now, prepare yourself for your future, free from the curse."

Et sic, Nut spe renovata est, grata Thothi pro sua astutia et bonitate. Ra, sua maledictione elusa, tacite observavit, quid futurum esset ex his quinque diebus novis, mirans an fortasse sapientiam suam superare possit amor.

And so, Nut's hope was renewed, grateful to Thoth for his cunning and kindness. Ra, his curse evaded, silently watched, wondering what would come of these five new days, and whether perhaps love could surpass his wisdom.

Hoc capitulum finit, monstrans ingenium et sapientiam Thothis contra severitatem et potentiam Ra, et spem quae etiam in difficillimis temporibus inveniri potest.

This chapter ends, showing the ingenuity and wisdom of Thoth against the severity and power of Ra, and the hope that can be found even in the most difficult times.

Deorum Nativitas

In his quinque diebus magicis, Nut quinque liberos peperit. Primo die, Osirim, futurum deorum hominumque regem, enixa est. Secundo die, Horum Seniorem, deum caeli, genuit. Tertio die, Seth, deum chaos et tempestatum, mundo adiecit. Quarto die, Isis, dea magiae et sanationisque, nata est. Quinto die, Nephtys, dea mortis et renascentiae, in lucem venit.

In these five magical days, Nut gave birth to five children. On the first day, she bore Osiris, the future king of gods and men. On the second day, she gave birth to Horus the Elder, the god of the sky. On the third day, Seth, the god of chaos and storms, was added to the world. On the fourth day, Isis, the goddess of magic and healing, was born. On the fifth day, Nephthys, the goddess of death and rebirth, came into the light.

Cum prima lux diei novi oriretur, Nut, matre praeclara, Osirim aspiciebat. "O fili," inquit, "tu regnum nostrum ad gloriam ducere destinatus es."

As the first light of the new day arose, Nut, the proud mother, looked at Osiris. "Oh my son," she said, "you are destined to lead our kingdom to glory."

Osiris, vix natus, oculis plenis sapientiae, susurravit, "Mater, regnum iustum et pacem aeternam polliceor."

Osiris, barely born, whispered with eyes full of wisdom, "Mother, I promise a just reign and eternal peace."

Proximo die, Horus, oculos in caelum levans, inquit, "Ego caeli custos ero, ut lux solis semper in terra nostra refulgeat."

The next day, Horus, lifting his eyes to the sky, said, "I will be the guardian of the sky, so that the light of the sun always shines upon our land."

Tertio die, Seth, spiritus ferus et indomitus, clamavit, "Ego vim tempestatum regam. Nemo meam potestatem contemnet."

On the third day, Seth, a wild and untamed spirit, shouted, "I will rule the force of storms. No one will disregard my power."

Quarto die, Isis, suam vim magicam iam sentiens, inquit, "Per magiam sanationem et protectionem afferam his qui me invocant."

On the fourth day, Isis, already feeling her magical power, said, "Through magic, I will bring healing and protection to those who call upon me."

Quinto die, Nephtys, silentio plena et mysteriosa, murmuravit, "Ego mortis portas custodiam, animas ad novam vitam ducens."

On the fifth day, Nephthys, full of silence and mystery, murmured, "I will guard the gates of death, leading souls to new life."

Nut, liberos suos amplexa, dixit, "Vos novum aevum incepturi estis. Singuli vestrum munus habetis in ordine mundi conservando."

Nut, embracing her children, said, "You are about to begin a new era. Each of you has a role in maintaining the order of the world."

Et sic, in his quinque diebus extra temporis fluxum, Nut non solum maledictionem Ra superavit sed etiam fundamenta posuit pro futuro deorum Aegyptiorum et hominum. Hoc capitulum finit, ostendens quomodo ex amore et sapientia, etiam sub pressura deorum maiorium, nova vita et spes nasci possunt.

And so, in these five days outside the flow of time, Nut not only overcame Ra's curse but also laid the foundations for the future of the Egyptian gods and humans. This chapter ends, showing how from love and wisdom, even under the pressure of the greatest gods, new life and hope can be born.

Hereditas Nutis

Nut venerabatur ut mater deorum et custos caeli. Aegyptii eam celebrabant ut protectoram mortuorum, animas in alteram vitam ducentem. Noctu in precationibus invocabatur pro sua tutela somni. Templis et sepulcris saepe decorabatur imago eius, stellis ornata et vigilans. Legenda Nutis et familiae eius origines cosmos Aegyptii explicabat. Nut et Geb semper pariter figurabantur, caeli terraeque unionem aeternam symbolizantes. Dea caeli in mythologiis creationis figura centralis erat, caelestem arcum infinitum repraesentans. Eius fabula Aegyptiis vitam, mortem, renascentiamque cyclos reminiscebat. Nut in festis celebrabatur, quae stellas et caelestia corpora honorabant. Praesentia eius in mythologia Aegyptia harmoniae et aequilibrii in universo momenti sublineabat.

Nut was venerated as the mother of the gods and the guardian of the sky. The Egyptians celebrated her as the protector of the dead, leading souls into the afterlife. She was invoked at night in prayers for her protection over sleep. Her image, adorned with stars and watchful, often decorated temples and tombs. The legend of Nut and her family explained the origins of the Egyptian cosmos. Nut and Geb were always depicted together, symbolising the eternal union of the sky and the earth. The sky goddess was a central figure in creation myths, representing the infinite celestial arch. Her story reminded the Egyptians of the cycles of life, death, and rebirth. Nut was celebrated in festivals that honoured the stars and celestial bodies. Her presence in Egyptian mythology emphasised the importance of harmony and balance in the universe.

In templi sanctissimo loco, sacerdos ante altare stetit, Nutem invocans. "O Nut, caeli domina," sacerdos oravit, "tutela tua nobis

In the most sacred part of the temple, the priest stood before the altar, invoking Nut. "O Nut, lady of the sky," the priest prayed, "your protection gives us light in the darkness. You show the way for souls to eternity."

Sub caelo nocturno, familia Aegyptia simul stellis contemplabatur. "Videte," pater suaviter dixit, "Nut nos omnes custodit, ducens nos per noctem ad lucem novi diei."

Under the night sky, an Egyptian family gazed together at the stars. "Look," the father said gently, "Nut watches over us all, guiding us through the night to the light of a new day."

In magnis festis, populus adorabat, cantus et preces ad Nutem dirigens. "Nut, mater stellarum," canebant, "gratias tibi agimus pro protectione et amore tuo."

At great festivals, the people worshipped, directing songs and prayers to Nut. "Nut, mother of the stars," they sang, "we thank you for your protection and love."

Nut et Geb in arte sacra depicti, manu in manu, aeternum amorem et unitatem caeli terraeque demonstrabant. "Haec unio," magister artis explicavit, "nos docet de amore et harmonia quae omnia sustinet."

Nut and Geb, depicted in sacred art, hand in hand, demonstrated the eternal love and unity of the sky and the earth. "This union," the art master explained, "teaches us about the love and harmony that sustains everything."

Nut, non solum dea sed etiam mater, in corde Aegyptiorum vivebat, eos docens de vitae mysteriis, mortis, et renascentiae perpetuae. Eius legenda, aevum transiens, adhuc mentes cordeque hominum illuminat, memoria perpetua harmoniae quae in universo regnat.

Nut, not only a goddess but also a mother, lived in the hearts of the Egyptians, teaching them about the mysteries of life, death, and eternal rebirth. Her legend, passing through the ages, still illuminates the minds and hearts of people, a lasting reminder of the harmony that reigns in the universe.

Hoc capitulum claudit fabulam Nutis, non solum ut mythi narratio sed ut perpetua sapientiae et amoris fons, demonstrans quomodo antiquae deae legenda adhuc in vita cotidiana Aegyptiorum resonare potest, universi comprehensionem profundam offerens.

This chapter closes Nut's story, not only as a myth but as a perpetual source of wisdom and love, showing how the legend of the ancient goddess can still resonate in the daily lives of the Egyptians, offering a deep understanding of the universe.

Narratio Osiridis Deique Resurrectionis

Imperium Osiridis

Osiris, deus benignus, Aegyptum cum iustitia et concordia regebat. Agriculturam, leges, et cultum deorum humanis docebat. Isis, eius uxor, imperium cum eo participabat, amorem et magiam symbolizans. Simul, prosperitatem et stabilitatem Aegypto attulerunt. Seth, frater Osiridis invidus, thronum cupiebat.

Osiris, a kind god, ruled Egypt with justice and harmony. He taught humans about agriculture, laws, and the worship of the gods. Isis, his wife, shared the power with him, symbolising love and magic. Together, they brought prosperity and stability to Egypt. Seth, Osiris' envious brother, desired the throne.

In regni aula, Osiris ad populum suum loquebatur: "Nobis, o cives, est vivere in harmonia cum natura et deis. Doctrinas vobis trado ut meliorem vitam agatis."

In the royal hall, Osiris spoke to his people: "It is for us, oh citizens, to live in harmony with nature and the gods. I pass down teachings to help you lead better lives."

Isis, adstante, inquit, "Amor et magia nos ducant. Una, prosperitatem ad nostram terram feremus."

Isis, standing by, said, "Let love and magic guide us. Together, we will bring prosperity to our land."

Subito, Seth, angulo tenebroso insidias struens, sibi susurravit, "Regnum Osiridis meum esse debet. Consilium perfectum habeo ad eum deponendum."

Suddenly, Seth, plotting in a dark corner, whispered to himself, "The kingdom of Osiris should be mine. I have the perfect plan to overthrow him."

Interim, Osiris et Isis, nihil de consiliis Seth scientes, in sua benevolentia et cura pro Aegypto perseverabant. Sed umbrae conspirationis iam super regnum se extendebant, futurum incertum praenuntiantes.

Meanwhile, Osiris and Isis, unaware of Seth's plans, continued in their benevolence and care for Egypt. But the shadows of conspiracy were already spreading over the kingdom, foreshadowing an uncertain future.

Hoc capitulum initium ponit fabulae plenae magiae, proditoriae, et quaestus aeterni, ubi amor et iustitia in facie adversitatis testantur. Osiris, rex iustus et sapiens, et Isis, regina amoris et magiae, exemplar vitae et regni aequi praebebant, sed invidia et avaritia in corde Seth latent, minae magnae et tumultus futuri semina iaciunt.

This chapter sets the stage for a tale full of magic, betrayal, and the quest for eternity, where love and justice are tested in the face of adversity. Osiris, the just and wise king, and Isis, the queen of love and magic, provided an example of a fair life and reign, but envy and greed lay hidden in Seth's heart, sowing the seeds of great danger and future turmoil.

Proditio Seth

Seth, callidus et dolosus, contra Osirim consilium cepit, regem fraude deponere molitus. Convivium magnum in honorem Osiridis paravit, omnes deos invitans. Sarcophagum splendidum ostendit, pollicitus se id donaturum ei qui in eo perfecte decumberet.

Seth, cunning and deceitful, devised a plan against Osiris, attempting to overthrow the king through trickery. He prepared a great banquet in honour of Osiris, inviting all the gods. He displayed a splendid sarcophagus, promising to give it to whoever fit perfectly inside.

In magnifico aulae spatio, Seth, voce plena insidiae, inquit, "Hoc donum cui convenit, regiae dignitatis est signum. Quis audet se in sarcophagum ponere?"

In the magnificent hall, Seth, with a voice full of deceit, said, "This gift, to whom it fits, is a symbol of royal dignity. Who dares to lie in the sarcophagus?"

Osiris, fide plenus nec dolos suspicatus, respondit, "Ego tuum munus experiri velim." Et in sarcophagum decubuit.

Osiris, full of trust and suspecting no deceit, replied, "I would like to try your gift." And he lay in the sarcophagus.

Seth, vultu occultato gaudium malum, celeriter sarcophagum clausit et, adiuvante suis, in Nilum proiecit. "Sic," sibi susurravit, "de throno Osirim removeo."

Seth, his face hiding wicked joy, quickly closed the sarcophagus and, with the help of his followers, threw it into the Nile. "Thus," he whispered to himself, "I remove Osiris from the throne."

Isis, absentia Osiridis perculsa, exclamavit, "Quid factum est Osiridi, meo carissimo?" Anubis, deus funerum, adstitit, "Seth proditor est. Invenire Osirim debemus."

Isis, struck by Osiris' absence, exclaimed, "What has happened to my beloved Osiris?" Anubis, the god of funerals, stood by, "Seth is a traitor. We must find Osiris."

Isis, lacrimis oborta, dixit, "Viam inveniam, Osirim meum a tenebris revocabo. Seth poenas dabit."

Isis, with tears in her eyes, said, "I will find a way. I will bring my Osiris back from the darkness. Seth will pay."

Seth, regnum suum nunc arbitratus, non intellexit quantam vim amorem Isis pro Osiride haberet, nec quanta magia Isis uteretur ad maritum suum salvandum. Proditio eius initium est historiae plenae magiae, quaestus et ultionis, in qua amor et veritas in extremis adversitatibus clarissime luceant.

Seth, now considering the kingdom his, did not understand how strong Isis's love for Osiris was, nor how much magic she would use to save her husband. His betrayal is the beginning of a story full of magic, quest, and revenge, where love and truth shine brightest in the face of extreme adversity.

Hoc capitulum finit, profundam tristitiam et proditoriam actionem revelans quae cor fabulae tangit. In umbra proditio et dolor, spes tamen et amor in corde Isis ardent, promittentes futurae narrationis vim et passionem.

This chapter ends, revealing deep sorrow and a treacherous act that touches the heart of the story. In the shadow of betrayal and pain, hope and love still burn in Isis's heart, promising strength and passion in the story yet to come.

Quaestio Isis

Isis, Osiridis sui amissione devastata, in eius quaerendum profecta est. Per Aegyptum transivit et ultra, dilectum suum quaerens. Sarcophagum denique in arbore apud Byblum inventum est. Corpus in Aegyptum rettulit ut honores funebres redderet. Cum Anubis auxilio, corpus Osiridis embalsamavit, primum ritum mummificationis creans.

Isis, devastated by the loss of her Osiris, set out to search for him. She travelled across Egypt and beyond, seeking her beloved. At last, the sarcophagus was found in a tree near Byblos. She returned the body to Egypt to perform funeral honours. With the help of Anubis, she embalmed Osiris' body, creating the first ritual of mummification.

In solitudine magnae Aegypti, Isis, lacrimis obruta, clamat: "Osiris, ubi es?" Nusquam responsio auditur, nisi venti susurrus et arenarum motus.

In the solitude of the great Egyptian desert, Isis, overwhelmed with tears, cried out: "Osiris, where are you?" No answer was heard, only the whisper of the wind and the shifting of the sands.

Iter longum et arduum, per urbes et deserta, Isis pergit. "Non desistam," in corde suo dicit, "donec te, Osiridis mei, inveniam."

On a long and arduous journey through cities and deserts, Isis continued. "I will not stop," she said in her heart, "until I find you, my Osiris."

Apud Byblum, in loco secreto, sarcophagum in alto arboris ramo celatum invenit. "Hic est," Isis exclamat, "amor meus, tandem inventus!"

At Byblos, in a secret place, she found the sarcophagus hidden high in the branches of a tree. "Here it is," Isis exclaimed, "my love, finally found!"

Corpus Osiridis cum veneratione in Aegyptum reportat, ubi cum cura et amore, honores ultimos parat. "In terra tua, Osiris, te honorabo," Isis dicit.

She reverently carried Osiris' body back to Egypt, where she lovingly prepared his final honours. "In your land, Osiris, I will honour you," said Isis.

Anubis, funerum deus, advenit: "Isis, tibi in hoc tristi opere adero. Scientiam meam de embalsamatione tibi do."

Anubis, the god of funerals, arrived: "Isis, I will assist you in this sorrowful task. I give you my knowledge of embalming."

Isis, Anubis gratias agens, dicit: "Gratias tibi, Anubis. Cum tua sapientia, Osiridis corpus aeternum conservabimus."

Isis, thanking Anubis, said: "Thank you, Anubis. With your wisdom, we will preserve Osiris' body for eternity."

Et sic, sub Anubis ductu, Isis primum ritum mummificationis exsequitur, Osiridis corpus ad vitam post mortem praeparans. "Per hoc," Isis dicit, "Osiris, non solum in memoria nostra, sed in Aegypto aeterna vivet."

And so, under the guidance of Anubis, Isis performed the first mummification ritual, preparing Osiris' body for life after death. "Through this," Isis said, "Osiris will live not only in our memory but eternally in Egypt."

Hoc capitulum finit, monstrans immensum amorem et devotionem Isis ad Osirim, necnon ingentem eius laborem ad amatum redintegrandum. Etiam initium ritus sacri mummificationis introducit, quod essentiale erit in cultura Aegyptia ad vitam aeternam assequendam.

This chapter ends, showing the immense love and devotion Isis had for Osiris, as well as her great effort to restore her beloved. It also introduces the sacred ritual of mummification, which will be essential in Egyptian culture for achieving eternal life.

Resurrectio Osiridis

Isis, magia sua usus, Osirim resuscitare conata est, sed inter vivos regnare non potuit. Osiris rex mundi subterranei factus est, animas mortuorum iudicans. Horus, filius Osiridis et Isis, educatus est ut patrem ulcisceretur et contra Seth pugnaret. Certamen inter Horum et Seth ordinem et chaos significabat. Osiris, in inferis, immortalitatis et renascentiae symbolum fiebat.

Isis, using her magic, tried to resurrect Osiris, but he could not rule among the living. Osiris became the king of the underworld, judging the souls of the dead. Horus, the son of Osiris and Isis, was raised to avenge his father and fight against Seth. The battle between Horus and Seth symbolised order and chaos. Osiris, in the underworld, became a symbol of immortality and rebirth.

In secreta Aegypti camera, Isis ad Osiridis corpus accedit. "Per hanc magiam," susurrat, "te, Osiris, ad vitam revocabo, non ut inter vivos regnes, sed ut mundi subterranei rex sis."

In a secret chamber of Egypt, Isis approached the body of Osiris. "Through this magic," she whispered, "I will bring you back to life, not to rule among the living, but to be the king of the underworld."

Cum verbis magicis et gestibus sacris, Osiris paulatim ad vitam redit, oculos aperit. "Isis," voce gravida amoris et gratitudinis inquit, "quid mihi accidit?"

With magical words and sacred gestures, Osiris gradually returned to life, opening his eyes. "Isis," he said with a voice full of love and gratitude, "what happened to me?"

"Carissime," Isis respondet, "a Seth proditus es. Nunc regnum subterraneum tibi est, ubi iustitiam mortuorum servabis."

"My dearest," Isis responded, "you were betrayed by Seth. Now the underworld is yours, where you will uphold justice for the dead."

Horus, iuvenis fortis et decisus, ad eos accedit. "Mater, Pater, me ad ultionem paravi. Seth me non terrebunt."

Horus, a strong and determined young man, approached them. "Mother, Father, I have prepared for revenge. Seth will not frighten me."

Osiris, Horum intuens, dicit, "Fili mi, certamen tuum non solum de potentia est sed etiam de mundo meliore faciendo. Ordinem ex chao creare debes."

Osiris, looking at Horus, said, "My son, your battle is not only about power but also about making a better world. You must create order out of chaos."

Horus, pugnae se praeparans, inquit, "Promitto, non desistam donec iustitia restituta sit. Seth sciet verum ordinis significatum."

Horus, preparing for battle, said, "I promise, I will not stop until justice is restored. Seth will learn the true meaning of order."

Osiris, iam in sua nova regna descendens, dicit, "Ego, etsi in umbra regno, semper vobiscum ero, dux et protector. Immortalitas nostra in renascentia et iustitia vera est."

Osiris, now descending into his new realm, said, "Though I rule in the shadows, I will always be with you, as a guide and protector. Our immortality lies in rebirth and true justice."

Hoc capitulum finit, ostendens non solum physicam Osiridis resurrectionem sed etiam spiritualem eius victoriam super mortem, eiusque novum munus ut iudex inferorum. Horus, nunc proelium suum contra Seth paratus, non solum patris mortem sed etiam maioris ordinis et iustitiae causa pugnat. Osiris, licet in aeternum mutatus, immortalitatis et renascentiae potentiam demonstrat, sperantibus et credentibus viam praebebat.

This chapter ends, showing not only Osiris's physical resurrection but also his spiritual victory over death, and his new role as the judge of the underworld. Horus, now prepared for battle against Seth, fights not only for his father's death but for the greater cause of order and justice. Osiris, though changed forever, demonstrates the power of immortality and rebirth, offering a path to those who hope and believe.

Hereditas Osiridis

Osiris ut deus mortis, renascentiae, vitaeque aeternae venerabatur. Aegyptii ritus funebres in honorem eius celebrabant, sperantes se ad aeternitatem ut ille pervenire. Templa Osiridi sacra loca cultus et peregrinationis erant. Ceremonia Osiridis, mortem et resurrectionem eius celebrans, eventus magni momenti habebatur. Osiris docebat iustitiam et moralitatem claves esse ad pacem post mortem. Mythus eius spem et fiduciam in vitam post mortem inspirabat, religionem Aegyptiam alte influens.

Osiris was worshipped as the god of death, rebirth, and eternal life. The Egyptians celebrated funeral rites in his honour, hoping to reach eternity as he had. Temples dedicated to Osiris were sacred places of worship and pilgrimage. The ceremony of Osiris, celebrating his death and resurrection, was considered an event of great importance. Osiris taught that justice and morality were the keys to peace after death. His myth inspired hope and confidence in life after death, deeply influencing Egyptian religion.

In templo magnifico, sacerdotes parati, summus sacerdos dixit, "Hodie Osiridis sacra mysteria celebramus. Eius via nos doceat de vita, morte, renascentia."

In the magnificent temple, with the priests prepared, the high priest said, "Today we celebrate the sacred mysteries of Osiris. May his path teach us about life, death, and rebirth."

Fideles undique conveniunt, animis pleni spe et reverentia. Multi in corde suo murmurant, "Osiris, doce nos transire per mortem ad vitam aeternam."

Believers gathered from everywhere, their hearts filled with hope and reverence. Many murmured in their hearts, "Osiris, teach us to pass through death to eternal life."

In ceremonia, effigies Osiridis portatur, circum templa gestatur, fideles eius viam et victoriam super mortem commemorantes. Summus sacerdos proclamat, "Per haec sacra, Osiris semper inter nos vivit, nobis viam ad iustitiam et aeternitatem monstrans."

During the ceremony, the effigy of Osiris was carried, paraded around the temples, with the faithful commemorating his path and victory over death. The high priest proclaimed, "Through these sacred rites, Osiris lives among us always, showing us the way to justice and eternity."

Post ritus, congregatio silentium tenet, orantes, "Osiris, nobis pacem et iustitiam affer, ut in vita et morte tibi fideles simus."

After the rites, the congregation held a moment of silence, praying, "Osiris, bring us peace and justice, so that we may remain faithful to you in life and death."

Osiris, etsi in inferis regnat, per ritus et preces fidelium in mundo vivorum praesens manet. "Ego," inquit in corde cuiusque, "via, veritas, vita sum. Qui in me credit, etiamsi mortuus fuerit, vivet."

Osiris, though he reigns in the underworld, remains present in the world of the living through the rites and prayers of the faithful. "I," he says in the heart of each one, "am the way, the truth, and the life. Whoever believes in me, even if they die, shall live."

Hoc capitulum finit, profundum Osiridis legatum illustrans, non solum ut deus inferi sed etiam ut magister vitae, mortis, et renascentiae. Eius doctrinae et mysteria, per saecula, spem et lucem Aegyptiis in tenebris praebebant, demonstrantes quomodo antiqua fides adhuc modernos sensus et quaestiones de vita et aeternitate tangit.

This chapter ends, illustrating the profound legacy of Osiris, not only as the god of the underworld but also as a teacher of life, death, and rebirth. His teachings and mysteries, through the ages, provided the Egyptians with hope and light in times of darkness, showing how ancient faith still touches modern feelings and questions about life and eternity.

Mythus Phoenicis et Symbolismus eius in Cultura Aegyptia

Legenda Phoenicis

In antiquis temporibus, sub lumine solis et ignis potentia, avis mirabilis, Phoenix nomine, vivebat. Hic in vasto Arabiae deserto habitabat, longe ab mortalium conspectu. Quinque centenis annis, mirum spectaculum fiebat: Phoenix se ipse in rogum sponte incendebat, et ex cineribus suis renascebatur.

In ancient times, under the light of the sun and the power of fire, a marvellous bird named Phoenix lived. It dwelled in the vast desert of Arabia, far from the sight of mortals. Every five hundred years, a wondrous event would occur: the Phoenix would ignite itself on a pyre and be reborn from its ashes.

"Hoc est aeternitatis et regenerationis signum," Phoenix aliquando voce clara dixit, flammis circumdatus. "Mors mea non est finis, sed initium novae vitae."

"This is the sign of eternity and regeneration," the Phoenix once said in a clear voice, surrounded by flames. "My death is not the end, but the beginning of a new life."

Sic mortem et renascentiam suam celebrabat, immortalitatis et victoriae contra mortem symbola praebens. Hominibus, avis haec veneratio erat, quasi deus quidam, resurrectionis potentiam demonstrans.

Thus, it celebrated its death and rebirth, offering symbols of immortality and triumph over death. To humans, this bird was revered as a kind of god, demonstrating the power of resurrection.

Progressione capituli, narratio ad solem et Phoenix vinculum flectitur. Phoenix, Ra, solis deo, arcte coniunctus erat. "Salve, Ra, lux et vita mundi," Phoenix in aurora cantabat, colores aurorae in plumis suis mirabiliter reflectens. Hoc ritu quotidiano, iter solis per caelum et Phoenix renascentiam ad vitae novae principium coniungebat.

As the chapter progresses, the story turns to the bond between the sun and the Phoenix. The Phoenix was closely connected to Ra, the sun god. "Hail, Ra, light and life of the world," the Phoenix sang at dawn, reflecting the colours of the sunrise in its feathers. Through this daily ritual, the sun's journey across the sky and the Phoenix's rebirth were linked to the beginning of new life.

Cum finis vitae appropinquaret, Phoenix nidum ex aromatibus et ramis construebat, et, alis suis vehementer pulsatis, ignem incitabat. Ex igne sacro, novus Phoenix emergebat, purificationis et renovationis ritu completus.

As the end of its life approached, the Phoenix built a nest from aromatic herbs and branches, and by beating its wings vigorously, it ignited a fire. From the sacred flames, a new Phoenix emerged, completing the ritual of purification and renewal.

"In hac renascentiae actione," novus Phoenix dixit, "vitae cyclum acceptamus, et nosmet ipsos purificamus."

"In this act of rebirth," the new Phoenix said, "we accept the cycle of life and purify ourselves."

In cultura Aegyptia, Phoenix, Benu avem sacram repraesentans, magni momenti erat. Benu, mundi creationem adiuvans et in arte Aegyptia saepe depictus, solis radiis et creationis potentia coniungebatur. Aegyptii Phoenix, velut Ra animam, venerabantur, et eius resurrectionem ut immortalitatis et continuitatis signum celebrabant.

In Egyptian culture, the Phoenix, representing the sacred bird Benu, was of great importance. Benu, assisting in the creation of the world and often depicted in Egyptian art, was associated with the rays of the sun and the power of creation. The Egyptians revered the Phoenix as the soul of Ra and celebrated its resurrection as a symbol of immortality and continuity.

Sic, Phoenix mythus non solum imaginem mortis et renascentiae praebet, sed etiam aeternitatis et regenerationis potentiam in culturis antiquis, praecipue in Aegyptia, demonstrat. Huius mythi legatum per saecula manet, inspirationem et spem praebens.

Thus, the myth of the Phoenix not only offers the image of death and rebirth but also demonstrates the power of eternity and regeneration in ancient cultures, particularly in Egypt. The legacy of this myth endures through the ages, providing inspiration and hope.

Phoenix et Sol

Cum primum lux diei terram tangit, Phoenix, avis mirabilis, ex somno evigilat. Hic avis, Ra, deo solis, valde coniunctus, nova luce gaudet et honorem deo fert. "Salve, Ra, vitae dator," Phoenix in matutino cantu clamat, "tua lux me renovat et vires mihi praebet."

As the first light of day touches the earth, the marvellous bird, Phoenix, awakens from sleep. This bird, closely connected to Ra, the sun god, rejoices in the new light and brings honour to the god. "Hail, Ra, giver of life," the Phoenix cries in its morning song, "your light renews me and gives me strength."

Plumae eius, solis radiis similes, mirum in modum colores caeli matutini reflectunt. Rubrum, aurum, et caeruleum in plumis eius ludunt, quasi pictura vivens de sole ipso.

Its feathers, like the rays of the sun, wonderfully reflect the colours of the morning sky. Red, gold, and blue play across its feathers, as if a living painting of the sun itself.

Itaque, Phoenix per aetherem volat, magnificum spectaculum praebens. "Vide," incolae dicunt, "Phoenix iter facit, sicut sol in caelo." Hoc volatu, Phoenix non solum solis iter imitatur sed etiam significat vitae renovationem et aeternitatis spem.

And so, the Phoenix flies through the air, presenting a magnificent spectacle. "Look," the people say, "the Phoenix makes its journey, like the sun in the sky." Through this flight, the Phoenix not only imitates the sun's path but also symbolises the renewal of life and the hope of eternity.

Unus dies, dum Phoenix altum in caelo volat, vox parva ad eum pervenit. "Quid tu facis, o avis mirabilis?" passer, parvus avis, interrogat.

One day, while the Phoenix is flying high in the sky, a small voice reaches him. "What are you doing, oh marvellous bird?" asks a sparrow, a small bird.

"Imitor iter solis," Phoenix respondet, "et meae renovationis mysterium celebro. Sicut sol omni die renascitur, sic ego ex cineribus meis renascor."

"I imitate the journey of the sun," the Phoenix responds, "and I celebrate the mystery of my renewal. Just as the sun is reborn every day, so I am reborn from my ashes."

Passer, hoc audito, miratur. "O mirum! Tu ergo aeternus es?"

The sparrow, hearing this, marvels. "Oh, wonderful! So you are eternal?"

"Sic," Phoenix dixit, "per mortem et renascentiam, aeternitatis arcanum teneo. Hoc me docet acceptare vitam ut est, cum eius finibus et novis principiis."

"Yes," said the Phoenix, "through death and rebirth, I hold the secret of eternity. This teaches me to accept life as it is, with its endings and new beginnings."

In hoc dialogo, Phoenix non solum suum nexum cum sole et renovatione exprimit, sed etiam profundiorem veritatem de vita et natura universi. Omnia in mundo cyclica sunt, morte et renascentia perpetua.

In this dialogue, the Phoenix not only expresses its connection with the sun and renewal but also a deeper truth about life and the nature of the universe. Everything in the world is cyclical, with death and rebirth being eternal.

Ita Phoenix, solis et vitae symbolus, nos docet ut vitam celebremus, eius mutationes accipiamus, et in aeternitatis mysterio confidamus. Hic mythus, per saecula narratus, aeternam veritatem de renovatione et spe continet.

Thus, the Phoenix, a symbol of the sun and life, teaches us to celebrate life, to accept its changes, and to trust in the mystery of eternity. This myth, told through the ages, contains an eternal truth about renewal and hope.

Ritus Renascentiae Phoenicis

Tempus advenit, ut Phoenix, avis antiqua et mirabilis, finem vitae suae sentiret appropinquare. Non tristitia aut metu affectus, sed cum dignitate et spe, opus ultimum suum incepit. In deserto secreto, locum elegit ubi nidum ex incenso et ramis aromaticis construxit. "Haec domus mea nova erit," Phoenix dixit, "ubi ex novo nasci possum."

The time came when the Phoenix, an ancient and marvellous bird, felt the end of its life approaching. Not affected by sadness or fear, but with dignity and hope, it began its final task. In a secret desert, it chose a place where it built a nest of incense and aromatic branches. "This will be my new home," the Phoenix said, "where I can be reborn."

Cum omnia parata essent, Phoenix alas suas fortiter movit, scintillas excitans quae nidum in flammam verterunt. Flammae sacrae circumdabant, corpore suo consumpto. "Per ignem," Phoenix voce clara exclamavit, "purificatio mea et renovatio fient."

When everything was ready, the Phoenix moved its wings vigorously, sparking flames that turned the nest into fire. Sacred flames surrounded it, consuming its body. "Through fire," the Phoenix exclaimed in a clear voice, "my purification and renewal will come."

Miraculum fit: ex calore ignis et virtute flammae, ex cineribus nidus, novus Phoenix nascitur, pulcher et vivus, sicut antea nunquam fuerat. "Ego sum," inquit novus Phoenix, "simul et idem et novus. Vita mea, iterum incepta, testimonium est aeternitatis et mundi renovationis."

A miracle happened: from the heat of the fire and the power of the flames, from the ashes of the nest, a new Phoenix was born, beautiful and alive, as it had never been before. "I am," said the new Phoenix, "both the same and new. My life, begun again, is a testimony to eternity and the renewal of the world."

Hoc ritu, Phoenix non solum se renovat sed etiam profundam veritatem docet: vitam esse cyclum mortis et renascentiae, in quo finis semper novi principii occasio est. "Videte," novus Phoenix passeribus et aliis avibus narrat, "mors non est finis sed via ad novum initium. Sic, in nostra vita, difficilem veritatem accipimus, quod post finem semper novum principium est."

Through this ritual, the Phoenix not only renews itself but also teaches a profound truth: life is a cycle of death and rebirth, where every ending is always an opportunity for a new beginning. "Look," the new Phoenix told the sparrows and other birds, "death is not the end but a path to a new start. So, in our lives, we accept the difficult truth that after every end, there is always a new beginning."

Passeres et aves, hoc audientes, admiratione pleni sunt. "O Phoenix," dicunt, "tu magister vitae et spei es. Tua historia nos docet ut vitam et eius mysteria cum amore et fortitudine accipiamus."

The sparrows and birds, hearing this, were filled with admiration. "Oh Phoenix," they said, "you are a teacher of life and hope. Your story teaches us to accept life and its mysteries with love and courage."

Sic Phoenix, per ritum suae renascentiae, non solum aeternitatem suam sed etiam omnium creaturarum potentiam ad renovationem demonstrat. Haec fabula, per saecula tradita, nos adhuc hodie docet ut vitae cyclos cum gratia accipiamus et in spe et amore semper vivamus.

Thus, the Phoenix, through the ritual of its rebirth, demonstrates not only its own eternity but also the potential of all creatures for renewal. This story, passed down through the ages, still teaches us today to accept life's cycles with grace and to always live in hope and love.

Phoenix et Cultura Aegyptiorum

In terris Aegypti, antiquae et mysticae, Phoenix, quem Aegyptii Benu vocant, in magna reverentia tenebatur. Hic avis, creationis et solis potentiae sacra, inter deos et homines medium locum tenebat. "Benu," sacerdos in templo Ra loquitur, "non solum avis est, sed etiam mundi creatio, ex primordiali chaos orta."

In the lands of Egypt, ancient and mystical, the Phoenix, whom the Egyptians call Benu, was held in great reverence. This bird, sacred to creation and the power of the sun, held a central place between gods and humans. "Benu," the priest in the temple of Ra says, "is not just a bird, but also the creation of the world, born from primordial chaos."

Benu, in arte Aegyptia saepe depictus, super ben-ben lapidem sedebat, qui solis radiis et creationis initio sacra erat. "Videte," sacerdos populo demonstrat, "Benu, solis spiritum gerens, nos docet de lumine et vita."

Benu, often depicted in Egyptian art, sat upon the ben-ben stone, which was sacred to the rays of the sun and the beginning of creation. "Look," the priest shows the people, "Benu, carrying the spirit of the sun, teaches us about light and life."

In illis diebus, Phoenix, sive Benu, non solum ut avis mirabilis sed etiam ut Ra animae symbolum colebatur. "Benu est ba Ra," sacerdos explicat, "quae est anima et spiritus solis dei. Per Benu, Ra in mundo nostro praesens est."

In those days, the Phoenix, or Benu, was worshipped not only as a marvellous bird but also as a symbol of Ra's soul. "Benu is the *ba* of Ra," the priest explains, "which is the soul and spirit of the sun god. Through Benu, Ra is present in our world."

Aegyptii magnos templos Benu dedicaverunt, ubi ritus et caerimoniae eius honori fiebant. "In his templis," sacerdos adulescenti discipulo narrat, "nos Benu resurrectionem celebramus, quae est signum continuitatis et immortalitatis nostrae."

The Egyptians dedicated great temples to Benu, where rituals and ceremonies were performed in his honour. "In these temples," the priest tells a young disciple, "we celebrate Benu's resurrection, which is a sign of our continuity and immortality."

Discipulus, hoc audito, miratur et quaerit, "Quomodo nos Benu resurrectione ad vitam nostram applicare possumus?"

The disciple, hearing this, marvels and asks, "How can we apply Benu's resurrection to our own lives?"

Sacerdos respondet, "Sicut Benu ex cineribus renascitur, ita nos debemus in vita nostra adversitates superare et semper ad meliorem nos renovare. Benu nobis exemplar est, quod, quamvis difficultates et mortem, vita semper victoriam et renovationem invenit."

The priest responds, "Just as Benu is reborn from the ashes, so too must we overcome adversities in our lives and always renew ourselves for the better. Benu is an example to us, showing that, despite difficulties and death, life always finds victory and renewal."

Per hanc fabulam, Aegyptii non solum cosmologiam et theologiae suae partes expresserunt sed etiam profundam philosophiam de vita, morte, et renascentia. Phoenix, sive Benu, in cultura Aegyptia, aeternum est symbolum quod adhuc hodie nos de aeternitate, lumine, et possibilitate in vita nostra renovanda docet.

Through this story, the Egyptians expressed not only parts of their cosmology and theology but also a deep philosophy about life, death, and rebirth. The Phoenix, or Benu, in Egyptian culture, is an eternal symbol that still today teaches us about eternity, light, and the possibility of renewal in our lives.

Phoenicis Legatum in Aegypto

In antiqua Aegypti terra, ubi flumen Nilus per deserta et campos fertiles serpit, Phoenicis mythus profundas in animis hominum radices egit. "Phoenicis," sacerdos in templo narrat, "non solum nobis est avis mirabilis, sed etiam aeternitatis nostrae spes."

In the ancient land of Egypt, where the Nile River winds through deserts and fertile fields, the myth of the Phoenix took deep root in the minds of the people. "The Phoenix," the priest in the temple says, "is not only a marvellous bird to us, but also the hope of our eternity."

Pharaones, reges magni Aegypti, in morte sua Phoenicis ritum renascentiae imitari cupiebant. "In nostris ritibus funerariis," sacerdos adulescenti discipulo explicat, "sicut Phoenicis ex cineribus renascitur, ita speramus regem nostrum ad vitam novam venire."

Pharaohs, the great kings of Egypt, in their death, wished to imitate the ritual of the Phoenix's rebirth. "In our funerary rites," the priest explains to a young disciple, "just as the Phoenix is reborn from the ashes, so we hope our king will come to new life."

Populus, hoc credens, amuleta et talismanos Phoenicis formam habentes gestabat. "Haec amuleta," mercator in foro dicit, "te a malis defendent et vitam tuam renovabunt, sicut Phoenicis renascitur."

The people, believing this, wore amulets and talismans in the shape of the Phoenix. "These amulets," a merchant in the market says, "will protect you from evil and renew your life, just as the Phoenix is reborn."

Poetae et musici, Phoenicis laudes in versibus et cantibus extollebant. "Audi," poeta in via recitat, "carmen de Phoenice, qui sua morte et resurrectione nos docet de vita et spe."

Poets and musicians praised the Phoenix in verses and songs. "Listen," a poet recites in the street, "to a poem about the Phoenix, who through its death and resurrection teaches us about life and hope."

Phoenicis, per saecula, in cultura Aegypti manet symbolus potens renascentiae, eius historia in arte, litteris, et religionis ritibus intexta. "Phoenicis nobis est magister," sacerdos conclamit, "qui per suum exemplum nos docet mortem non esse finem, sed viam ad novum principium."

Through the centuries, the Phoenix remained a powerful symbol of rebirth in Egyptian culture, its story woven into art, literature, and religious rites. "The Phoenix is our teacher," the priest exclaims, "who through its example teaches us that death is not the end, but a path to a new beginning."

Discipulus, sacerdotis verba meditans, inquit, "Ergo, Phoenicis non solum de ave fabulosa narrat, sed etiam de nobis, de nostra vita, de nostra spe renascentiae."

The disciple, pondering the priest's words, says, "So, the Phoenix does not only tell the story of a mythical bird, but also of us, of our life, of our hope for rebirth."

Sic Phoenicis legatum vivit, non solum in Aegypti historia sed etiam in corde humanitatis, ut monitum aeternum de virtute, spe, et possibilitate renovationis nostrae in facie adversitatum. Hoc mytho, antiqui nos docuerunt quamvis in vita difficilia et mortem experiamur, semper est spes renascentiae et novae vitae.

Thus, the legacy of the Phoenix lives on, not only in the history of Egypt but also in the heart of humanity, as an eternal reminder of strength, hope, and the possibility of our renewal in the face of adversity. Through this myth, the ancients taught us that although we experience difficulties and death in life, there is always hope for rebirth and new life.

Legenda Serpentis Apophis et Pugna Contra Ra

Origo Apophis

In profundis tenebris mundi subterranei, quod Duat appellatur, serpens ingens, nomine Apophis, habitabat. Hic serpens, chaos et tenebras corporans, diu expectabat tempus ut se in Ra, solem deum, inmitteret. "Ecce," Apophis sibi susurrat, "nox mea est, quando Ra vulnerabilis est, et ego, in tenebris regnans, eum superare possum."

In the deep darkness of the underworld, called Duat, lived a giant serpent named Apophis. This serpent, embodying chaos and darkness, long waited for the moment to strike against Ra, the sun god. "Behold," Apophis whispered to himself, "this is my night, when Ra is vulnerable, and I, ruling in darkness, can defeat him."

Nocte una, cum Ra barcam suam solarem per obscura Duati flumina navigabat, Apophis ex umbris emersit, intentans impetum. "Hodie," inquit Apophis, "Ra, te in tenebras aeternas demergam."

One night, as Ra was navigating his solar barque through the dark rivers of Duat, Apophis emerged from the shadows, ready to strike. "Today," said Apophis, "Ra, I will plunge you into eternal darkness."

Sed Ra, licet in periculo, numquam sine defensione erat. "Apophis," Ra voce tonante respondet, "etsi fortis es, numquam ordinem et lucem, quam ego porto, superabis."

But Ra, though in danger, was never without defence. "Apophis," Ra thundered in reply, "though you are strong, you will never overcome the order and light that I carry."

Magna cum vi, Apophis barcam solarem aggreditur, eius immensa corporis mole et viribus pugnam ferocem faciens. Tamen, Ra, cum lumine et virtute solis gerens, non facile victus erat.

With great force, Apophis attacked the solar barque, using his immense body and strength to wage a fierce battle. However, Ra, wielding the light and power of the sun, was not easily defeated.

"Semper tenebris resistam," Ra exclamat, "et tu, Apophis, licet numquam plene vinceris, semper repulsus eris." Sic in aeternum, Apophis, quamvis potens, semper in fine certaminis a Ra et eius lumine repellebatur.

"I will always resist the darkness," Ra exclaimed, "and you, Apophis, though you may never be fully vanquished, will always be repelled." Thus, for eternity, Apophis, though powerful, was always driven back by Ra and his light at the end of the battle.

Hac fabula, antiqui Aegyptii non solum de cosmogonia et deorum virtutibus narrabant sed etiam profundam veritatem de vita, de lucta inter ordinem et chaos, lucem et tenebras docuerunt. Et quamvis Apophis noctu renascitur, semper spes est in ortu solis, qui tenebras superat, ordinem restituens et vitam renovans.

Through this story, the ancient Egyptians not only told of cosmogony and the virtues of the gods but also taught a profound truth about life, about the struggle between order and chaos, light and darkness. And although Apophis is reborn each night, there is always hope in the rising sun, which overcomes the darkness, restoring order and renewing life.

Ra in Itinere

In caelo clarissimo, sub aurea luce solis, Ra, magnus deus solis, cotidie iter faciebat, mundum lumine suo implens. Sed cum sol occideret et nox caelum obtegeret, in mundum alterum, Duat appellatum, descendebat. Hic in tenebris, pericula innumera et hostes terribiles, praecipue Apophis, serpentem ingentem chaosque ipsum repraesentantem, inveniebat.

In the bright sky, under the golden light of the sun, Ra, the great sun god, made his daily journey, filling the world with his light. But when the sun set and night covered the sky, he descended into another world, called Duat. Here, in the darkness, he encountered countless dangers and terrible enemies, especially Apophis, the giant serpent representing chaos itself.

"Ecce iterum in tenebras descendimus," Ra dixit, barcam solarem parans. "Nocte hac, ut semper, Apophis nos oppugnabit."

"Here we descend into darkness once again," Ra said, preparing the solar barque. "Tonight, as always, Apophis will attack us."

Comites dei, inter quos Set etiam, deserti dominus, fortis audaxque, se ad proelium parabant. "Non timeo," Set exclamat, "Apophis hodie vincetur, sicut semper ante."

The gods who accompanied him, among them Set, the lord of the desert, brave and bold, prepared for battle. "I do not fear," Set exclaimed, "Apophis will be defeated today, as always before."

Dum barca solis silentio per tenebrosas aquas Duat navigat, subito, immenso fragore, Apophis apparuit, oculis ardentibus corporeque vasto, qui noctem ipsam terroremque repraesentabat. "Ra, hodie te et tuam lucem devorabo," Apophis minitans dixit.

As the solar barque silently navigated through the dark waters of Duat, suddenly, with a massive roar, Apophis appeared, his eyes burning and his enormous body representing night and terror itself. "Ra, today I will devour you and your light," Apophis threatened.

Sed Ra, non territus, respondit: "Numquam cedemus tibi, Apophis. Ordo et lux semper chaos tenebrasque superabunt."

But Ra, unafraid, replied: "We will never yield to you, Apophis. Order and light will always overcome chaos and darkness."

Cum Apophis adgressus est, Set, coram stans, lanceam suam levavit. "Pro Ra, pro luce!" clamavit et in serpentem magnum impetum fecit. Alii dii, magia et viribus suis utentes, Apophim repellebant, dum Ra sollemniter pericula et hostem superabat, mundum rursus ad lucem ducens.

As Apophis attacked, Set, standing in front, raised his spear. "For Ra, for the light!" he shouted and charged at the great serpent. Other gods, using their magic and strength, repelled Apophis, while Ra solemnly overcame the dangers and the enemy, leading the world back to light once more.

"Gratias tibi, Set, et omnibus qui mecum stant," Ra post victoriam dixit. "Una, tenebras semper superabimus et ordinem servabimus."

"Thank you, Set, and to all who stand with me," Ra said after the victory. "Together, we will always overcome the darkness and preserve order."

Ita, nocte quaque, Ra et comites eius contra Apophis et chaos pugnabant, victoriam lucis super tenebras semper renovantes. Haec certamina non solum de potestate et virtute erant sed etiam de spe et fide in luce perpetua, quam Ra ad mundum omni mane reportabat.

Thus, every night, Ra and his companions fought against Apophis and chaos, continually renewing the victory of light over darkness. These battles were not only about power and strength but also about hope and faith in the eternal light, which Ra brought back to the world every morning.

Pugna Sine Fine

Nox iterum super Aegyptum descendit, et cum stellis, tenebrae et silentium regnant. Sed sub hac tranquillitate, proelium immensum inter deum solem Ra et horrendum serpentem Apophis exardescit. In profundis mundi subterranei, ubi mortales oculi non perveniunt, fatescens pugna aeternum ordinem et chaos decidit.

Night falls once again over Egypt, and with the stars, darkness and silence reign. But beneath this tranquillity, an immense battle between the sun god Ra and the dreadful serpent Apophis flares up. In the depths of the underworld, where mortal eyes cannot reach, the fading battle determines the eternal struggle between order and chaos.

"Ecce, Apophis rursus advenit," Ra dicit, suam barcam solarem per tenebras Duat dirigens. "Parati sumus, ut semper, eius impetus repellere."

"Behold, Apophis returns once again," Ra says, steering his solar barque through the darkness of Duat. "We are ready, as always, to repel his attack."

Cum magna ira, Apophis in barcam solem irruit, flammis oculorum suorum et veneni halitu minans. Sed dii protectores, magicae artis periti, statim ad defensionem accinguntur. "Hodie non praevaleris, serpens," unus ex diis exclamat, magicae vires in Apophim dirigens.

With great fury, Apophis rushes toward the solar barque, threatening with the flames of his eyes and the breath of venom. But the protective gods, skilled in magical arts, immediately prepare for defence. "Today you will not prevail, serpent," one of the gods exclaims, directing his magical powers at Apophis.

Set, deserti dominus, ante omnes stabat, lancea in manu tenens. "Pro Ra! Pro lumine!" clamavit, Apophim audacter aggrediens. Eorum certamen, tam violentum quam fulgur nocturnae tempestatis, silentium caeli subterranei rumpit.

Set, the lord of the desert, stood at the forefront, holding a spear in his hand. "For Ra! For the light!" he shouted, boldly attacking Apophis. Their battle, as violent as lightning in a nocturnal storm, breaks the silence of the underworld's sky.

Simul, in terra Aegypti, sacerdotes et populus, sensu periculi moti, ad templa currunt, deorum auxilium invocantes. Incantationibus et precationibus, suam fidem et spem in Ra renovant. "O Ra, vincas tenebras, ut lux rursus nascatur," sacerdos in templo orat, fumum incensi ad caelos ascendente.

Meanwhile, on the land of Egypt, priests and people, moved by a sense of danger, run to the temples, invoking the help of the gods. With incantations and prayers, they renew their faith and hope in Ra. "Oh Ra, may you conquer the darkness so that light may be born again," a priest prays in the temple, as the smoke of incense rises to the heavens.

Nocte post noctem, quamvis Apophis fortis et perseverans sit, semper fine carens, dii et magicae artes eum repellant. Set, praesertim, in proelio contra Apophim praestans, barcam solarem protegit, quae sine intermissione iter suum pergit.

Night after night, although Apophis is strong and persistent, always unrelenting, the gods and their magical arts drive him back. Set, in particular, excelling in the battle against Apophis, protects the solar barque, which continues its journey without interruption.

"Vincimus iterum," Ra post proelium dicit, "sed scimus Apophim rursus rediturum. Ita pugna nostra aeterna est, sicut ordo et chaos quae mundum regunt."

"We have won again," Ra says after the battle, "but we know Apophis will return. Thus, our fight is eternal, like the order and chaos that rule the world."

Hac fabula, Aegyptii non tantum cosmologiam suam exprimunt sed etiam profundam veritatem de vita: lucem et tenebras, ordinem et chaos, in perpetuo certamine esse, sed semper spem esse in aurora, quae tenebras vincit.

Through this story, the Egyptians express not only their cosmology but also a profound truth about life: light and darkness, order and chaos, are in perpetual struggle, but there is always hope in the dawn, which conquers the darkness.

Significatio Pugnae

In Aegypto antiqua, sub caelo semper mutante, fabula de Ra et Apophis non solum narratio deorum erat, sed etiam profundum symbolismum tenebat. Hoc certamen magnum inter deum solem et serpentem malum, ordini et chaos, luci et tenebris dedicatum erat.

In ancient Egypt, under the ever-changing sky, the tale of Ra and Apophis was not just a story about the gods but also held deep symbolism. This great battle between the sun god and the evil serpent was dedicated to order and chaos, light and darkness.

"In hac lucta," sacerdos in templo explicat, "videmus constantem naturae et humanitatis conflictum. Ra, per suum iter diurnum et nocturnum, spem et victoriam nobis praebet."

"In this struggle," the priest in the temple explains, "we see the constant conflict of nature and humanity. Ra, through his daily and nightly journey, gives us hope and victory."

Quotidie, cum sol in caelum ascendit, Aegyptii victoriam lucis super tenebras celebrabant. "Vide," puer ad patrem dicit, spectans solem orientem, "Ra iterum vicit, et lux tenebras superavit."

Every day, as the sun rose into the sky, the Egyptians celebrated the victory of light over darkness. "Look," a boy says to his father, watching the rising sun, "Ra has won again, and light has overcome the darkness."

Populus, hanc historiam intellegens, magnum solacium in ea inveniebat. "Quamvis nox longa et tenebrosa sit," mater filiae narrat, "lux semper redit. Haec est promissio Ra, promissio vitae."

The people, understanding this story, found great comfort in it. "Though the night is long and dark," a mother tells her daughter, "the light always returns. This is Ra's promise, the promise of life."

In arte et cultura Aegyptia, Apophis saepe depictus est in statu victo, subiectus potentiae Ra et ordinis. "Haec imago," artifex in officina sua dicit, "non solum deum nostrum glorificat, sed etiam nos de virtute perseverantiae et spe docet."

In Egyptian art and culture, Apophis was often depicted in a defeated state, subjected to Ra's power and order. "This image," an artist says in his workshop, "not only glorifies our god but also teaches us about the virtue of perseverance and hope."

Ritualia et incantationes ad Ra protegendum et Apophim superandum ubique erant, in templis et domibus. "Per haec verba sacra," sacerdos ante altare stat, "nos Ra in eius pugna adiuvamus, et nostram partem in aeterno ordine et lumine servando facimus."

Rituals and incantations to protect Ra and defeat Apophis were everywhere, in temples and homes. "Through these sacred words," the priest stands before the altar, "we help Ra in his battle, and we do our part in preserving eternal order and light."

Ita, per has historias et ritus, Aegyptii non tantum deorum suorum virtutes celebrabant, sed etiam profundiores vitae suae veritates explorabant. Certamen Ra et Apophis, in sua essentia, nos docet de aeterna spe et luce quae tenebras, quamvis fortes et minaces, semper superat.

Thus, through these stories and rituals, the Egyptians not only celebrated the virtues of their gods but also explored deeper truths about their lives. The battle between Ra and Apophis, in its essence, teaches us about the eternal hope and light that always overcomes the darkness, no matter how strong and menacing it may be.

Legati Aeterni

In antiqua Aegypti terra, ubi Nili fluenta per arva et urbes leniter fluunt, fabula de Ra et Apophis non solum in mentibus sed etiam in corde cultus Aegyptiorum profundas radices misit. Haec narratio, plus quam mythus, modum vivendi et credendi formavit.

In the ancient land of Egypt, where the waters of the Nile flow gently through fields and cities, the story of Ra and Apophis took deep root not only in the minds but also in the heart of Egyptian worship. This tale, more than just a myth, shaped their way of living and believing.

"Videsne, discipule," sacerdos, templi magni parietibus incisos textus ostendens, inquit, "hic sunt gesta Ra adversus Apophim. Non solum historiae sunt, sed etiam sapientiae nostrae fontes."

"Do you see, disciple," the priest says, showing the texts carved into the walls of the great temple, "here are the deeds of Ra against Apophis. These are not just stories, but sources of our wisdom."

In templorum atriis, quae Ra et eius defensoribus sacra erant, magnificae inscriptiones et picturae victorias deorum super chaos depictae sunt. "Quaelibet imago, quaelibet linea nos docet de luce contra tenebras pugnandi importantiam," sacerdos explicat.

In the courtyards of temples, sacred to Ra and his defenders, magnificent inscriptions and paintings depicted the gods' victories over chaos. "Each image, each line teaches us the importance of fighting for light against darkness," the priest explains.

Inter Aegyptios, amuleta et talismani magni pretii erant, non solum ut ornamenta sed etiam ut verae protectionis media. "Hoc amulettum," mercator in foro tenens et Setis imaginem monstrans, dicit, "te in periculis tutum servabit, sicut Set Ra servavit."

Among the Egyptians, amulets and talismans were of great value, not only as ornaments but also as real means of protection. "This amulet," says a merchant in the market, holding up an image of Set, "will keep you safe in danger, just as Set protected Ra."

Festivitates et celebrationes, quae fabulam magnam recreabant, in tota terra frequentes erant. Populus, actores spectans qui deorum et Apophis pugnas agebant, non solum delectabantur sed etiam sacrorum mysteriorum participes fiebant. "Per has fabulas," sacerdos ad populum in festo loquitur, "memores sumus luminis nostri in tenebris semper renasci posse."

Festivals and celebrations that re-enacted the great story were common throughout the land. The people, watching actors perform the battles between the gods and Apophis, were not only entertained but also became participants in the sacred mysteries. "Through these stories," the priest says to the people at the festival, "we are reminded that our light can always be reborn in the darkness."

Haec legenda, per saecula transmissa, Aegyptiis non tantum recordatio erat deorum magnitudinis sed etiam monitum de vita ipsa: in mundo ubi ordo et chaos in perpetuo certamine sunt, homines, sicut dii, in lumine et harmonia semper laborare debent. "Sic," sacerdos, caelum nocturnum spectans, susurrat, "legenda de Ra et Apophis nos docet de aeterno equilibrio mundi et nostro loco in hoc universo mirabili."

This legend, passed down through the centuries, was not only a reminder to the Egyptians of the greatness of the gods but also a lesson about life itself: in a world where order and chaos are in perpetual conflict, people, like the gods, must always strive for light and harmony. "Thus," the priest whispers, gazing at the night sky, "the legend of Ra and Apophis teaches us about the eternal balance of the world and our place in this wondrous universe."

Legenda Scarabaei et Symbolismus eius in Religione Aegyptiaca

Origines Scarabaei

In antiqua Aegyptia, scarabaeus animal magni momenti habebatur, quod renascentiae et regenerationis symbola gerebat. Deus quidam, Khepri nomine, qui solis ortum repraesentabat, saepe in scarabaei forma depictus est. Ferunt Kheprim ipsum solem per caelum cotidie volvere, sicut scarabaeus sphaeram stercoream volvit. Hoc actum scarabaei, solis cursum aeternum et vitae cyclum significabat.

In ancient Egypt, the scarab was considered an animal of great importance, as it carried symbols of rebirth and regeneration. A certain god, named Khepri, who represented the rising of the sun, was often depicted in the form of a scarab. It is said that Khepri rolled the sun across the sky every day, just as the scarab rolls its ball of dung. This act of the scarab symbolised the eternal course of the sun and the cycle of life.

In lucem solis orientis, Khepri, conversus ad scarabaeum, dixit: "Ecce, meum opus cotidianum incipit, solis sphaeram per caelum movens, ut homines vitam et lucem habeant."

In the light of the rising sun, Khepri, turning to the scarab, said: "Behold, my daily task begins, moving the sun's sphere across the sky, so that humans may have life and light."

Scarabaeus, terrae adhaerens, respondit: "Et ego, simili modo, meam sphaeram stercoream volvo, vitam ex morte creans. Nonne mirabile est quomodo nostra opera, quamvis diversa, ad vitae cursus contribuant?"

The scarab, clinging to the earth, replied: "And I, in a similar way, roll my dung ball, creating life from death. Isn't it remarkable how our works, though different, both contribute to the cycle of life?"

Khepri, solis radiis circumdatus, assensus est: "Vere, in tuo labore, principium et finem vitae videre possumus. Tu es magister regenerationis et symbolus potentiae vitae quae in natura invenitur."

Khepri, surrounded by the rays of the sun, agreed: "Indeed, in your work, we can see the beginning and end of life. You are the master of regeneration and a symbol of the power of life found in nature."

Cum scarabaeus suam sphaeram prae se moveret, Khepri continuavit: "Tuum exemplum populum Aegyptium docebit de renovatione et immortalitate animae. Amuleta in tua effigie facta vires et protectionem ferent, et in ritibus funeribus te ut symbolum renaissance utentur."

As the scarab rolled its ball before it, Khepri continued: "Your example will teach the Egyptian people about renewal and the immortality of the soul. Amulets made in your image will bring strength and protection, and in funerary rites, you will be used as a symbol of rebirth."

Scarabaeus, in humo laborans, sensum honoris et propositi sensit, agnoscens se partem esse magni cycli naturae et humanitatis culturae.

The scarab, working in the soil, felt a sense of honour and purpose, recognising itself as part of the great cycle of nature and human culture.

Ita, per conversationem inter deum et parvum insectum, profundae vitae veritates revelatae sunt. Scarabaeus non solum in natura sed etiam in cordibus hominum, per amuleta et artes, vitam novam semper spirabat. Et sic, per aetates, legenda scarabaei, symboli potentis renascentiae et regenerationis, in cultura Aegyptiaca perpetuo mansit.

Thus, through the conversation between a god and a small insect, profound truths about life were revealed. The scarab not only lived in nature but also in the hearts of humans, through amulets and art, always breathing new life. And so, through the ages, the legend of the scarab, a powerful symbol of rebirth and regeneration, remained ever-present in Egyptian culture.

Scarabaeus in Vita Cotidiana

In vita cotidiana Aegyptiorum, scarabaeus non modo animal venerandum erat, sed etiam in usum quotidianum veniebat. Amuleta scarabaei formam habentia ad protectionem et fortunam bonam gerebantur. Hi, qui talia Amuleta portabant, se fortes et audaces sentiebant, credentes se divina protectione muniri.

In the daily life of the Egyptians, the scarab was not only a revered animal but also had a practical use. Scarab-shaped amulets were worn for protection and good fortune. Those who carried such amulets felt strong and brave, believing they were endowed with divine protection.

Quodam die, Aegyptius nomine Ammon, mercator opulentus, filium suum, Sethum, ad forum duxit ut donum speciale emeret. "Fili mi," Ammon dixit, "hodie amulettum scarabaei tibi emam, ut te in omnibus itineribus tuis protegat et fortunam bonam afferat."

One day, an Egyptian named Ammon, a wealthy merchant, took his son, Seth, to the market to buy a special gift. "My son," Ammon said, "today I will buy you a scarab amulet, so that it may protect you on all your journeys and bring you good fortune."

Sethus, oculis magnis, respondit: "Pater, vere credis in potentiam harum amulettorum?"

Seth, wide-eyed, responded: "Father, do you truly believe in the power of these amulets?"

"Sane, fili. Non solum nos protegunt, sed etiam virtutem et audaciam nobis conferunt. Etiam in ritibus funeribus magni momenti sunt, viam ad aeternam vitam aperiunt," Ammon explicavit.

"Of course, son. They not only protect us but also grant us courage and strength. They are also important in funeral rites, as they open the way to eternal life," Ammon explained.

Cum ad tabernam pervenissent, artifex, Amuleta scarabaei prae se habens, coepit: "Vide, quam pulchra! In his amulettis, verba sacra incisa sunt, quae divinam protectionem invocant."

When they arrived at the shop, the artisan, holding scarab amulets, began: "Look, how beautiful! On these amulets, sacred words are inscribed that invoke divine protection."

Sethus, amulettum tractans, mirabatur: "Quam mirum est cogitare, quod haec parva imago scarabaei nos a malis defendere possit."

Seth, handling the amulet, marvelled: "How amazing it is to think that this small image of a scarab can protect us from harm."

Ammon, filium suum intuens, addidit: "Et memoriale est potentiae naturae et divinitatis. Scarabaeus, in arte et in vita, symbolum est solis, vitae, et resurrectionis."

Ammon, looking at his son, added: "And it is a reminder of the power of nature and divinity. The scarab, in art and in life, is a symbol of the sun, life, and resurrection."

Postea, domum revertentes, Ammon et Sethus in via colloquebantur de variis modis quibus scarabaeus in vita Aegyptiorum integratus est. "Pater, cur etiam in ritibus funeribus scarabaeus tam magni momenti est?" Sethus rogavit.

Later, as they returned home, Ammon and Seth talked on the way about the various ways the scarab was integrated into Egyptian life. "Father, why is the scarab so important in funeral rites as well?" Seth asked.

Ammon, sermone continuo, explicavit: "Scarabaei in corde defuncti collocantur ut renascentiam in alio mundo assecurarent. Creduntur enim animam mortui protegere et ei viam in aeternam vitam monstrare."

Ammon, continuing the conversation, explained: "Scarabs are placed on the heart of the deceased to ensure rebirth in the next world. They are believed to protect the soul of the dead and show them the way to eternal life."

Sethus admiratione plenus, inquit: "Itaque, scarabaeus non solum protector noster est in vita sed etiam dux noster ad vitam post mortem?"

Seth, filled with admiration, said: "So, the scarab is not only our protector in life but also our guide to life after death?"

"Exacte," Ammon affirmavit. "Per scarabaeum, Aegyptii intellegunt mortem non esse finem sed transmutationis partem ad novam vitam."

"Exactly," Ammon confirmed. "Through the scarab, Egyptians understand that death is not the end but a part of the transformation to a new life."

Cum ad domum suam pervenissent, Sethus amulettum suum spectavit, nunc non solum ut ornamentum sed etiam ut symbolum profundiorum veritatum vitae et mortis. In momento quieto, Ammon dixit: "Vide, fili mi, quamvis technologiae et tempora mutantur, quaedam symbola, sicut scarabaeus noster, aeternam sapientiam et consolationem nobis afferunt."

When they arrived home, Seth looked at his amulet, now seeing it not just as an ornament but as a symbol of the deeper truths of life and death. In a quiet moment, Ammon said: "Look, my son, though technology and times change, some symbols, like our scarab, bring us eternal wisdom and comfort."

Nocte illa, sub stellis claris, Sethus cogitavit de scarabaeo non solum ut de amuleto vel symbolo sed etiam ut de magistro qui perennes vitae lectiones docebat. Per scarabaeum, sensum profundiorem vitae, mortis, et regenerationis comprehendere coepit, sicut antecessores sui Aegyptii per milia annorum fecerant.

That night, under the bright stars, Seth thought of the scarab not only as an amulet or a symbol but also as a teacher, imparting eternal lessons about life. Through the scarab, he began to understand a deeper sense of life, death, and regeneration, just as his Egyptian ancestors had done for thousands of years.

Ita, in corde Sethi et in cultura Aegyptia, scarabaeus, praeclarus renascentiae et regenerationis nuntius, perpetuo manebat, pontem inter praeteritum, praesens, et futurum constituens, semper docens de immortalitate animae et de cyclis vitae quae sine fine sunt.

Thus, in Seth's heart and in Egyptian culture, the scarab, a renowned messenger of rebirth and regeneration, remained forever, forming a bridge between past, present, and future, always teaching about the immortality of the soul and the cycles of life, which are without end.

Scarabaeus et Creatio

In principio, mundus ex chaos natus est, obscuritas et confusio ubique regnabant. In hoc vasto tenebrarum mari, scarabaeus, creatura parva sed potens, vitam ex morte, ordinem ex disordine creabat. Aegyptii credebant scarabaeum non solum animal esse, sed etiam divinum nuntium transformationis et renovationis.

In the beginning, the world was born from chaos, and darkness and confusion reigned everywhere. In this vast sea of darkness, the scarab, a small but powerful creature, created life from death, order from disorder. The Egyptians believed the scarab was not just an animal but also a divine messenger of transformation and renewal.

Certa die, in horto secreto, ubi deorum colloquia fieri solebant, Khepri, deus creationis, apparuit, forma scarabaei accepta. "Mira vis scarabaei," inquit Khepri, "exemplum est potentiae vitae renovandae. Sicut scarabaeus sphaeram suam stercoream volvit, sic ego solem per caelum moveo, diem noctemque creo."

One day, in a secret garden where the gods used to converse, Khepri, the god of creation, appeared, taking the form of a scarab. "The wondrous power of the scarab," Khepri said, "is an example of the power of life's renewal. Just as the scarab rolls its dung ball, so I move the sun across the sky, creating day and night."

Prope arborem sacram, sacerdos Aegyptius, Iset nomine, verba Khepri audivit et admirans accessit. "O deus magnus, quomodo nos, mortales, tuam sapientiam de creatione et renovatione in vita nostra adhibere possumus?" rogavit Iset.

Near a sacred tree, an Egyptian priest named Iset heard Khepri's words and approached in admiration. "O great god, how can we mortals apply your wisdom of creation and renewal in our lives?" asked Iset.

Khepri, radiis solis circumlatus, respondit: "Observa scarabaeum, Iset. In eius labore quotidiano, mysterium vitae aeternae invenies. Sicut scarabaeus ex stercore vita generat, ita vos debetis invenire viam ad vitam meliorem creandam ex difficultatibus et chaos."

Khepri, surrounded by the rays of the sun, replied: "Observe the scarab, Iset. In its daily work, you will find the mystery of eternal life. Just as the scarab generates life from dung, so you must find a way to create a better life from difficulties and chaos."

Iset, capite inclinato, meditabatur. "Ergo, scarabaeus non solum creatura est, sed etiam magister qui nos docet de potentia transformationis et spei."

Iset, with bowed head, reflected. "So, the scarab is not just a creature, but also a teacher who shows us the power of transformation and hope."

"Recte dicis," affirmavit Khepri. "In hoc mundo mutabili, scarabaeus remindet vos, quod semper est spes, semper est possibilitas ad meliorem futurum creandum. Ita, in arte vestra, in ritibus vestris, scarabaeum celebrate, symbolum creationis, ordinis, et vitae perpetuae."

"You speak correctly," Khepri affirmed. "In this ever-changing world, the scarab reminds you that there is always hope, always the possibility to create a better future. So, in your art, in your rituals, celebrate the scarab, the symbol of creation, order, and eternal life."

Iset, animo affecto, promisit verba Khepri inter populum suum divulgaturum esse, ut omnes memoriae tenerent scarabaeum non solum animal esse, sed etiam sacrum symbolon quod viam ad renovationem et spem aperit.

Iset, moved in spirit, promised to spread Khepri's words among his people, so that all would remember the scarab was not just an animal, but also a sacred symbol that opens the path to renewal and hope.

Et sic, per saecula, legenda scarabaei et eius conexio cum creatione et ordine in cultura Aegyptiaca pervigil mansit, semper monens homines de potentia quae in transformatione et renovatione inest.

And so, through the ages, the legend of the scarab and its connection with creation and order remained ever-present in Egyptian culture, always reminding people of the power that lies in transformation and renewal.

Symbolismus Scarabaei

In regno Aegypti, ubi solis cursus et fluminis Nili undae vitae ritus dictabant, scarabaeus magis quam simplex animal reputabatur. Symbolum erat perseverantiae et resistentiae, immortalitatis signum et animae regenerativae potentiae.

In the kingdom of Egypt, where the course of the sun and the waves of the Nile dictated the rites of life, the scarab was considered more than a simple animal. It was a symbol of perseverance and resilience, a sign of immortality and the regenerative power of the soul.

Aulam regis ingressus, pictor regius, Necho nomine, Pharaoni, Horo regnanti, novam picturam revelavit. Imago magnifica scarabaei in medio solis radiis depicti erat. "Hoc opus, o rex," incepit Necho, "scarabaei virtutem et tuam aeternam potentiam repraesentat."

Entering the royal hall, the court painter, named Necho, unveiled a new painting to Pharaoh Horus, who reigned. The magnificent image of a scarab was depicted in the centre, surrounded by rays of the sun. "This work, O king," Necho began, "represents the power of the scarab and your eternal strength."

Horus, regalis et augustus, opus admirans, respondit: "Scarabaeus, ut videmus, non solum in natura sed etiam in regno nostro aeternus est. Sicut sol omni die renascitur, ita nos, per scarabaeum, de immortalitate et animae renovatione meminimus."

Horus, regal and majestic, admiring the work, replied: "The scarab, as we see, is eternal not only in nature but also in our kingdom. Just as the sun is reborn every day, so we, through the scarab, are reminded of immortality and the renewal of the soul."

In templi sanctissimo loco, sacerdos maior, Anubis nomine, de scarabaei significatione docebat. "Fratres et sorores," exclamavit Anubis, "scarabaeus nos docet, etiam in difficillimis temporibus, sperare et perseverare. In amulettis et ornamentis nostris, scarabaeus non solum nos protegit, sed etiam ad vitam meliorem aspirare monet."

In the holiest place of the temple, the high priest, named Anubis, taught about the significance of the scarab. "Brothers and sisters," Anubis exclaimed, "the scarab teaches us, even in the most difficult times, to hope and persevere. In our amulets and ornaments, the scarab not only protects us but also encourages us to aspire to a better life."

Inter artifices, qui ad templum convenerant, mulier nomine Isis, artifex peritissima, novam collectionem monilium scarabaei formam habentium praesentabat. "Per haec ornamenta," explicavit Isis, "non solum decorem nostrum augemus, sed etiam divinae vitae principia celebramus. Scarabaeus in his gemmis et auro inclusus, solis vitamque potentiam nobis quotidie memorat."

Among the artisans gathered at the temple, a woman named Isis, a most skilled artist, was presenting a new collection of jewellery in the shape of scarabs. "Through these ornaments," Isis explained, "we not only enhance our beauty but also celebrate the principles of divine life. The scarab, encased in these gems and gold, reminds us daily of the power of the sun and life."

Ad finem diei, Horus, Anubis, Isis, et cives omnes in magnam celebrationem conveniebant, ubi cantus, saltationes, et historiae de scarabaeo et eius symbolismo narrabantur. "Hodie," proclamavit Horus, "recognoscimus scarabaeum non tantum ut naturae miraculum, sed etiam ut nostrae culturae et spiritualitatis centrum."

At the end of the day, Horus, Anubis, Isis, and all the citizens gathered for a great celebration, where songs, dances, and stories about the scarab and its symbolism were told. "Today," Horus proclaimed, "we recognise the scarab not only as a wonder of nature but also as the centre of our culture and spirituality."

Et ita, per aetates, Aegyptii scarabaeum venerati sunt, non solum pro eius naturali virtute sed etiam pro eius profundo symbolismo: signum perseverantiae, immortalitatis, et divinae connexiones. In arte, in regno, et in corde populi, scarabaeus aeternus mansit, sempiternus vitae et solis nuntius.

And so, through the ages, the Egyptians venerated the scarab not only for its natural virtues but also for its profound symbolism: a sign of perseverance, immortality, and divine connections. In art, in the kingdom, and in the hearts of the people, the scarab remained eternal, an everlasting messenger of life and the sun.

Hereditas Scarabaei

Per saecula, fascinatio hominum cum scarabaeo non minuitur. Hic parvus, sed potentissimus animal, culturam Aegyptiam trans tempora formavit, eiusque mysterium adhuc in corde humanitatis pulsat.

Through the centuries, humanity's fascination with the scarab has not diminished. This small but powerful creature shaped Egyptian culture across time, and its mystery still beats in the heart of humanity.

In museo, ubi antiquitates Aegyptiae conservantur, curator, Aten nomine, adulescentibus visitatoribus narrat: "Ecce mille amuleta scarabaei formam habentia, quae in antiquis sepulcris inventa sunt. Haec nos docent quanti Aegyptii scarabaeum aestimaverint, non solum ut amulettum sed etiam ut symbolum aeternae vitae."

In a museum where Egyptian antiquities are preserved, a curator named Aten explains to young visitors: "Behold, a thousand scarab-shaped amulets, which were found in ancient tombs. These teach us how highly the Egyptians valued the scarab, not only as an amulet but also as a symbol of eternal life."

Dum per expositionem ambulant, Iulia, studiosa archaeologiae, amico suo Marco dixit: "Miror, quomodo scarabaeus, tam parva creatura, tam magnam partem in cultura et religione Aegyptia habuerit. Inspiratio eius in arte, litteris, etiam in vestitu hodierno inveniri potest."

As they walk through the exhibition, Julia, a student of archaeology, says to her friend Marcus: "I marvel at how the scarab, such a small creature, held such a large role in Egyptian culture and religion. Its inspiration can be found in art, literature, and even in modern fashion."

Marco, arte et historia captus, respondit: "Ita vero. Scarabaeus transformationis et renovationis symbolon est. Mythes et legenda de eo non solum nobis de Aegyptiorum vita et credentiis narrat, sed etiam universales veritates de vita et morte, chaos et ordine."

Marcus, captivated by art and history, replied: "Indeed. The scarab is a symbol of transformation and renewal. Myths and legends about it not only tell us about the lives and beliefs of the Egyptians, but also universal truths about life and death, chaos and order."

Ad alteram partem musei, artifex qui moderna opera inspirata antiquitate creavit, explicavit: "In hoc opere meo, scarabaeum uti volui ad nostrae aetatis quaestiones de identitate et mutatione explorandas. Sicut Aegyptii olim, etiam nos renovationem et spem in symbolo scarabaei invenimus."

In another part of the museum, an artist who created modern works inspired by antiquity explained: "In this work of mine, I wanted to use the scarab to explore the issues of identity and change in our era. Just as the Egyptians once did, we too find renewal and hope in the symbol of the scarab."

In aula magna, ubi conferentia de hereditate culturali Aegypti habebatur, orator principalis, Cleopatra nomine, audientibus dixit: "Scarabaeus, trans millennia perseverans, nos admonet de sapientia et mysteriis nostrorum antecessorum. Hic nos docet, ut in perpetuo mundi mutatione, semper est locus pro renovatione et spe."

In the grand hall, where a conference on Egypt's cultural heritage was being held, the keynote speaker, named Cleopatra, said to the audience: "The scarab, persevering through millennia, reminds us of the wisdom and mysteries of our ancestors. It teaches us that in the perpetual change of the world, there is always room for renewal and hope."

Et sic, hereditas scarabaei pergit illuminare mentes et animas hominum, aeternum pontem inter praeteritum et praesens, inter mortalem vitam et divinam sapientiam formans. Scarabaeus, symbolus vetustus, adhuc novas generationes ad inspirationem, ad mirationem, ad profundam vitae comprehensionem vocat.

And so, the legacy of the scarab continues to enlighten the minds and souls of people, forming an eternal bridge between the past and present, between mortal life and divine wisdom. The scarab, an ancient symbol, still calls new generations to inspiration, wonder, and a deeper understanding of life.

Lingua Latina

111 Interlinear

Latin – English Conversations

More books

More ressources

Endorsements by leading Latinists

All on discoverlatin.com